THE KILLER IN THE ATTIC

And More True Tales of Crime and Disaster from Cleveland's Past

D1065873

Also by John Stark Bellamy II:

The Corpse in the Cellar
The Maniac in the Bushes
They Died Crawling

THE KILLER IN THE ATTIC

And More True Tales of Crime and Disaster from Cleveland's Past

John Stark Bellamy II

GRAY & COMPANY, PUBLISHERS
CLEVELAND

The Killer in the Attic

Gray & Company, Publishers
1588 E. 40th St.
Cleveland, OH 44103
(216) 431-2665

Library of Congress Cataloging-in-Publication Data
Bellamy, John Stark.
Killer in the Attic / John Stark Bellamy II.
p. cm.
ISBN 1-886228-57-4
1. Crime—Ohio—Cleveland—History—Anecdotes.
2. Crime—Ohio—Cleveland—History—Case studies.
3. Cleveland (Ohio)—History—Anecdotes. I. Title.
HV6795.C5 B447 2002
364.1'09771'31--dc21
2002002430

This book is the fourth volume in a series of books on
the Cleveland of yesteryear. Narrative slide shows
chronicling some of the chapters are available for a fee,
and additional slideshows are under development. For
more information or bookings, contact John Stark Bellamy II via e-mail (jstarkbII@aol.com) or by mail via
the publisher of this book.

ISBN 1-886228-57-4

Printed in the United States of America

10 9 8 7 6 5 4 3 2 1

With love to my
beautiful wife Laura,
Soul's companion
and the answer to the
question of my life

CONTENTS

CONTENTS, *continued*

ACKNOWLEDGMENTS

Chapter 1 ("Smithereen Street") was written for and originally appeared in *Dick Goddard's Almanac for Northeast Ohio, 2002* (Gray & Company, Publishers, Cleveland). Chapter 15 ("I Am Settling For All Past Wrongs . . .") is reprinted from the author's Internet-only publication *By The Neck Until Dead: A History of Hangings in Cuyahoga County* (http://web.ulib.csuohio.edu/spec-coll/bellamy); an alternate version of it appeared in the September 2000 issue of *Northern Ohio Live.* Chapter 24 ("Shot in His Own Bed") is also reprinted from the author's *By The Neck Until Dead: A History of Hangings in Cuyahoga County* (copyright 2000, John Stark Bellamy II).

Many of the stories told in the author's Cleveland crime-and-disaster books are also the subjects of slide shows he presents throughout Northeast Ohio. For a catalog of slide shows (or details of his notorious trolley tours of Cleveland murder and disaster sites), see the Gray & Co. Web site (www.grayco.com) or e-mail the author directly at: jstarkbII@aol.com.

PREFACE

Why another book on Cleveland crime and disaster? The answer, of course, is because it's there. There will always be people who are fascinated by the romance of miseries past, and what could be more alluring to Clevelanders of such tastes than more Forest City violence, both planned and accidental?

As I may have mentioned a few million times or so, I am one of those happily morbid Clevelanders. And this book, like its three predecessors, is a celebration, if you will, of some of the more melodramatic moments, events, and personalities (often but not always malign) of Northeast Ohio's yesteryears. It is true that I had not intended to perpetrate another Cleveland book so soon after the last one, but I confess that I have been irresistibly impelled to the dread act by an importunate public. Like Conan Doyle with his Sherlock Holmes, I have discovered that I could not stifle my melodramatic tale telling even if I wanted to—and the frank truth is that I don't.

My more constant readers may wonder how this collection differs from its predecessors. In most ways it doesn't: like the contents of *They Died Crawling, The Maniac in the Bushes,* and *The Corpse in the Cellar*, these are some of my favorite Cleveland stories, and I cherish them all equally as my own varying but beloved literary creations. Perspicacious readers will note, however, that most of the tales included here are somewhat briefer than is my wont. Their relative shortness was dictated by two considerations. The first is that I wanted to squeeze in as many great stories as possible. The second is that many of these quirky, disquieting subjects are best served by a more concise treatment than the big warhorse narratives (such as the Sheppard murder, the Torso murders, and the Collinwood School fire) of my earlier books. Many of these stories, I flatter myself, are completely unknown to most Clevelanders, even those of a historical/criminal bent, and I welcome the opportunity to introduce to them an unprecedented array of outré tales and peculiar characters.

As ever, my obligations are immense and unrecompensed. I never would have begun my criminous writing career without the example of George Condon, the dean of Cleveland writers, best of all Cleveland historians, raconteurs, and friends. Another Cleveland historian, Peter Jedick, showed me the way (by example) to writing Cleveland history for periodicals, and creating and performing slide shows about such topics.

Particular thanks are due to *Northern Ohio Live* editor Dennis Dooley for the serial publication of the Adin murder tale in the September 2000 issue of that esteemed periodical and to Cleveland's First Meteorologist, the inimitable Dick Goddard, for including the West 117th explosion story in *Dick Goddard's Almanac for Northeast Ohio, 2002.* I am likewise grateful to William Barrow, Webmaster Supremo over at the Cleveland State University Library, for posting my Internet-only book—*By The Neck Until Dead: A History of Hangings in Cuyahoga County*—on the Cleveland Digital Library Web site (http://web.ulib.csuohio.edu/speccoll/bellamy). The Adin and Skinner murder narratives first appeared there, and insatiable Cleveland crime (or capital punishment) enthusiasts will find in it five additional murder stories that have never been published elsewhere. Not to mention that charming hangman's rope that scrolls continually with you as you read them . . .

The present collection of local horrors would not have been possible without the help of those dedicated Cleveland archivists and librarians who preserve the antique materials of which it is ultimately composed. I would like to thank in particular: William Barrow, William Becker, Lynn Bycko, and Joanne Cornelius at the Special Collections branch of the Cleveland State University Library; David Holcombe and Alan Coates at the Cleveland Police Historical Society; Noah Himes and Carol Bellina at the Western Reserve Historical Society; and Dr. Judith Cetina and her wonderful staff over at the Cuyahoga County Archives. The institutions they serve, along with the Photograph Department at the Cleveland Public Library, are the uncelebrated but real stars in Cleveland's historical firmament.

My co-workers at the Cuyahoga County Public Library have earned my enduring gratitude for their failed but sincere conspiracy to keep me humble. They include: Mary Erbs, Catherine Monnin, Christy Wiggins, Clara Ballado, Nick Cronin, David Soltesz, Avril McInally, Daniel Jezior, Mary Ryan, Abbey O'Neill, Marty Essen, Jennifer Gerrity, Rebecca Groves, Pamela DeFino, Judy

Vanke, Mary Ann Shipman, Nancy Pazelt, Christy Igo, Holly Schaefer, Dave McNally, Roberta Tyna, Lynne Cipriani, Laurie Evanko, Karen Rabatin, and Victoria ("The Vixen") Richards, for whom the story entitled "An Unquiet Grave" was written, but not exactly inspired by.

As ever, I am inadequately grateful to my mother Jean Dessel Bellamy, who made my late-blooming career as a chronicler of gloom possible; my brother Stephen Paul Bellamy and his wife Gail Ghetia, who nurtured my fledgling literary efforts; and to my sister-in-law Joan Patrici, who finally put me in touch with my inner Corpse in the Cellar.

Finally, it is safe to say that I wouldn't even be alive, must less a serial Cleveland author, but for the incredible unstinting love and support of my wife, Laura Ann Serafin. This book may be a peculiar one, but it is above all a valentine to her.

THE KILLER
IN THE ATTIC

And More True Tales of Crime
and Disaster from Cleveland's Past

Chapter 1

SMITHEREEN STREET

The 1953 West 117th Street Explosion

All Cleveland disasters are not created equal. Especially, it would seem, if they happen on the West Side. You don't believe it? Consider, then, the 1953 West 117th Street disaster. In just a few seconds of unexpected violence it destroyed an entire mile of a heavily industrialized Cleveland thoroughfare. It killed one person and put 64 more in hospitals. The force of its explosions catapulted at least a dozen cars high above the street, along with their stunned occupants. It lifted hundreds of huge concrete slabs into the air and then rained them down on terrified motorists and pedestrians. It bounced 100 weighty manhole covers into the sky, whence they descended to penetrate vulnerable homes and apartments. It smithereened 5,000 feet of road, damaged and disrupted two railroads and a trolley line, not to mention pulverizing the water, sewer, and gas infrastructure along the border of two cities. It caused $5 million in damage and stimulated half that amount again in lawsuits. And the odds are that, if you don't hail from the West Side, you've never heard of it.

It was the height of the Cleveland rush hour and the traffic light at West 117th and Madison was about to turn red when the first blast came at exactly 5:15 P.M. on September 10. Investigators later pinpointed its genesis at the intersection of Detroit Avenue and West 117th. Owing to the nature of the explosion, however, the upheaval from the blast instantaneously transmitted itself both north and south on West 117th via the six-foot sanitary sewer that ran along the western edge between Lake Avenue and Berea Road. Finding additional fuel as it raced through the disintegrating sewer,

West 117th Street at the New York Central railroad tracks, epicenter of the explosion.

the blast reached the peak of its destruction at the intersections of West 117th Street with Berea Road, Madison Avenue, and Lake Avenue. The first and most obvious result was that much of the surface of West 117th was suddenly thrust upward several feet with incredible force, trampolining at least a dozen cars into the air. The second, and more lethal, effect was the shattering of the adjacent sidewalks and retaining walls, especially in the area by the New York Central Railroad overpass (the current site of the West 117th Street RTA station). What goes up must come down, and even as the first automobiles crashed to the street, airborne concrete chunks—some of them as large as 20 feet by 10 feet—began to descend. For those unlucky humans on the scene, it became an instant hell on earth.

Charles Flickinger's experience was typical for motorists in the area. Waiting for the light at Clifton Boulevard and West 117th, he heard a "sudden bang." The next thing he knew, he was lying in the street, looking at his car smashed into a bus. Worse yet was the ordeal of Robert Hudson. He heard "a big explosion and saw a pink flash," the pyrotechnic prelude to having his car thrown 15 feet into the air, where it collided with another auto and then crashed down. And there were several drivers who shared the fate of Herman

Ground Zero on Smithereen Street: West 117th Street at the New York Central railroad bridge.

Heppner, who remembered it this way: "I heard an explosion and everything went black. The next thing I knew my car was upside down on top of another car and four men were chopping my windshield to get out."

It could have been worse—and it was for Katherine Szabo, 42, and Eleanor Rinaldi, 24. Katherine, driving in a borrowed car with her brother Robert, had just cleared the New York Central overpass when the street exploded. Her car, at the epicenter of the catastrophe, was one of the first hurled into the air and probably the first to be crushed by the concrete fallout from the blast. Seconds later, the car caught on fire. Robert managed to crawl out of the wreckage and the fire was soon extinguished. But Katherine didn't make it, dying of her injuries shortly after she was taken to St. John's Hospital. Amazingly, she was the only fatality of the rush-hour disaster. But Eleanor Rinaldi came close to joining her in death. She was motoring with her husband, Angelo, when the first blast caught them by the overpass, and she was trapped when a huge concrete slab smashed through the car roof and crushed the dashboard area into her legs. While firemen desperately labored to extricate her smashed body, Father James O'Brien, a priest from the nearby Sts. Philip and James parish, consoled the still-conscious Rinaldi and administered the last rites of the Roman Catholic Church to her. Astonishingly, Rinaldi survived her ordeal and could not remember anything after her car cleared the underpass.

Things weren't much better for the hapless pedestrians in the five-block explosion area. Margaret Calvey was waiting for the bus

at Berea Road when "the ground shook and the sidewalk rose up and struck me in the face. I was blown right out of my shoes." Joy Moore was leaning against a delicatessen window when she heard the first blast and then watched in stupefied horror as a rain of bricks, pavement, and streetcar tracks began to fall around her. One of the most seriously injured was Joyce Bauer, 22, who was standing with two other women in front of the Glidden Company plant at West 117th and Berea Road when the street detonated. Caught in the sudden shower of concrete and miscellaneous debris, she finished her day in critical condition at Lakewood Hospital.

Top: From out of the jaws of death: safety forces try to extricate Eleanor Rinaldi from her car, September 10, 1953. Bottom: Smashed automobile.

Among those who endured a different kind of fright were Sue Townsend of 1497 West 117th and Edwin Hood of 11708 Detroit Avenue. As they abruptly learned, the force of the multiple explosions had sent 100 heavy metal manhole covers temporarily skyward. Townsend was preparing dinner in her second-floor flat when she heard a noise like an auto crash. As she ran to the window, a manhole cover came through the kitchen ceiling and smashed halfway through the floor. About the same moment, another bored through the top of Hood's fourth-floor apartment, took off his living room door, and drilled into an unoccupied third-floor apartment.

There were at least four explosions in all, although the worst of the violence and damage was wrought within the first few seconds at 5:15 P.M. Within minutes, safety forces poured into the stricken area. Much of the locale was flooded by broken water mains pouring millions of gallons into the ruins, a torrent that threatened to aggravate the public health peril of the wrecked sanitary sewer system. East Ohio workers began capping gas lines exposed by the blasts, and Red Cross workers began distributing water and sandwiches. Indeed, for the most part, the disaster spectacle over the next 48 hours was a showcase of Cleveland at its finest, with the terrors and challenges of the tragedy bringing out the best in all. All except, naturally, the crowds of thousands of unappeasable spectators, who continually impeded safety forces. After touring the ruins, Mayor Thomas Burke, in high dudgeon, vented civic spleen: "I was disgusted when I saw men and women taking little children into the explosion area. It was undoubtedly thoughtlessness on their part but they blocked rescue work."

Within a week, the sewers were rebuilt, roadway repairs were under way, and most of the victims had left the hospital. The cities of Cleveland and Lakewood, which shared the West 117th Street boundary, were now free to concentrate on discovering what exactly had occurred there. As is typical of Cleveland disasters, they didn't succeed very well.

It wasn't for lack of resources or expertise. Coroner Sam Gerber was put in charge of the official probe, and he immediately recruited Dr. George W. Barnes, Dr. Leon W. Weinberger, and Professor George Blum from Case Institute of Technology. These appointments augured well, especially as Barnes had headed the probe into the 1944 East Ohio Gas Company fire, and the team enjoyed additional resources provided by experts from the U.S. Bureau of Mines. But the formal report of the Gerber team, issued in March 1954, failed to answer the question of exactly who and what were responsible for the disaster. Ruling out escaping natural gas (either from East Ohio lines or the numerous abandoned gas wells that dotted—and still dot—the West 117th area) or sewer gas (which had caused two East Side explosions just previous to the West 117th blast), Gerber's probers focused on the evidence of flammable industrial waste and gasoline found in the shattered sanitary sewer lines. Their conclusion was that area plants had been illegally dumping such hazardous wastes for some time before they ignited on September 10, 1953. What had pushed them to critical mass was a hot, dry summer, which curtailed the normal flushing action of the sewers. By September 10, it was just a disaster waiting to happen. In all probability, a chance friction spark or a carelessly thrown cigarette had triggered the initial explosion.

Gerber's report further noted that there were 194 area plants using flammable substances, but it refused to speculate on the exact origins of whatever blew up five blocks of city street.

Automobile crushed by flying concrete near the New York Central Railroad overpass, September 10, 1953.

The last word about the tragedy, inevitably, belonged to the lawyers. Gerber & Co. may have embraced a masterly ambiguity about the source of the explosions, but the lawyers who brought the 91 personal injury lawsuits filed were uninterested in such coyness. Lawyers for injured plaintiffs brought suits totaling $2.5 million against Sun Oil, Shell Oil, White Sewing Machine, Union Carbide, Ferbert-Schorndorfer, and the cities of Cleveland and Lakewood. The five firms were accused of dumping flammable substances that caused the disaster, and the cities were held liable for permitting such illegal practices. In the end, however, four years later, the plaintiffs got little for their troubles. Under the persuasive aegis of Common Pleas Court judge William K. Thomas, attorneys reached an out-of-court settlement in June of 1957. With both cities agreeing to pay a third apiece and the five firms dividing the last third of the payment, the victims settled for a total of $205,000. One of the smallest amounts, $3,000, went to Julius Szabo, who had suffered the greatest loss of all, his wife Katherine. No fault whatsoever was admitted by any defendant. And so ended one of the West Side's worst, and undeservedly obscure, disasters. Let us hope that the present guardians of our public safety are more alert than those caught snoozing on September 10, 1953.

Chapter 2

FRIDAY ON HIS MIND

The 1948 Spanish Fly Killer

Ace *Cleveland News* crime beat writer Howard Beaufait described it as almost the perfect crime. All it took was a little chemistry and a little play-acting, and it should have come off flaw-lessly. Unfortunately for Clark Hill—1948's "Spanish Fly Killer"—his knowledge of both chemistry and acting was rudi-mentary at best. Instead of getting away with the "perfect" murder, Hill came within a whisper of sitting in the electric chair.

No one in Medina County, it is safe to say, had a higher opinion of Clark Hill than he himself as the spring of 1948 blossomed. Although the Medina High School graduate had flunked out of Ohio State University after his first year, he seemed content to live with his doting parents and to work on the foundry shift at the Henry Furnace Company. The 19-year-old Clark's chief interest, moreover, lay neither at work nor at home. As the boastful Clark would tell anyone willing to listen, he had "quite a way with women." He was notorious for not allowing his engagement to his high school sweetheart to interfere with burnishing his reputation as at least the loudest Lothario in Medina County. Just two years out of high school, Clark was still frantically living up to his year-book entry for the Last Will and Testament of the Class of June, 1946: "My rumble seat to any pretty girl who will ride in it."

Most Medinans would have agreed that 17-year-old Jeanette Weimer of Mogadore, Ohio, was pretty—and she was more than willing to occupy Clark's rumble seat. Brown eyes, brown hair, and a sparkling personality complemented the attractive, if mildly plump appearance that made her popular with all, especially those young men like Hill who hung out at the "Huddle," the drive-in restaurant on Route 42 where Jeanette had worked since dropping

 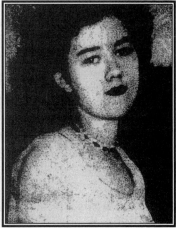

He called himself "The Sheik,"   Before the fatal milk shake:
the law called him a murderer: Jeanette Weimer.
Clark Hill, The "Spanish Fly"
Killer.

out of school three months before. Nor did Jeanette let her engagement to high school sweetheart Alden Mohler interfere with her
blooming relationship with Clark. The teenaged stranger from
Summit County must have been lonely, and the handsome, blue-
eyed, brown-haired Hill had become quite a fixture in Jeanette's
social life by the second week of April 1948. Indeed, Clark's
shabby black 1939 Chevy did heroic service in his wooing of
Jeanette that week. They went out on Tuesday night, Wednesday
night, and Thursday night. True, Clark had to get her back home
early on Wednesday so she could see her fiancé, but that didn't stop
her from necking with Clark on the Bagdad Road "lover's lane,"
several miles outside Medina. Engaged or not, she seemed headed
for a rapid seduction by Clark Hill, the boy with the "fast"
reputation.

Apparently—and tragically—Clark's relationship with Jeanette
wasn't moving fast enough for him. The next evening, Friday, April
9, he picked Jeanette up after her shift at the "Huddle," and they
drove to Lodi to see Wallace Beery in the movie *Alias A Gentle-
man*. Afterward they repaired to the restaurant next door for a
snack. Just as their milk shakes arrived at the table, Clark got up
and began playing the pinball machine. After about a minute, he
asked Jeanette to try her luck at it. As she turned her back to him

and engaged the flippers, Clark quickly and stealthily poured the contents of a small cardboard box into her milk shake. Clark Hill, whatever his claims as the irresistible Medina Casanova, was not willing to wait for Jeanette Weimer to succumb to his charms. What he poured into her drink was a powerful dose of animal cantharis—that alleged sexual stimulant known to generations of adolescent boys as "Spanish Fly." Clark was nervous as he watched Jeanette down her milk shake. His veterinary student friends, from whom he had requisitioned the drug, had warned him that its taste was bitter. But Jeanette noticed nothing amiss, and they were soon speeding back to resume their activities at the Bagdad Road "lover's lane."

For whatever reason, Jeanette was quite responsive that night, and Clark quickly, as the prosecuting attorney would later put it, "accomplished his purpose." But Clark was horrified when Jeanette immediately lapsed into unconsciousness and began breathing heavily. Whether Clark really thought she was dying will never be known. He would later give conflicting accounts of what went through his mind as he stared at the stupefied girl in the front seat of his car. But he was definitely terrified: he knew the drug he had used was illegal and he was "scared she'd tell on me" if she survived. What was he to do now?

What he in fact did was to pick up a five-foot-long rubber hose he had in the back seat and step out of the car. Wriggling underneath the rear exhaust pipe, he carefully punctured a hole and inserted one end of the hose into the tailpipe. Snaking the other end the length of the Chevy, he brought it up through the floorboard and between Jeanette's thighs. Then he rolled up the windows, turned on the ignition, and went for a long walk. When Clark returned an hour later, Jeanette was clearly dead. Clark removed the hose and initiated the second phase of his cover-up plan, which was to pretend that carbon monoxide fumes had "accidentally" overcome both of them. He would just sit there next to Jeanette's corpse with his eyes closed until some compassionate passerby found the "unconscious pair."

Alas for his clever plan. Clark sat next to Jeanette's dead body for 16 hours on Bagdad Road but no one stopped, except some children who knew Clark and said hello to him before walking on. About 4 P.M. the next day, Clark finally gave up and drove to the highway patrol barracks in Medina. His speech slurred and inco-

Medina Love Potion Death Revealed by Boy Friend, 19

Cleveland Press, April 15, 1948.

herent, he told the patrolmen there his sad tale of a faulty exhaust system and a tragic accident before they rushed him and the dead Jeanette to Medina Community Hospital. Within minutes the practically mute Clark was under an oxygen tent with intravenous needles and a catheter shoved into him.

Clark's imaginative cover-up began to disintegrate almost the moment he arrived at the hospital. Resident physician Frederick Kornfield noted that while Jeanette's stiffened corpse bore the telltale scarlet hue of a carbon monoxide victim, Clark did not, nor did he suffer the labored breathing or incontinence associated with that condition. And nurse Edith Escott noted that Clark seemed reluctant to have his blood sampled and that he seemed to be feigning unconsciousness only when he thought someone was looking. A suspicious Medina County coroner Theodore Gross soon sent blood samples from both Clark and Jeanette off to his good friend Cuyahoga County coroner Samuel Gerber. Gerber called the next day to relay the bombshell news that while Jeanette's blood showed a 70 percent carbon monoxide saturation (50 percent being sufficient to cause death), Clark's blood showed none whatsoever. Even as Gerber asked that Jeanette's body be rushed to Cleveland for autopsy, Medina County lawmen stepped up their intense interrogation of Clark Hill.

As happened by chance, Everett L. McSavaney of the Ohio State Bureau of Criminal Investigation was in town, and it was he who eventually wrenched a confession out of the beleaguered Hill on Wednesday, April 16. Although he had no evidence that Hill had used a "love drug" on Jeanette, he had "experience" with such misbehavior, and he casually asked Hill if he knew about Spanish Fly. Hill knew that the toxicology report on Jeanette was imminent, so he soon blurted out, "If I tell the truth will I get the electric chair?" McSavaney replied that he didn't know, but that he thought Hill would "feel a lot better" if he got it off his chest. Minutes later, in the company of witnesses who had overheard McSavaney's skillful interrogation, Hill dictated a 23-page confession. The next day he made a few corrections, read and signed each page, and was taken back to jail. That evening Gerber reported finding a dose of a cantharis substance in Jeanette's stomach sufficiently toxic to kill 30 people. On April 17, Hill was arraigned, and at the May session of the Medina grand jury he was indicted on three counts of first-degree murder: (1) premeditation of murder; (2) malicious killing by means of a poisonous gas; and (3) murder in the act of attempted perpetration of rape.

Although there was intense antagonism to Hill in the Medina area, he got a fairer trial than he probably expected, despite his unconvincing display of cocky bravado. Defended by Raymond B. Bennett and H. Dennis Dannley, Hill was prosecuted by William G. Batchelder Jr. before a three-judge panel after Hill's attorneys waived a jury trial. By the time proceedings opened on October 18, 1948, Hill had repudiated his confession, claiming it was procured under duress, and returned to his original scenario of two unlucky teenagers falling victim to a faulty automobile exhaust system. Prose-

> **Youth Says He Gave Girl 'Love Potion'**
>
> *Cleveland News,*
> April 15, 1948

cutor Batchelder quickly demolished Hill's preposterous defense. Witnesses from the police and hospital testified to Hill's unconvincing performance as a "carbon monoxide victim." Sam Gerber and chemist Erhard J. Kunde took the stand to explain their meticulous analysis of the blood samples and the contents of Jeanette's stomach. Perhaps the most devastating witnesses were four children, twins Patsy and Nancy Heiss, Robert Ferguson, and William Golder. They had passed by the death car twice and spoken to Hill at times when he claimed he was unconscious in the car seat next to Jeanette.

Bennett lost his legal battle to exclude Clark's voluminous confession and Dr. Kornfield's testimony on grounds of doctor–patient confidentiality. Defense quibbling as to the condition of the muffler previous to the fatal night only further emphasized Hill's desperate position.

In the end, Hill got better than he deserved. On the third day of the five-day trial, the judges threw out the count charging murder pursuant to rape. And when his judgment came, after four hours and 15 minutes of deliberation on October 21, Hill was convicted only on the second count, of poisoning by gas. Sitting silently slumped in his chair, Hill was found guilty of first-degree murder—but with a recommendation of mercy that meant a life term in prison. Still whining that he was the innocent victim of gas fumes and police bullying, he was led off to the Ohio Penitentiary.

Clark Hill's bid for a new trial failed the next month. In 1950, attorney Emile Reiss, representing an unofficial "Court of Last Resort," which in that era espoused bleak causes such as Hill's, took up his case. But Governor Frank Lausche and the Ohio Parole Board would have none of it, and Clark Hill stayed in prison. He was released from the Marion Correctional Institution in 1973, having served 25 years, and he has not been heard from since. As far as is known, he never acknowledged his responsibility for Jeanette Weimer's sordid death.

Chapter 3

A GANGSTER'S GANGSTER

The Improbable Story of "Big Jim" Morton (1884–1960)

"Jim, I can't understand you. You're a good-looking man. You've got brains. Then why are you a criminal?"

—*Unknown social worker to Big Jim Morton while interviewing him in prison*

Every Cleveland crime buff has his favorite bygone gangster. For some it remains the last of the breed, cocky Danny Greene, whose roughneck swagger ended in the bomb-shattered ruins of his luxury car in 1977. Older enthusiasts still treasure memories of "Shondor" Birns, whose cobra-like charm failed to mask the ruthlessness that made him Cleveland Public Enemy Number One between 1931 and 1975. Veteran readers of this author's antique chronicles may vote for "Blinky" Morgan, the 19th-century desperado who long tormented Cleveland lawmen and whose exploits inspired dime novels of his day. Still others may plump for George "Jiggs" Losteiner, the terror of post–World War I Cleveland and probably the most deadly psychopath ever to walk Forest City streets. But for my money, the best of them all is still Big Jim Morton, a flashy career criminal worthy of standing in a lineup with any notable gangster of any era. For sheer improbability alone, his saga is a matchless tale.

Born to respectable middle-class parents in a small town north of Chicago on May 19, 1884, James Franklin—the alias "Morton" would come later—grew to adolescence steeped in the habits of honest thrift and hard work in a preurbanized America. His father, a carpenter, died when James was four, and his mother when he

Big Jim Morton, 1925.

was nine, but he was immediately adopted by the loving family of a maternal uncle. His new family also took in his two brothers and two sisters, all of whom went on to lead productive, blameless lives. Given this supportive family background, there was no obvious reason, as James himself eventually admitted, for his becoming a thief, although he would sing a different song about his "unhappy" childhood to successive, gullible parole boards during his long criminal career. But become a thief he did at the tender age of 15, shortly after he quit school to take a job as the driver of a delivery wagon. Two of his friends decided to steal some copper and lead scrap from his employer, and James agreed "not to tell" for the fee of $1.50. Alas, his two pals were soon caught, immediately squealed on him, and he was arrested for abetting their robbery. Advised by a policeman to plead guilty, he did so—and found himself serving a sentence of 1 to 20 years in the Illinois State Prison at Joliet. Paroled a year later, James soon found it advisable to leave Illinois after perjuring himself to support a friend's alibi. After bumming around the country for a few months, he returned to Illinois, only to be imprisoned as a parole violator when one of his friends turned him in for the $10 reward. From this point on, James Franklin dedicated himself to a full-blown life of crime.

After escaping from Joliet in 1904, Franklin drifted to California. Arrested for burglary there on January 4, 1905, he served three years at Folsom Prison before his discharge in August 1908. Three months later he was arrested for burglary in Carson City and subsequently served three years in Nevada prisons. Released in 1911, he was free for only five months before he entered the Utah State Prison in Salt Lake City on a robbery rap. By the time he was released in 1912, he had become the complete career criminal. Specializing in bank robbery and safecracking, he was already revered as one of the best operatives in his profession. He burnished his flashy public image with fancy clothes, impeccable grooming, expensive living, and the company of attractive women. Sometimes working alone but more often with experienced criminal confederates, Morton was highly successful at his dubious craft, taking in as much as $500,000 in one three-year period. By his twenties, the six-foot-one James Franklin had acquired the nickname "Big Jim" from one of his many girlfriends and adopted "Morton" as his most frequently used surname. The memorable moniker would stick to him to the end of his life.

Big Jim continued to cultivate his prison résumé. Arrested in 1914 in Nevada, again for burglary, he was paroled on April 27, 1916. Four months later he was pinched for car theft in Minneapolis, Minnesota, but avoided further unpleasantness by jumping his $5,000 bail. These World War I years were Morton's salad days, highlighted by a $28,000 heist of the Commonwealth State Bank in Detroit on March 28, 1918. The next month Morton was picked up on suspicion in Toledo but released before Minneapolis authorities were notified that their much-sought-for bail-jumper had been found. It was then that Morton turned his attention to Cleveland—with historic results.

The employees of the West Cleveland Banking Company at West 101st Street and Detroit Avenue knew they were dealing with professionals from the moment Morton's gang walked through the corner door at 2:30 P.M. on June 16, 1919. Quickly herding the five bank employees and three patrons against the wall, the five undisguised robbers moved quickly but without haste, grabbing the paper currency and Liberty Bonds but avoiding the silver. Although they threatened to shoot, especially when savings teller Lucile Shirkey reached for her gun, they remained calm right up to the moment they vanished out the front door and ran to their getaway car at West 103rd Street. One witness would recall the unflappable Morton telling his men, "Take your time, boys. Can't afford to get excited on a job like this." Minutes later, puzzled West Side residents watched as the fleeing yeggs threw their shabby work clothes

JUST GUESS WHO THIS "HERO" IS

Cleveland Press, January 1, 1923.

Diagram of the West Cleveland Bank, Big Jim's biggest Cleveland heist. *Cleveland Press*, June 17, 1919.

out of the car as it sped south down West 100th Street toward Lorain Avenue The discovery the following day of their hideout at the Franklin Apartments at 5601 Franklin Avenue and the recovery of the stolen auto used in the robbery further served to alert the Cleveland police that this was one of the most professional heists in Cleveland history. So was the take: an unprecedented $65,000.

Unfortunately for Morton, the West Cleveland bank employees had gotten a good look at his handsome, unmasked face. Moreover, they had also noticed during those few, tense minutes of the robbery that he was the obvious leader of the gang. Several weeks later, "Wanted" circulars were issued furnishing excellent descriptions of four of the five bank robbers. Morton was most accurately described as being six feet, one inch, possessing a florid complexion, dark chestnut eyes, dark brown hair, blue eyes, and two facial scars. On August 31, Morton was arrested on suspicion in Toledo and identified as the chief robber by bank employees five days later.

Morton's trial was held in the old County Courthouse in January 1920 under circumstances of unprecedented security. Owing to the discovery of several escape plots contrived while Morton was awaiting trial and a violent Toledo jailbreak on December 25, 1919, Big Jim was guarded in court by two armed deputies, the courthouse halls and entrance were ringed with armed police, and no spectators were allowed in Judge Frank C. Phillips's courtroom. Morton's attorney, Patrick J. Mulligan, accused the state of using the guards to "coerce and intimidate the jurors into believing Morton is guilty."

Unfortunately for Morton and Mulligan, the jury needed little help, as there was already an embarrassing wealth of incriminating evidence. The star witness was peppery Lucile Shirkey, who strode from the witness box over to Morton and said, "I recognize him. Perfectly. That's Mr. 'Big Jim' Morton. I only got one good look at him but I shall never forget his face." The imperturbable Ms. Shirkey's identification of Morton was seconded by teller E. L. Stafford and Catherine Fay, the custodian of the Franklin Apartments, who identified Morton as the man who had rented the Franklin Avenue hideout from her. (Readers of these chronicles may recall Ms. Fay as one of the witnesses subsequently indicted for perjury after one of Judge William McGannon's trials.) Nor did Morton help himself in his own appearance on the witness stand. He blandly denied that he had ever been in Cleveland before his September arrest but airily volunteered that he had served five prison terms and used a wide range of aliases, including "James Morton," "Magnus Olsen," "James Farmer," "Frank Wilson," and "Joe Murray." The highlight of his testimony came on January 7, when Prosecutor Stephen Young interrogated him about his lengthy prison record:

Young: When were you released
from the State Reformatory?

Morton: I wasn't released; I escaped.

Wanted Poster for "Big Jim" and his gang (Morton 3rd down). *Cleveland Press*, July 4, 1919.

Morton's only defense against the compelling testimony of no fewer than eight eyewitnesses was his alibi that he had been in Chicago the day the West Cleveland Bank was robbed. But no credible witness came forward to support that claim, and Ohio law prevented the imprisoned Morton from obtaining depositions from persons in Illinois whose testimony, Morton insisted, would exonerate him. Sensing the inevitable, defense counsel Mulligan pulled out the rhetorical stops in his final plea to the jury, piously averring: "I have often wondered how 'he without sin' is convicted but it is all very plain to me now." On January 9, following Morton's conviction on the bank robbery charge, Judge Phillips smacked him with a 1- to 15-year sentence in the Ohio Penitentiary. Characteristically, Morton didn't move a muscle as both the verdict and sentence were pronounced. Immediately spirited away to the Ohio Penitentiary, Morton waved jauntily to the crowd of well-wishers at the West 9th Street Union Depot and shouted, "I will be back in two months." Interestingly, despite the arrests of three of the four other robbers, Morton was the only person ever convicted of the West Cleveland Bank robbery.

Judge Phillips must have suspected something was rotten in the state of Ohio justice, for why else would he have added these prophetic words after sentencing Morton to prison: "If, during the 15 years you are confined there, the State Board of Clemency acts in your favor, the people of the state, knowing of your crime, will be entitled to feel a deep contempt for that board." How prescient Judge Phillips proved to be. On July 5, 1922, Morton's budding career as a shirt maker in the Ohio Penitentiary factory was interrupted when the Ohio Supreme Court overturned his trial verdict on the grounds that the law prohibiting the taking of Morton's Illinois depositions was unconstitutional. It is incontestable that Ohio Supreme Court justice R. M. Wannamaker spoke for thousands of outraged jurists and citizens when he commented on the Court's ruling in a withering dissent: "A score of witnesses from Morton's friends in Chicago would not have changed the verdict of guilty . . . If the court had permitted Morton to take depositions from his friends in Chicago it would have been permitting perjury." Warming to his theme, Wannamaker penned a character sketch of Morton remarkable for its concise accuracy: "As far as anyone can tell, Morton has never done an honest day's work nor earned an honest dollar."

Morton wasn't the kind to take such personal criticism lying down. Two days later, he issued a statement setting out the mendacious, sanctimonious credo that would serve him well before many a parole board in the future:

> My whole conviction was obtained as the result of a frame-up on the part of [Cuyahoga County] Sheriff [Edward J.] Hanrattay and Police Inspector [Charles N.] Sterling of Cleveland. True, I am, or rather have been a crook, but it's my past record that is counting against me this time. I blame no one but myself for my downfall. I am the only crook in the family but I got started wrong. I was sent to a reformatory when I was 16 and there I learned all my bad habits. Reformatories should be abolished and the money spent for community playgrounds, so that the youths could be kept off the streets.

Although many, including Cuyahoga County prosecutor Edward Stanton, were dubious that Morton could be convicted a second time, the course of the second trial in January 1923 proved otherwise. With visiting judge Harry W. Jewell of Delaware County presiding and Stanton prosecuting, seven heavily armed deputies guarded Morton with shoot-to-kill orders in the event of any escape attempt. Miss Catherine Fay, already sought for perjury in the McGannon case, turned up missing but the West Cleveland Bank employees reprised their testimony perfectly, as did witnesses from the Franklin Apartments. Although the depositions from Morton's Illinois friends were allowed, Judge Jewell rejected Morton's request that he be allowed to travel to Marquette Prison in Michigan to obtain depositions from inmates William Wilson and W. E. Harris,

Morton in the Cuyahoga County jail. *Cleveland Press*, November 7, 1922.

who were serving life terms for the murder of a deputy sheriff. (Their testimony, naturally, was that a conveniently dead inmate, Frank Adams, had confessed responsibility for the West Cleveland job and that the accusations against Morton were just an unfortunate case of mistaken identity.) Even Morton knew it was over when his girlfriend refused to support his Chicago alibi on the stand. But he retained his suave, upbeat manner even as he was convicted again on January 19, 1920, and Judge Jewell slapped him with another 1- to 15- year sentence the following morning. To Judge Jewell, Morton simply said, "I am as innocent now as anyone in this courtroom," and left the room, shouting a jaunty "So long, everybody!" to the considerable throng of his fans. George W. Spooner, Morton's attorney, immediately filed a motion for a new trial, but virtually no one was surprised when it was turned down by the Court of Appeals eight months later. Once again, it looked like the end of the line for Big Jim.

As usual, Morton's considerable list of enemies had once again underestimated his persistence and guile. Over his many years in prison—more than 20 by 1925—Morton had taken the time to educate himself in prison libraries. In his autobiography he would claim that it was the effect of a prisoner sermon that moved him to do so. Indeed, he would boast that he had mastered the works of Aristotle, Plato, Gibbon, Swift, Tolstoy, and other kindred intellects while in stir. He had also developed both a persuasive rhetorical manner and a fluent writing style. He now applied himself to writing honeyed epistles to Ohio governor Vic Donahey and the members of the Ohio Board of Clemency. In these fawning, flattering letters he emphasized the unfairness of his conviction, his completely reformed character, his declining health (he claimed the heat of Columbus summers was particularly inimical to his delicate constitution), and the alleged background of privation, orphanage, and bad companions that had impelled him to a life of crime. As he put it so eloquently in one wheedling missive:

> I am not the vicious criminal that I am sometimes pictured. The life that I have led is unexplainable by me. I have tried to find out why I have been such a sucker as I really work harder in prison than I would have to work for wages as a free man on the outside.

As for Governor Donahey's virtues, Big Jim just couldn't say enough:

> This state and especially the wards of this state are very fortunate indeed that the present governor of this great state is of such great force and character. Filled as he is with compassion for the failings of his fellowmen, he is ever ready to right a wrong and

despite the "unmerited" criticism heaped upon his every act (by
newspapers of this state of opposite political faith), he steadfastly refused to be swerved against her principles he so ably sets
forth.

For whatever reasons—Big Jim would always insist that no
money changed hands—the Board of Clemency and Governor
Donahey were eventually moved to compassion by his insistent
pleas. On August 5, 1925, Big Jim was granted a conditional pardon by Governor Donahey on the Clemency Board's recommendation and released to Michigan authorities to stand trial in Detroit
on the 1918 Commonwealth Bank robbery charge. It is interesting
to note, despite their later equivocations, that Morton's pleas to the
Board for parole were supported both by Cuyahoga County prosecutor Edward Stanton and Judge Harry Jewell.

The crux of the parole deal was that Morton would plead guilty
to the Michigan bank robbery charge and promise never to return
to Ohio on pain of imprisonment. This seemed to satisfy everyone,
as Michigan juries were reputed to be tougher on bank robbers than
Ohio juries. The official rationale was that Ohio would be rid of a
disagreeable prisoner and Morton would end up serving even more
prison time. So imagine the surprise of embarrassed Ohio officials
when: (1) Morton pleaded not guilty at his preliminary criminal
hearing in Detroit; (2) the chief witness against him in the Commonwealth robbery case turned up missing; and (3) Morton's
lawyer, Thomas Chawkey, requested and received eight continu-
ances in the proceedings against his client.

It was too much for the mortified Governor Donahey, who had
already formally revoked his imprudent commutation of Morton's
sentence. Donahey was under considerable public pressure, especially after the Cleveland Association for Criminal Justice released
the correspondence between Morton and Ohio officials in early
December. And so, on the morning of December 14, 1925, just
minutes after a smirking Morton received his ninth continuance in
a Detroit criminal court, Donahey, acting in collusion with Michigan governor Alex J. Grosbeck, decided to rectify his compassionate mistake. As Morton left the courtroom he was lured into a side
room, where handcuffs and leg irons were slapped on him. Seconds
later he was hustled into a waiting car and taken to the Ohio border. There, he was turned over to waiting Ohio officials, who took

him back to a cell in the Ohio Penitentiary. Lawyer Chawkey made
the expected protests when he discovered what had happened to his
client, but it was a done deal. As Detroit prosecutor Robert M.
Toms said to him, "He's gone, isn't he? What are you going to do
about it?" No one except Morton was inclined to pursue the embarrassing matter further. The official record stated that he had simply
been rearrested as a "parole violator." The 1925 Annual Report of
the Ohio Board of Clemency didn't even mention the name of Big
Jim Morton.

More years of prison routine rolled by. In 1926 Morton almost
died from the effects of drinking wood alcohol with some other
prisoners. He implausibly insisted he had merely quaffed some
discarded cans of cherry juice, but the emphatic beverage did permanent damage to his digestive system. He continued his legal
efforts to get out of prison, working through former Ohio attorney
general C. C. Crabbe to pursue a habeas corpus suit on the basis of
his 1925 "kidnapping." In 1929, in one of his last acts of office,
Governor Donahey again granted clemency to Morton. There was
another public firestorm of protest, again spearheaded by the
Cleveland Association for Criminal Justice. This time, however,
Morton backed down, ultimately rejecting Donahey's conditional
clemency and insisting on his unconditional freedom on the basis
of his 1925 parole.

Not even Big Jim Morton could have predicted the turn his
improbable life now took. On Easter Monday, 1930, a fire swept
the Ohio State Penitentiary in Columbus, killing 324 prisoners. Big
Jim was one of the unexpected heroes of the tragedy, spurning
escape opportunities to help free as many as 40 prisoners who were
trapped in their cells by the advancing flames. In recognition of his
bravery, not to mention his time already served, Morton was finally
freed in 1931. He was 47 years old, with bad feet, a ruined stomach, no wife, no kids, and no visible means of support. How was he
going to start his life over again?

It would be heartwarming to record that Big Jim Morton made
the best of his new shot at a decent life. But the sordid truth is that
he soon returned to his familiar haunts, erstwhile acquaintances,
and timeworn avocations. Already expert at "soaping" safes and
cooking nitroglycerin for bank jobs, he now enrolled in trade
school classes to perfect his technique with a safecracking blow-
torch. Soon, after a brief stint as a bodyguard in the Capone orga-

nization, it was back to business as usual, as Big Jim and divers criminal associates cut a wide swath through the country's banking system. He would later boast that during those Depression years he did "jobs" in every part of the country except New England, Mississippi, Louisiana, and Arkansas. His luck ran out temporarily in 1935, when he was pinched for possession of burglary tools in Georgia and sentenced to six years on a chain gang. But Morton walked off that chain gang a year later, courtesy, he later claimed, of Governor Eugene Tallmadge, who was anxious to curry favor with some of Morton's august criminal associates.

Morton's luck ran out for the last time in 1937. Arrested for burglary by federal postal authorities in South Carolina, he opted to plead guilty to an outstanding federal bank rap in South Bend, Indiana. But as soon as he finished that four-year term in 1941, who should show up but vindictive officials from the Illinois State Penitentiary at Joliet? It seems that Morton was still wanted for the 1901 parole violation charge and his subsequent prison escape. In 1941 he began his last prison term in Joliet, 41 years after he had begun his first term there.

By the time Morton got out of prison in February 1949 he was 65, a broken, penniless, and defeated man. But life had one more improbable role left for him. In early 1950, while Morton was visiting the offices of the *Cleveland Press*, editor Louis B. Seltzer spotted him. "Aren't you 'Big Jim' Morton?" said Seltzer, and a friendship soon sprang up between the two. The upshot was that Seltzer contacted friends at the *Saturday Evening Post* and convinced them that Morton's life story was worth telling in their pages. Morton's three-part autobiography, entitled "I Was the King of Thieves," and coauthored by David G. Wittels, appeared in the magazine over three weeks in August 1950. In it, Morton frankly confessed to doing over 200 major "jobs" during his criminal career, including the West Cleveland Bank heist, a crime he had hitherto steadfastly denied. Altogether it was a very sad story in which the emphasis, properly, was placed on how little Morton had to show for his seemingly glamorous life: no money, no family, no future, and a life of almost 40 years behind bars. To his credit, Morton blamed no one but himself and admitted that he had only wised up during his last stretch in Joliet. It seems he had met a 17-year-old doing his first stretch there, and the resemblance between the youth and his memories of himself at that age moved him to try and persuade the young felon to go straight. Of course, being Big Jim, he couldn't resist noting, with considerable professional pride, that he had never been caught—not even once—in the actual commission of his well-planned heists.

Considering his outlaw past, Morton's last years were good ones. Although prospects for a full-length autobiography and a movie dramatization never materialized, the national exposure from the *Post* series brought him a new circle of rich and influential friends. One of them was South Carolina banker Ralph Bowden, who invited Morton to be a pampered guest at his palatial mansion. There, in the lap of luxury, Morton offered Bowden knowledgeable advice on how to deter bank thieves. The completely captivated Bowden described Morton to reporters as "the best company I've ever had—the most versatile and loquacious of men." Indeed, the courtly Bowden waxed veritably sentimental in his evaluation of the thief who had once robbed his bank:

> About the only experience I have not had in the banking business has been the privilege of sitting down in some isolated spot with a jug of wine and a loaf of bread . . . and talking to a one-time professional yeggman. I might mention in connection with the torch job on me that [Morton] displayed a Christian and most gentlemanly characteristic by placing paper weights on the papers in the shelves of my vault, so, apparently, to disturb me as little as possible. By doing this he could not have told me in plainer English that I was a nice, sleek and fat old banker; that he hated to pester me; but that he was a yeggman simply pursuing his profession, whose only interest was in the contents of his safe.

Other bankers followed Bowden's lead in lavishing hospitality on Big Jim, and he subsequently worked on the publicity campaign for Stanley Kramer's film *My Six Convicts* as a "crime expert." As a reformed criminal celebrity, Morton also appeared on radio programs and was the star of "Big Jim's Clinic," a special presentation on WEWS-TV moderated by Dorothy Fuldheim.

When Big Jim Morton finally died on July 16, 1960, at Doctors' Hospital in Cleveland Heights, he had long since become a sort of "grand old man" of Cleveland crime enthusiasts. He was well known around town as a Cleveland character and raconteur, especially to habitués of Sonnahalter's Restaurant at East 55th and

Euclid Avenue, where he held court in his "retirement." Content in his sunset years to fill modest jobs as hotel clerk and newsstand vendor, the oft-interviewed and always quotable Big Jim expressed genial contentment with the way his life had turned out and soberly cautioned youngsters to avoid the temptations to which he had succumbed. He especially liked to stress that he had never fired a shot in all his decades of armed robbery. But every now and then, Big Jim had a nostalgic twinge when he thought about the old days, as he once admitted to a reporter:

> You know, it isn't easy. Even now, when I go by some of these small banks I can't help looking them over—thinking: this would be an easy one—no one can see you from the street, you can park your car around the corner.

Big Jim Morton Dies, Helped Steal a Million

Cleveland Press, July 16, 1960.

Chapter 4

CUYAHOGA DEATH TRIP

The 1896 Willow Bridge Scow Disaster

The Flats and the lakefront were no place for sissies in late-19th-century Cleveland. Cleveland was first and foremost a city of hard, brutal work. Men labored long, often dangerous hours, toiling their lives—and often their health—away at the manufacturing and shipping occupations of a still largely unmechanized economy. And perhaps no line of work was tougher and more brutalizing than what was done on Whiskey Island. For this is where much of the iron ore—the rusty gold that turned Forest City skies orange and built so many Mather and Hanna mansions—was unloaded by sweating, ill-paid men from the cavernous holds of Rockefeller-owned fleets to feed the satanic steel mills farther down the Cuyahoga River.

Which is why, no doubt, the day-shift men at the Cleveland & Pittsburgh ore docks were in such haste to get off Whiskey Island that hot summer evening of July 16, 1896. They had been working all day emptying tons of heavy ferrous metal from the hold of the *Sir Henry Bessemer.* Most of them were German immigrants who lived in the Clark Avenue-Selden Avenue (West 43rd Street) neighborhood, and they were anxious to get back to their homes and families. Until recently, they had used the Willow Street bridge, which spanned the Old Riverbed just south of Whiskey Island and took them to the near West Side. But the city had razed the old bridge, and the men now preferred being ferried across the Old Riverbed, rather than walking a few hundred feet more to the Valley Railway bridge, which the Cleveland & Pittsburgh firm had leased for their convenience. Chipping in a few pennies apiece, the ore workers had purchased a wooden scow from the nearby Murphy and Miller shipyard. The young boys hired to bring water to

Cleveland Press, July 17, 1896.

the parched men throughout the day were also expected to row them homeward across the Old Riverbed after each shift ended.

Given their work patterns and their makeshift commuting arrangements, the tragedy that occurred was probably inevitable. For one thing, the scow itself was an unstable, unsafe, and frail craft. Perhaps 26 by 5 feet, it was not built to hold as many men as it usually carried, and the relatively new craft was already leaking "green slime" in several places. It wouldn't take much motion to upset such a boat, and the Old Riverbed sustained a more or less chronic commotion as feisty tugboats, leviathan bulk carriers, and divers craft of all descriptions and motive power jostled for space at all hours in the crowded, 250-foot-wide waterway. So no lethal element was lacking as the doomed men downed their tools at 7 P.M. sharp and ran for the scow that would carry them toward hearth and home.

Ed Patten was one of the first into the scow at the Whiskey Island dock. It was his custom to help water boy Martin Corrigan with the heavy oar. But he began to have second thoughts as a group of at least 40 men, virtually all of them carrying their lunch pails, jumped into the scow after him. As Corrigan prepared to cast off, Patten noticed that the sides of the scow were only several inches above the river. At the last possible second he hurled himself out of the scow and just managed to land on the dock. Right behind him was a young man named Ed Savage, who shared Patten's lucky premonition.

The problem began with the *Lagonda*. The big steamer was being towed eastward toward the main Cuyahoga channel by the tugboats *W. D. Cushing* and *Chamberlain*. But the men in the scow couldn't see either the *Lagonda* or its tugs, as they were blocked from view by the *Bessemer* to the right of the scow as it pushed off on its southwest, diagonal course from Whiskey Island. Nor could the crew of the lead tug *Cushing* see the scow, then about 100 feet away from the northeast shore. The first mutual sighting occurred at the same moment that the first surging wave, generated by the tug's powerful screw, turned the scow sideways and emptied into the overloaded boat.

It all happened so fast. Because of the scow's filthy condition, most of the men were already standing up, many of them on top of the three long seats that ran the length of the narrow craft. As the tug's wave filled the boat almost full of water, the men began to scream and shout with fear as the boat rocked from side to side. Seconds later, some of them rushed to the far side of the scow, further destabilizing the craft. Then, one of the men doffed his coat and jumped into the waters of the Old Riverbed.

It was as if the other frightened men had been waiting for a signal. By ones, then twos, and then in larger groups, they began leaping into the water, most of them clutching their lunch pails and hats as they did so. Some of them immediately sank like stones to the bottom, about 18 or 19 feet deep in that area of the Old Riverbed.

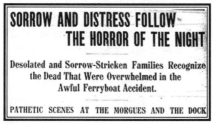

Cleveland World, July 17, 1896.

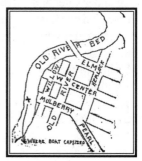

The Plain Dealer,
July 17, 1896.

Searching for the bodies of victims.
Cleveland Press, July 17, 1896.

Most of the others, screaming and struggling, grabbed onto their fellows, a desperate act that only intensified the general peril and added to the mass hysteria. Seconds later, the scow flipped over and the few men still left in it joined their companions in the water.

The experience—if not the fate—of Bernard Patton, 16, was typical. Unlike most of the men, he could swim, but he not gotten more than four feet from the overturned scow when four desperate men grabbed him. He kicked and struggled against them, but it was only when they all sank together that he was able to kick his way free underwater and get to the south shore. Another workman, John Perew, did even better. An excellent swimmer, Perew quickly made it to shore, only to reenter the water to save two men who were all but dead. Perhaps even more heroic was the example of Pat McGinty. Like Perew, he swam to shore and then returned to his struggling companions. Swimming to a life preserver, he gave it to a drowning man, and then repeated the action with another before swimming to shore.

Perew and McGinty had plenty of help in their efforts to save the men in the water. As those on board the *Bessemer, Lagonda, Chamberlain,* and *Cushing* became aware of the developing tragedy, they threw life preservers, ropes, and anything that would float, especially wood, at the vortex of struggling men. A fireman named Dwyer even leaped into the water from the *Cushing* and saved two men. Richard Masten, however, was one who didn't need such help. Along with four or five others, he had the presence of mind to remember that the overturned scow would still float. So while most of the men were pulling each other to a wet death, Masten's group stayed underneath the scow until they were rescued.

It was over in less than five minutes. Virtually all the witnesses agreed that quite a number of the men sank for good as soon as they hit the water. Others struggled for two or three minutes, fighting to hold on to their equally terrified and doomed companions. But by 7:15 P.M. the only apparent evidence of the tragedy was the overturned scow and the mute evidence of a dozen workingmen's hats floating on the surface of the Old Riverbed. All of the victims were later found on the riverbed bottom within a 20-foot radius of where the scow had overturned. Evidence of the blind terror that possessed the victims was furnished by the first body pulled from the river. As the body broke the surface of the water, horrified spectators could clearly see the hands of a second corpse, still clasped in desperation around its neck.

The aftermath of the scow disaster, like that of the Central Viaduct tragedy eight months before (see "Horror of All Horrors" in the author's *They Died Crawling*), furnished scenes unflattering to human character as found in Cleveland. Until an irate policeman read them the riot act, ambulance men from the many competing private morgues of Cleveland fought for possession of the bodies, even fighting with the bereaved relatives. Within scant minutes of the disaster, hundreds of Clevelanders lined the shores of Whiskey Island and the south shore, gawking at the drowned corpses as they were reclaimed and interfering with Cleveland's safety forces. Most fitting was the fate of William Buelow, 28, a curious printer. Hearing of the disaster, he gathered some friends and rushed to the scene. But while running along the dock area at the foot of Detroit Street, he fell off and quickly drowned. He left a wife and two children. Buelow's death might well have been what one of the clergymen who preached funeral orations for the scow dead had in mind when he moralized: "[The disaster] demonstrates the uncertainty of life and shows that we ought always to make the best use of our time."

Although the authorities could never be sure (many of the Ger-

The Plain Dealer,
July 18, 1896.

man laborers' identities were only vaguely known or documented), probably 16 men drowned in the scow disaster. Twenty-seven men survived and most of them, albeit bruised and scratched, were back unloading ore at the C. & P. dock the very next day. All 16 of the identified dead were brought up by crews working with grappling hooks, taken to nearby morgues, and given proper funerals by their grieving families. Most of them left widows, many children, and little savings.

Coroner Arbuckle's inquest the following week was as perfunctory as expected. It simply reiterated conclusions already formed, including: (1) the frail scow was overloaded; (2) most of the men could not swim; (3) mass panic paralyzed most of them; and (4) the skin, hair, and clothes of the ore workers were so impregnated with iron that they might as well have been carrying metal weights when they leaped overboard. Certainly the *Plain Dealer* spoke for established opinion with its editorial the day after the tragedy and even before the inquest opened:

> Recklessness of the men who were anxious to reach their homes was responsible for the terrible disaster Thursday evening. Common prudence would have told these men that the scow was unsafe for so many to ride upon . . . The accident . . . is worse than the viaduct disaster [as] in the present case there will be no person or corporation to pay damages.

So ended the worst, and one of the most obscure, of Cleveland's transportation disasters. It might be a good idea for some labor group to put up a memorial to these dead someday, but in any case, it's something to think about the next time you're motoring past Whiskey Island on the Shoreway or grumbling about how the Cleveland rush hour is just plain murder . . .

Chapter 5

THE MAN WITH THE TWISTED LIFE

The Sad Saga of
Ernst Watzl (1929–1930)

How many people really live the lives they want to live? How many us, stunted or stymied in our jobs or intimate relations, dream of an alternate life in which we are free to claim what experience—often bitter experience—has tutored us to desire? It matters not, of course, how unrealistic and unobtainable such a life might be—what counts is the intensity and desperation of the deferred dream. Gustave Flaubert famously wrote of Emma Bovary, condemned to mundane provincial monotony and ultimately brought to ruin and death by her fantasies of romantic love (and ample pin money). Some decades later, Sir Arthur Conan Doyle articulated a male version of such a reimagined life in the Holmesian tale of "The Man with the Twisted Lip." Like *Madame Bovary*, it was the story of a double life motivated in part by economic need: the narrative of Neville St. Clair, a penurious journalist who discovers he can make a better living by secretly assuming the identity of a pathetic beggar. More comically, James Thurber celebrated a similar escapist fantasy a generation later with his burlesque about Walter Mitty, a henpecked Milquetoast who soothes his shattered *amour propre* with daydreams of masculine derring-do and swashbuckling bravado. Such fantasies are a common human preoccupation and, like thoughts of suicide, help many a tortured man and woman carry on through dreadful nights to face more bleak days.

Every once in a while, however, someone really *does* try to escape to that newly invented, newly perfect, and newly satisfying life so long denied. It may happen more in literature than in reality. It may happen more now than it used to—especially given the decreased social and financial sanctions on divorce and bankruptcy enjoyed by us moderns. But it does happen and always did, at least to those who were willing to take the risks.

Dr. Ernst Watzl was just such a person. He dreamed of a better life and a more passionate, purer love than he had ever known. He dreamed and dared to bring that life and love to pass—and he paid the price with his life and reputation when it came crashing down around his ears. While the tale of Dr. Watzl may not be an edifying one, it will not be found wanting in human drama or those aspects of the freakish beloved by students of human affairs.

The man with the twisted life: Ernst Watzl, 1929.

As far as the public was concerned, the Watzl affair began at 6:37 on the evening of Wednesday, November 6, 1929. Several passengers on a Reading Railroad passenger coach were looking out the windows of the Philadelphia-bound train at that hour when they noticed an automobile in flames on the banks of the nearby Schuylkill River. It was dark, the spot was out in the middle of nowhere, and the railway passengers, including Dr. Raymond Blesgen, Leonard Howard, John Tyson, and Joseph Statler, thought little of the burning auto. Their thoughts were focused on their impending arrival in Pottstown, Pennsylvania, four miles north, and they thought no more of it at the time than a Clevelander would of seeing an object aflame in the desolation of Kingsbury Run through the view afforded by an RTA window seat.

The burning car was brought forcefully back to their minds, however, when police officials from Pottstown and the nearby town of Royersford discovered its burnt wreckage the next day. There wasn't much of it left: the fire had burned so fiercely that its glass windshield, windows, and instrument panel had completely melted, and much of its steel frame had been fractured by the heat. There was no trace of a driver or passenger in the ruins of the car, but, disquietingly, there was a set of distinct footprints leading right into the Schuylkill River . . . and not returning. It looked bad, and the discovery of four suspicious-looking cans in what was left of the back seat immediately suggested to the Pottstown and Royersford police that the fire had been spurred by an accelerant. The only other evidence, other than the four train witnesses who soon came forward, was the rear license plate, still intact and readable. Traced to Cleveland by Royersford chief of police Jesse Neiman, the car was found to be registered to Dr. Ernst Watzl of 1719 Preyer Road, Cleveland Heights. But there was no trace of Watzl, except perhaps the ominous tread of the footprints leading to the river, fully 500 feet wide at the site of the wrecked auto.

The news of his disappearance came as a shock to both the doctor's family and friends. Well known in the Cleveland professional community, chemist Ernst Watzl had carefully earned an esteemed reputation in both scientific and social circles during his three years in Cleveland. Respected by such civic figures as City Manager

Scenes from Ernst Watzl's fatal attraction.
Cleveland News, April 25, 1930.

William R. Hopkins and Republican party mogul Maurice Maschke, the 41-year-old scientist had worked for the Cleveland Water Department and was considered a world authority on the subject of water purification and filtration. Reputed to be a tireless experimenter, he owned several patents and was considered a genius by virtually all who knew him. Indeed, Hopkins had only recently been considering Watzl's newly invented "American Dechlor" purification process for Cleveland, admiring the effectiveness of the charcoal filtration but rejecting it on the ground of its considerable cost.

But there was much more to Dr. Ernst Watzl than just his image as a sort of exotically foreign Gyro Gearloose of Cleveland. Born in 1888, the scion of an Austrian military family, the suavely charming Ernst had been educated during the early years of the century at the University of Heidelberg and later at a graduate chemistry school in Zurich, Switzerland. Always a passionate man, it was said that the ever-monocled, always heel-clicking Ernst sported dueling scars from those student days, not to mention a few more grievous wounds earned in real affairs of honor. Watzl's scientific brilliance had been recognized from an early age, and in 1912 he was recruited by the Austrian government to emigrate to the United States and learn all that he could about scientific and manufacturing techniques with military applications. His efforts eventually brought him to Cleveland, where in 1913 he married Marie Cahill. A year later, their daughter Herta was born.

When the First World War broke out in August 1914, Ernst and his wife returned to Austria. He spent the next four years in a liquid fire unit, developing and using flamethrowers against Italian troops in the fighting that raged on Austria's Alpine frontier. In a 1928 speech to a Cleveland meeting of the Army Officers Association, Watzl would recall with pride the occasion when he demonstrated flamethrowers to the German Kaiser, Wilhelm III, and his entourage, all present being dressed in asbestos suits. By the time the war ended in disaster for his native country, Watzl had become a major, come close to being court-martialed for refusing to fight against American troops, and acquired enough grisly memories to give him vivid nightmares for the rest of his life. After the war, he plunged himself back into scientific work, gradually achieving some repute—if not riches—as an expert on water treatment and, in particular, the use of carbon in filtration technology. Another daughter, Jane, was born in 1921, and in 1926, 38-year-old Ernst brought his family to Cleveland, hoping to find there the fame and fortune that had eluded him in Europe.

Although Ernst always maintained a brave public front, it would be clear, at least in retrospect, that things didn't quite work out for him in Cleveland. Working incessantly, often for days and nights on end without sleep, Watzl burnished his reputation as a water purification expert and managed to patent a number of his ideas. President of the Watzl-Schweitzer water filtration company, he worked as a consulting engineer for the Grasselli Chemical Company, the Bailey Meter Company, and the Cleveland utilities department while he tried hard to sell his American Dechlor purification process to municipal water systems around the country. But he never seemed to achieve the success that he desired or thought commensurate with his worth and with the quasi-aristocratic status he had enjoyed in his fatherland.

Not that anyone in Cleveland knew of his seething discontent. Mixing in the highest social and political circles, Dr. Ernst Watzl was well known as a sophisticated, witty, and learned bon vivant, painter, aviation enthusiast, fencer, and linguist. He was affable and courteous to a fault to all who met him in Cleveland and elsewhere. Such persons would discover only after his death that the good doctor despised almost all Americans, dismissing them harshly as "mostly hypocrites."

No one, seemingly, was more surprised at Watzl's disappearance than his wife Marie. She told police that he had left home on Sunday, October 27, on a business trip to Philadelphia. Watzl's journey had two supposed purposes. One was to conduct some tests of his new filtration process on some "dirty" water he hoped to find in secluded areas of the Pennsylvania countryside near Philadelphia. For that purpose, Watzl had loaded his car with chemicals necessary for the tests. His other goal was to secure employment as a consulting engineer with the Philadelphia Water Department. Ernst told Marie he had reason to believe that he could get a $12,000-a-year position there. The catch was that he needed to pay a $5,000 bribe to persons with political influence in the City of Brotherly Love. He also told Marie that he hoped to sell city officials the rights to his new filtration process. Marie would recall that he seemed confident of success on both counts, and to that end he borrowed the $5,000 from a banker friend—offering no security—and departed for Philadelphia in his automobile early on the afternoon of Sunday, October 27.

The next person to see Watzl was Walter Rudge, a 22-year-old Youngstown resident. He was standing on the corner of Euclid Avenue and East 105th waiting for the Youngstown bus when

Watzl beckoned to him and asked if he needed a ride. The surprised Rudge accepted the stranger's offer, and he listened with curiosity during the next two hours as the courtly Watzl boasted of his plans and expected success. "I'm on my way to Philadelphia," he told Rudge. "There's a contract as consulting engineer to the city waiting for me and I'm going to sign it. You'll also be seeing several articles about me in the Cleveland newspapers." He further related his contempt for most Americans and blamed his lack of deserved professional success in Cleveland on political interference and antiforeign prejudice.

Rudge was so impressed with Watzl that he invited the scientist to dinner at his house when they got to Youngstown. After the meal, just before he left, Watzl told Rudge he was going to meet with a German friend in Philadelphia who had come all the way from Switzerland to meet him. Watzl's farewell was a memorable set piece, well known to Cleveland acquaintances familiar with the doctor's Continental style. "When he said goodbye to my mother," Rudge recalled, "he clicked his heels together, extended his hand, and bowed smartly from the waist. Gosh! It startled me."

Ernst had told his wife Marie that he was staying at the Vendig Hotel in Philadelphia and that he was going to visit a friend there, a Dr. Bennett Hill of 2514 Race Street. He also told Marie he was going to try to sell his services to the Mutual Water Company of Philadelphia. Investigators would later discover that Watzl never registered at the Vendig, that there was no Dr. Bennett Hill on Race Street, and that there was no Mutual Water Company anywhere near Philadelphia. Little more than that is known of Watzl's actual activities during his 10-day sojourn in Philadelphia except that he never talked to anyone in the city water department and that he bought four one-gallon canisters of oxygen from the Air Reduction Sales Company of Philadelphia the day before his burning car was found.

Whatever else Watzl was doing in Philadelphia between October 27 and November 6, he apparently did nothing to arouse his wife's suspicions. An almost daily stream of letters and telegrams sent to their Cleveland Heights home assured her that he was confident about the water department job and that his water purification experiments were going well. In his last letter to Marie, postmarked 2 P.M. on Wednesday, November 6, Watzl told Marie the job was finally nailed down. He was going out to a secluded

Schuylkill River area to procure the suitably "dirty water" he needed for what he termed "the greatest experiment" of his life. His last words were for his daughter, Herta, telling her that he would be home by Sunday with promised presents in hand.

After talking with Marie Watzl and learning of Ernst's Philadelphia quest, the local police, led by Chief Jesse Neiman of Royersford, began to formulate theories to fit their incomplete evidence. The first hypothesis was simple, accidental death: chemicals, probably the liquid oxygen canisters purchased by Watzl on Wednesday, had exploded in his car and Watzl had staggered alive out of the flames only to drown in the Schuylkill River. A variant theory was that Watzl had escaped both the flames and the water and was safe somewhere, perhaps suffering from amnesia or too badly injured to contact his family. The most popular and ominous theory, spurred by Marie's revelation that Ernst had left Cleveland with $5,000 in traveler's checks, was that Ernst had met with foul play. Criminal elements, Neiman reasoned, had deceived Watzl into thinking they represented the Philadelphia water department and had lured him to a remote area, robbed him, killed him, and set his car on fire to hide the evidence of their crime.

It's easy to see why Neiman and other local lawmen were quick to embrace the last and most lurid of their theories. Watzl was missing, his $5,000 was unaccounted for, the automobile fire had been one of uncommon ferocity, and there were no witnesses to whatever had happened by the riverbank, a location at least a mile from the nearest occupied dwelling. And the predatory gangster theory gained heft when Pottstown police patrolman James Laughead encountered a mysterious (and ultimately unidentified) stranger who told him of seeing two men pushing an automobile on the evening of November 6 on the deserted river road near where the burned auto was found. The theory was further amplified by Philadelphia engineer Ottamar Strange, who had talked to Watzl earlier in the week and suspected that he was dealing with "the wrong crowd." An ominous detail was added by Marie Watzl, who said that her husband always carried a pistol in his car, hidden between the front seats. There was no trace of the weapon in the wreck.

Both the gangster and accident theories collapsed utterly within three days. After reading about Watzl's disappearance in the newspapers, James Bernhard of 2233 North Leithgow Street in

Philadelphia contacted the police. He told them that he had been approached by a stranger resembling Watzl on the evening of November 1. The man had offered him $50 for use of his birth certificate and name.

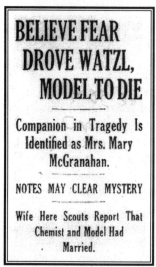

BELIEVE FEAR DROVE WATZL, MODEL TO DIE

Companion in Tragedy Is Identified as Mrs. Mary McGranahan.

NOTES MAY CLEAR MYSTERY

Wife Here Scouts Report That Chemist and Model Had Married.

Cleveland News,
April 25, 1930.

The stranger, who eventually displayed three passports to Bernhard, all of them made out to "Ernst Watzl," explained that he needed a false passport to get back into South America. He had been there before, Watzl explained, but had been kicked out and needed a false name and valid birth certificate to gain entry again. When Watzl returned the next day, Bernhard was unable to find the needed birth certificate, but Watzl flashed his roll of $5,000 in traveler's checks and told him his $50 offer still stood and that he would be back "one of these days." When Bernhard described his stranger as about 5 feet, 7 inches, 155 pounds, with a smooth, thin face, gray eyes, brown hair, tortoiseshell glasses, a gold plate in his upper jaw, and wearing a brown suit and brown hat, the Pottstown police knew they had their man. A day later, after learning that a man resembling Watzl had walked into the Bungalow Inn at 7 P.M. on Wednesday, November 6—just two miles from the site of the burned car—Chief Neiman and all the other Pennsylvania authorities called off their search. Deciding that Watzl had tried to fake his own death, Neiman expressed the official consensus that Watzl was "willfully missing." On Sunday, November 10, he wrote: "I have abandoned my previous belief that Dr. Watzl might have been murdered for the $5,000 he was carrying and think he has sailed under an assumed name to some foreign port and has not been the victim of an accident or foul play. Probably he took this means to avoid a row at home because I understand Mrs. Watzl objected to his leaving the country."

Two more pieces of news breaking that same weekend further bolstered the growing conviction that Ernst Watzl had tried to fake his own death. One was the discovery, apparently leaked by his friends, that Watzl had led something of a double life in Cleveland. For some time, it seems, he had maintained a secret art studio on

East 79th Street, where, under the name of "Ernst Vonderau," he had pursued his long-standing passion for painting. The revelation that his art sessions might have included the pursuit of other passions was suggested by the existence of a beautiful, blonde 20-year-old stenographer/model named Mrs. Mary Horvath McGranahan, who, it further developed, had been known to model nude for the good Dr. Vonderau. When Cleveland police interviewed her in mid-November, she seemed unconcerned and casually observed that she thought the missing Dr. Watzl would "be all right." The other revelation was that Dr. Watzl, or at least someone signing his name, had cashed all $5,000 of his traveler's checks on Wednesday, November 6.

Faced with these facts less than a week after his disappearance, the Pennsylvania police gave up their manhunt for Dr. Watzl, despite Marie Watzl's continuing insistence that he had been murdered or kidnapped. The newspapers, too, lost interest in Watzl's vanishing, not even mentioning the curious, unexplained disappearance of Mary McGranahan from Cleveland on December 8. But there were at least two parties still intensely interested in Watzl's fate: the John Hancock Insurance Company of Boston and the Equitable Life Insurance Company of New York. Between them, the two companies had carried a total of $60,000 on Watzl—neither of them excluding suicide—and they were naturally suspicious about his car fire, which had obviously been encouraged by the contents of the four oxygen canisters.

The suspicions of the insurance investigators were confirmed on December 24, when the two companies received policy renewal checks totaling $360 on Watzl's coverage. Mailed from New York, the valid checks were signed by "Charles Warner," but investigators proved to their satisfaction that they were typed on Dr. Watzl's personal typewriter. Handwriting experts assured them that the signatures were in a feminine hand. Insurance investigators now began to fan out to ports in North America, searching for evidence that the well-insured doctor had fled the country. By this time they were probably also looking for Mary McGranahan, who was still missing from Cleveland. They may even have talked to her estranged husband James at his house at 9622 Silk Avenue. If they did, it was not reported in the newspapers. But in early February 1930, two months after his wife's disappearance, James filed for divorce in Cuyahoga County Common Pleas Court. More interest-

ingly, he also filed a $100,000 alienation of affection suit against
the missing Dr. Watzl.

Whatever Marie Watzl may have said or thought, James
McGranahan was sure that his missing spouse had vamoosed with
her courtly employer. James and Mary had quarreled frequently
over her work for Dr. Watzl, especially the nude modeling sessions
in the East 79th Street studio. At one time he had persuaded Watzl
to promise that he would stop seeing Mary, but their meetings had
continued. In early 1929, Mary demanded a divorce but James
talked her out of it. In August she returned from a trip to Girard,
Pennsylvania, with Watzl and told her husband that they had sworn
a pact to throw themselves under the wheels of a locomotive, but
Watzl had backed out of the mutual suicide at the last moment.

If Marie Watzl knew anything about the relations between her
husband and Mary McGranahan, she preserved a reticent silence,
even after the lawsuits were filed. Clinging to the possibility that he
had amnesia or was held captive somewhere, she merely said, "My
husband counted heavily on the Philadelphia deal going through.
Its failure may have had very injurious effects on him." Meanwhile,
Mary's mother, Mrs. Julia Horvath, filed a cross-petition in her
own divorce suit against Mary's father, Paul Horvath, repudiating
Paul's assertion that she had encouraged her daughter's presumably wayward behavior with Dr. Watzl.

Four months of suspense ended on March 24, 1930, when a
cable from the police in Vienna, Austria, disclosed that Dr. Ernst
Watzl and Mary McGranahan had been found shot to death on a
bed in the Hotel Sacher there. Registered as "Johann Flassak and
wife" on March 20, Ernst and Mary had not been seen in 24 hours
when the suspicious hotel staff broke down the door of their suite.
When they entered, Mary was lying stretched out on the bed with
a bullet wound through her heart. Crumpled face down beside her
with his arm around her was Watzl, also dead from a bullet through
the heart. The bodies were quite cold. The bullet that had killed
Mary was found in the mattress beneath her; the slug that ended
Watzl's life was lying on the floor. Near it was the gun Watzl had
used on both of them, the 1915 Steyr high-caliber automatic that he
had carried during World War I. Strewn about the room were a
number of farewell notes explaining the details of their dramatic
elopement and suicide.

Watzl's farewell letter to Richard Bernkop, an Austrian government official and former army comrade, contained the fullest explanation of his dramatic end. In it he told of meeting Mary at a Cleveland art reception and falling "in love with her immediately." He admitted faking his fatal-looking accident in Pennsylvania but claimed it was done only so Marie and their two children would get the $60,000 in insurance money. Obtaining fake birth certificates and passports in New York after Mary joined him there in early December, the pair had been bigamously married in St. Louis on December 30 under the names of "Johann Flassak" and "Josefa Kropej" by justice of the peace Harry Pfeifer. They had tried to hide out in Canada, but after they were almost caught there by insurance detectives, they decided to leave the country. Boarding the Japanese passenger liner *Shidzuoka Maru* in Seattle on January 11, 1930, they had spent the next two months on a whirlwind "honeymoon" tour of Japan, Sumatra, India, Arabia, Egypt, Africa, France, Italy, and Austria.

By the time they arrived in Austria in late March, Ernst and Mary had nearly exhausted the $5,000 that Watzl had used to finance his disappearance. By Saturday, March 23, they were hard pressed to pay their bill at the Hotel Sacher. That afternoon they went for a walk in the romantic Vienna Woods and committed themselves to a mutual suicide pact. Wracked by guilt over his abandonment of Marie and his children, Ernst was only too aware that an insurance policy for $35,000 would lapse after March 25 due to nonpayment. So that afternoon, as they walked in the woods, they agreed to pay the last premium and then kill themselves together on the bed in their hotel room. As Watzl summarized it to Richard Bernkop, there was no other acceptable course of conduct:

> We were faced with two alternatives: Either go to my parents and relatives and ask assistance and confess my misdemeanors, or to commit suicide. I preferred the latter . . . Thus my wife will be robbed unless I die today.

Although he did not say so, Watzl's decision may have been prompted by word from his sister that the Austrian authorities were aware of his presence in Vienna and were about to arrest him and Mary for bigamy. And in a final gesture to her parents, Mary took out a $2,000 policy with the Vienna Municipal Insurance Company naming her mother as beneficiary. Unlike Watzl's policies, it would never be paid off, as it was bought under a false name and did not include suicide coverage.

Watzl's farewell letter to his wife expressed in emotional terms his horrible guilt at what he had done to her:

> I want to thank you for all your kindness, love and patience and loyalty that you have shown me for so many years. Forgive me if you can for what I did. I thought honestly that you and the children would be happier with me gone and some safe income, even if small, in case my "accident" had turned out luckily. As it didn't [because the insurance companies lacked proof of his death], I think I lost my head, made a thousand plans, foolishness, but could not drown that feeling of Ehre (honor) that somewhere must have been in my system all along. I have tried to keep Mary out of the unhappy ending, but she wants also to pay the price and thinks you wont think so harshly on her on that account. I hope that your children will make you happy. Goodby Dear, Ernst.

Mary's last letter to her mother was far more upbeat. Asserting that she loved Ernst "more than my life and I want to die with him," she went on to say that she had enjoyed "a delightful time" during their months of flight and that she did not fear death:

> Do not worry about me dying. It is really nothing. Ernst will go with me. Everyone has to die. I had a delightful time. We went all over the world. It was like heaven . . . I am very proud that I am not afraid of dying.

Referring to the subject of her recent world travels, she ended, "So you see I did live about 30 years in this three months. I was happier than I have ever been before."

Newspaper interviews with Mary's mother and sisters confirmed the sentiments in Mary's farewell missives. Claiming that Mary had endured an unhappy marriage, Julia Horvath defended both her daughter and Mary's older paramour:

> Mary met Dr. Watzl because she had to support herself. She advertised for home typing. Dr. Watzl gave her work to do. After Mary had sued her husband for divorce, he came back to Cleveland and persuaded her to come back to him again. Neither had

a job. Then Mary took a job as temporary stenographer with Dr. Watzl. Dr. Watzl was kind to Mary. He visited our home here sometimes. Mary's husband got jealous. Several times they separated. They were separated when Mary went away to join Dr. Watzl. She was not breaking faith with anyone. I do not blame her for falling in love with Dr. Watzl. Her sisters do not blame her. He was courteous and sympathetic . . . Mary has said that she wanted once to be happy and then she did not care what happened. I hope they will put their ashes together. They died together, in death they should be with each other.

Not everyone, of course, agreed with Mrs. Horvath's romantic interpretation of the matter. One of the dissenters was Franz Watzl, Ernst's horrified father, who had not even known his son was back in Vienna. Two days after the discovery of the bodies in the hotel room, he had Ernst's corpse cremated and interred in the family vault, in the Central Cemetery at Neusift. At the same time, Mary's body was quietly buried in consecrated ground, pending settlement of the bickering amongst her next of kin. Eventually, both families came around, and by the fall of 1930, the ashes of the dead lovers were mingled at last. In September of that year, Marie Watzl granted one last interview to an inquiring *Cleveland Press* reporter, in which she disclosed her plans to leave Cleveland forever, and admitted that she had known about Ernst's affair with Mary all along.

Maybe Ernst and Mary got what they wanted in the end. According to her family, Mary was quite sincere in her final protestations that she did not fear death. One of the letters found in their hotel room was a joint epistle to Udayasingh Rana, a mystic Hindu sage of Baroda, India. It seems that Ernst and Mary had visited him on their trip around the world and imbibed deeply of his reincarnation philosophies. Maybe—and maybe not. Dr. Ernst Watzl, whatever his internal conflicts, was a consummate actor, as proven by his construction of the double life he had lived during the last months of his life. Perhaps in the days after his Pottstown "accident" he suffered inklings that he had committed an act of irretrievable folly. In a letter to a Cleveland friend, James Kirby of the *Cleveland Press*, written shortly after his disappearance and purporting to be written by an anonymous "friend" of Dr. Watzl's, the tormented chemist wrote what may have been the real truth about his unhappy life and reckless affair:

This concerns the death of Dr. Ernst Watzl or Von Der Au as he called himself. I met him in a German restaurant only a week ago. Now I read in the newspapers that he has been murdered. This is his story: Unusual bringing up in a Viennese family, university in Switzerland, intellectual friends, artists and wanderlust which is in the family. Then a life of unrest, changing interests, invention, creating. Married to the finest woman in the world. Then the war. A vagabond, he called himself. The last year or so he discovered shortcomings in his makeup. He was sure to have been a failure. Only an inventor—a dreamer—not doing the right things for his family . . . He had tried a love affair, but the experience with a silly, dull youngster left him disgusted with himself. He had thought of quitting this life, but hated to go and have his wife and children thinking of him as a failure . . . Then he developed his death plan to me smilingly. He would write home that he had made a new and bigger discovery . . . would buy a gallon of liquid air openly and a shock from a small accident would explode this wonderful chemical, tearing him to shreds. He would die a pioneer and leave his family in better circumstances than when he had lived.

Dr. Ernst Watzl's gothic life came to an end in a Vienna hotel room, not in a burned automobile by the side of the Schuylkill River. And whether he repented of his rash scheme for a new life or his involvement with an uneducated woman only half his age is unknown. But he left behind a Cleveland legend to place beside that of his romantic and royal model, Crown Prince Rudolf of Habsburg, whose double suicide with his own inappropriate mistress, Marie Vetsera, shocked the well-born milieu of the newborn Ernst Watzl in 1889.

Chapter 6

"THEY'LL NEVER TAKE ME ALIVE!"

The 1906 Slaughter of Mary Shepard

If it had taken place in the hills of West Virginia, it would have made a great murder ballad, the kind of mournful hillbilly dirge revived by the likes of Doc Watson or the young Bob Dylan. It had all the awful elements: a good girl, a bad boy, love gone wrong, and a shocking denouement climaxing in murder and suicide. But it happened in the hills of Mayfield Township (now Mayfield Heights), not West Virginia. And it was back when Teddy Roosevelt was president and big-city Cleveland was a long way from Stop 16A on the Cleveland and Eastern Mayfield Road interurban line. As Mayfield evolved into a bedroom suburb, the saga was soon forgotten and filed away with other local antiquities like the 'ole swimming hole, and the flour mills once turned by the power of the Chagrin River. That's a shame, because the circumstances of the Mary Shepard murder were as sad and shocking as you could find in the annals of Cuyahoga County.

It should have been a storybook romance. Mary Shepard and Harry Smith met when they were 15. Fourth cousins, they were both the children of respectable farmers whose families had lived in the area for generations. Mary's father, Albert Shepard, was a hard-working widower who farmed on Orange Hill. Harry's father, James Smith, was a Warrensville Township trustee. Immediately smitten, Harry and Mary were inseparable from the start and considered "engaged" to each other by all. The attraction seemed natural enough: Mary was sweet, bright, and pretty, while Harry was good-looking and affable. But love's young bloom began to wither after Harry quit school and moved to Cleveland at the turn of the century. Unlike Mary, who believed in higher education, he was already working for the Phillips-Lander Dairy Company on Kins-

Scenes and characters from the Shepard tragedy.
Cleveland Press, October 11, 1906.

man Road in Cleveland and saw no need to better himself with further schooling. Mary, a graduate of Chagrin Falls High School, had
loftier goals and before long was teaching in the Chagrin, Orange,
and Mayfield Township schools. Whatever their feelings and intentions, they began to drift apart, and it wasn't just over Mary's high-
falutin' ambitions. City life had coarsened the susceptible Harry.
He began to drink to excess and use profanity freely, even in
Mary's company. He also grew fiercely jealous and began to
upbraid Mary for her supposed unfaithfulness. Before long, his
dissipated behavior and increasingly bellicose disposition had driven away all of his friends except Mary. She clung to him as long
as she could, despite his increasing brutality to her. But the last
straw came in late 1905, when an inebriated Harry struck her in a
jealous fit at a dance in Warrensville Township. When the bruised
Mary told her doting father, Harry was barred from the Shepard
house forever. Harry then began sliding into the emotional downward spiral that would doom them both.

Mary probably sensed what was coming. Her friends knew that she was terrified of the despondent Harry. He had already made some vague threats against her, and his heavy drinking was obvious to all who saw him during the last days of September 1906. But Harry's fatal decision probably wasn't made until he showed up at District Number 3 School, where Mary taught, just west of SOM Center on the south side of Mayfield Road. It was an early autumn afternoon and she had her children in recess outside. Visibly upset to see him, Mary stared for a moment, then turned and led the children back into the one-room schoolhouse. Students of Mary's murder would later conclude that it was the moment when Mary purposefully closed the door on Harry that he decided to kill her.

Wednesday, October 10, was a school day like any other for the 17 young pupils in Mary Shepard's classroom. Lunchtime was over, and the first-graders were reciting from their readers. At about 1:15 P.M., Marvin Parker was reading aloud his lesson for the day:

> The warm west will bring sunny hours.
> It will bring busy bees and—

Parker was interrupted by a loud knock on the door of the class vestibule. Mary paled visibly but said only, "Wait a minute, Marvin," and walked, trembling, to the door. Seconds later she was followed by Alden Hare, 10, who wanted to see who Mary's visitor was. He got to the door, but it was closed on him by a grim-looking stranger, who said, "Go back. Keep out of here." No more than a minute later, two shots shattered the dutiful quiet of the schoolroom.

The first thing the children heard after the shots was Mary Shepard's voice crying, "Oh, Maggie! Maggie!" (Maggie was one of her older students.) It was followed by another cry of "Oh, children! Children!" and then the frightened children heard the sound of Mary's body hitting the floor of the cloakroom next to the vestibule. Esther Leipmeyer was the first one to push her way into the cloakroom, where she stumbled over Mary Shepard's bloody, dead body. She began screaming and was soon joined in her noisy terror by her 16 classmates. Within seconds, the schoolhouse emptied as the frightened children ran for their homes as fast as they could.

MAYFIELD SCHOOL HOUSE, SCENE OF MURDER

Cleveland News, October 11, 1906.

Although none of the children had recognized Harry Smith, there was a posse looking for him only 15 minutes after he shot Mary Shepard twice through the head with a .38 caliber revolver. Harry was well known to the Mayfield Township farmers, and, as in any small community, they knew about his drinking and his poisoned relations with Mary. They might even have caught him in the schoolyard as he hung around there, revolver in hand, staring vacantly for some minutes after killing Mary. Finally, he was confronted by a truculently brave Alden Hare, who demanded, "What did you want with teacher?" "I've seen teacher," replied Harry, "and now you go." The exchange seemed to bring Harry to his senses, and he bolted toward the nearby woods.

It was easy for the armed Mayfield farmers to track Harry through the early October snow as he ran through patches of woods and meadow to the east. The first posse caught up to him three miles from the schoolhouse. When they told him to surrender, he answered with a fusillade from two revolvers. The six-man posse responded with an impressive barrage, but Harry had the best of it, putting a bullet through the hand of Frank Thorp. While the rest of the posse tended to Frank, Harry got away into the woods to the east. Several more miles brought him to Stop 25 on the Chagrin Falls interurban line.

Conductor R. H. Adams knew Smith well, so he wasn't surprised when the breathless Harry jumped aboard his westbound car at about 3 P.M. They chatted for some minutes until the car stopped at a switch. At that moment, a second posse came up in a buggy. Deputy Sheriff Frank Buckingham pointed frantically at Smith in the car window. When Adams asked Harry what they were pointing at, Harry whipped out his revolver. "I shot Mary," he said. "I had to do it." He forced Adams to put the car in motion and kept his gun aimed at the conductor as they pulled away and sped toward Cleveland.

Several miles later, Harry jumped off at Stop 21, practically in front of his father's Warrensville home. What occurred there afterward is a matter of dispute. Some sources claim that Harry's father and mother had already been telephoned with news of his crime. Other accounts insist that Harry broke the news to them, shouting, "I've done it now! She was false! They'll never take me alive!" At this point, although he would not admit it to the police later, Harry's father apparently struggled with his son for one of the revolvers. It went off, putting a bullet in the wall but injuring no one.

Harry was as good as his alleged word. Deputy Sheriff Buckingham and his posse got to James Smith's house about 5 P.M. James Smith handed his son one of his revolvers, then met the officers at the front door with a shotgun and said, "You can't come in here except over my dead body." Buckingham backed away and his men decided to wait it out. They didn't have to wait long. Harry watched from the house windows as more and more deputies arrived and positioned themselves with guns around the house. A few minutes after 5 P.M., Harry ran out the back door toward a small blacksmith shed at the back of the Smith lot. When he got there, he looked around to see an armed policeman only 10 feet away. Harry Smith put his revolver to his head—and blew his brains out. His mother, watching in horror at a house window, saw him do it. His lifeless body fell to the snow, where James Smith picked him up and carried him into the house.

The aftermath of the Shepard tragedy had touches worthy of its macabre climax. Bert Shepard, Mary's brother, arrived at the Smith house shortly after Harry killed himself. Refusing to believe that Smith was dead, he would not leave until a reluctant James Smith allowed him to see the bloody corpse. The funeral services for Mary and Harry were as quiet and dignified as possible under the lurid circumstances. But hundreds of curious strangers crowded

Harry's funeral at the Smith residence in Warrensville, where the Reverend George C. Griffin dwelt, understandably, on the grief of the parents, rather than the virtues of the deceased. The funerals were both originally scheduled for Saturday, October 13, but Harry's had to be bumped forward a day, as most of the mourners and even the pallbearers needed to attend both services. Harry was buried in the Warrensville East Cemetery, while Mary, after the biggest funeral in Mayfield Township history, was laid to rest in the Orange Hill cemetery not far from her father's home. Her 17 pupils were allowed to lead the funeral procession and accompanied her coffin to the grave.

Meanwhile, thousands of curious Clevelanders had already turned the District Number 3 schoolhouse into a muddy shambles, trampling in acres of mud and smashing furniture and fixtures in their mad haste to view the murder site.

Chapter 7

DEATH IN THE DEEP PIT

The 1928 Terminal Tower Tragedy

As Clevelanders we walk and motor through a death-drenched landscape. Progress never comes without a human price, and it is impossible to find a block in Greater Cleveland that does not have a tale of suffering and death somewhere in its history. (If you disbelieve that assertion, you might try one of the author's occasional trolley tours of Cleveland murder/disaster sites.) The construction of all the high-level bridges linking the East and West sides involved accidental deaths and injuries, from the genesis of the Superior Viaduct in the 1870s to the completion of the Main Avenue bridge in 1939. The erection of Cleveland's signature buildings, too, exacted their toll of dead and maimed, especially such illustrious structures as the Old Arcade, the Scofield Building, and the first Hollenden Hotel. But there is no more celebrated structure in Cleveland than the Terminal Tower—and it is therefore fitting that it was the site of the most sensational and poignant construction accident in Forest City history: the unintended concrete burial that took the lives of Patrick Toolis and Patrick Cleary.

It was, perhaps, inevitable, that some lives would be consumed in a project as large as the epic Terminal construction. It lasted seven years from groundbreaking to completion, requiring the razing of over a thousand existing structures. A mini-city of viaducts was created to support the network of streets (Ontario and Prospect for starters) that bounded the 52-story Union Terminal and its department store/hotel adjuncts. Much of the most dangerous toil involved the deep excavations for the Terminal, especially the 200-foot-plus borings down to the bedrock that supported the massive tower. Someone was going to get hurt sooner or later, and with record levels of cheap immigrant labor, it was likely to be sooner.

Southwest corner of the Terminal Tower excavation,
October 13, 1926.

An ominous harbinger of the 1928 tragedy came without warning at noon on June 9, 1926. Several men laboring in a concrete
well 192 feet deep had just returned to the surface at Ontario when
the entire Public Square area was shaken by a powerful explosion
originating in the well. The force of the blast knocked down workers within a 200-foot radius of the well. The central downtown area
was filled with noxious smoke. There were no fatalities, although
eight injured men were taken to the hospital as thousands of curious onlookers surged against police lines for a better look at the
damage. It was later surmised that one of the returning workmen
had lit a cigarette just as the elevator brought him to the surface,
igniting a seam of methane gas that his crew had discovered below
only minutes before. The wreckage was swept up, the gas pumped
out, and the enormous project ground on.

October 16, 1928, was a pleasant autumn day. It was already
dark at 7:30 P.M. as dozens of men toiled like so many purposeful
ants in the vast acreage of the Terminal excavation. Much of their

Desperate rescuers at the top of the Terminal death pit,
October 17, 1928

effort was devoted to digging deep shafts for the massive pillars
supporting the viaduct of the rerouted Prospect Avenue running
between Ontario Street and Superior behind the rising Terminal
Tower. (Cleveland folklore has it that the depth of the Terminal
support shafts was mandated by the presence of "quicksand" in the
area; it was not quicksand but rather varying levels of more or less
wet clay.) Seventy of the shafts had already been poured without
incident, so there was no reason for laborers Patrick Toolis, 29, and
Patrick Cleary, 27, to be alarmed. True, they were at the bottom of
their pit, 103 feet below the future junction of Prospect and Superior Avenue. But there was enough air to breathe for their scheduled stint, and they were just rounding out the bell-shaped bottom
of the shaft with their shovels so that its concrete fill could begin
and they could move on to another shaft.

Like most workplace accidents, theirs happened with sickening
suddenness. An identical 103-foot shaft next to the one holding
Toolis and Cleary was in the process of being filled with liquid con-

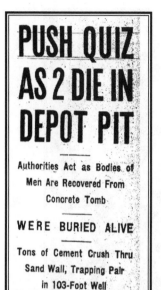

PUSH QUIZ AS 2 DIE IN DEPOT PIT

Authorities Act as Bodies of
Men Are Recovered From
Concrete Tomb

WERE BURIED ALIVE

Tons of Cement Crush Thru
Sand Wall, Trapping Pair
in 103-Foot Well

BURIED ALIVE

Cleveland Press,
October 17, 1928.

crete. All that lay between the two shafts was the lining of their own shaft, four feet of earth (which narrowed to two feet at the bottom), and the second shaft lining. As protection, it wasn't enough. At about 7:30 P.M., 150 tons of liquid concrete from the second shaft burst through its lining, drove through two feet of dirt, smashed through the second lining, and began pouring onto the stunned Cleary and Toolis. There was one startled cry from the bottom, heard by a man on a scaffold higher up in the shaft . . . and then nothing but ominous silence as the streaming concrete found its equilibrium, settled . . . and began to harden.

Reaction was instantaneous at the top of the dig. Cleary and Toolis's fellow workers rushed to the shaft and began descending, buckets in hand, in shifts of three. It was cramped and claustrophobic 60 feet down in the shaft where they were working, which was only six feet in diameter, and there were at least 40 feet of rapidly hardening concrete on top of Toolis and Cleary. But the work went on desperately all that night and into the day as word of the disaster spread and more and more workers arrived to lend a hand to rescue efforts. Deeper and deeper they penetrated, boring inch by inch, first with buckets, then with chisels, and finally with pneumatic drills as the concrete firmed to rocklike hardness. Frantic efforts to maneuver a steam shovel into place to speed up the concrete removal proved fruitless due to the terrain and mechanical congestion of the Terminal excavation.

Even the most optimistic of the rescuers must have known how it would end. (In fact, Toolis and Cleary probably died from suffocation within 15 minutes at the most.) Although unencumbered by 100 tons of concrete, the rescuers themselves could barely breathe in the thin, methane-contaminated air near the shaft bottom, and the digging crews were soon rotating in 15-minute, and then 10-minute, shifts as exhausted rescuers came gasping back to the top. Finally, after 15 hours of digging, the arm, then the head, and finally the torso of Patrick Toolis appeared. His cement-encrusted body was found hurled against the side of the shaft where the flood of concrete caught him. Toolis's brothers Edward and John and his sister Rita were among those who stared as his stiff corpse was finally unloaded topside. As the Reverend Lawrence Ahearn of St. Ignatius of Antioch Roman Catholic Church administered the last rites, Rita Toolis—who had to be physically restrained from joining the rescuers in the shaft—was led away sobbing from the terrible scene. Patrick was soon reburied, this time in a plot at Calvary Cemetery.

About an hour later, Patrick Cleary's body was uncovered. When the men found him he was standing upright in the shaft bottom, his right hand stretched upward, only inches away from a ring-bolt on a hoist that would have carried him to safety. He had been on the job for only three days when death took him for its own.

The aftermath of the Terminal shaft tragedy was the sour denouement typical of a Cleveland disaster. The first investigating official on the scene, Cleveland police sergeant William F. Moralevitz, filed a report after interviewing eyewitnesses and workers at the project. His report concluded that Toolis and Cleary had been innocent of any negligence and that the shaft collapse was due to faulty construction and bad judgment on the part of the project engineer used by the contractor, the firm of Spencer, White and Prentiss.

Spencer, White and Prentiss, unsurprisingly, conducted their own investigation, and more unsurprisingly still, insisted that the accident was "unavoidable" and probably caused by the unforeseen collapse of an undetected vein of sand.

The city of Cleveland, for its part, maintained its historically casual laissez faire attitude to such industrial/construction catastrophes. When asked whether the city should have insisted on a greater distance between the two shafts, city building commissioner William D. Guion sniffed, "That lies entirely with the engineers. We do not concern ourselves with such construction problems."

Such was not the opinion of Ohio deputy factory and building inspector J. P. Cummings, who noted that the accident could have been avoided if only the construction engineers had waited for the cement in the first shaft to harden before preparing the second. So ended a ghastly chapter in the painful record of those who really built the Cleveland we know today—except for the lawsuits and the $6,500 each awarded to the Toolis and Cleary families.

Cleveland News, October 17, 1928.

Chapter 8

"A QUIET, MIDDLE-AGED MAN"

The 1930 Assassination of Dr. Alfred P. Scully

It's an unkind truth that some people are far more interesting dead than they ever were alive. And there's nothing like an untimely, brutal murder to effect the sudden quickening of interest. Consider the case of Alfred P. Scully. Before the hour of 7:35 P.M. on March 3, 1930, he was just another middle-aged, portly, genial Cleveland physician. He was well liked by a wide range of friends, and admired for a panoply of interests that included art, golf, pugilism, travel, genealogy, radio, charitable giving, and haute cuisine. But no one seems to have found the good Dr. Scully exciting or of personal interest other than as an occasional dining companion or golf buddy. Even his best friend referred to him as "a little pudge of a man." But after 7:35 P.M. on that fatal day, he became the riveting cynosure of a murder mystery that thrilled Clevelanders of the Depression era and offers, to this day, an almost perfect model of the unsolved and insoluble crime.

It all began at the fatal evening hour stated, on the second floor of the Forest City Bank Building, then as now situated at the southwest corner of Detroit Avenue and West 25th. Fellow physician Frederick J. Wood was preparing for his evening appointments in Suite No. 6, when he heard a faint cry. It seemed to issue from Suite No.5 across the hall, where Dr. Scully had his combined living quarters and professional office. Seconds later, Dr. Wood heard a second cry, and he dashed into Scully's reception room. Normally, it was divided from Scully's bedroom by an elaborate partition screen. But the screen was now lying shattered in pieces on the floor, and Dr. Scully, also on the floor, was hardly in better condition. He was bleeding heavily from wounds in his left side and

The victim and his milieu. *Cleveland Press*, March 4, 1928.

head. Scully was still breathing, but Dr. Wood's practiced eye quickly told him that his colleague was beyond help. He immediately called the police, who found Scully dead when they arrived minutes later. On the table next to his body was the book he had been reading when surprised by death: *Ladies of the Underworld.*

Who had done this awful deed? Wood had seen no one in the second-floor hallway except his scheduled patients, Julia E. Kyle and Anna Savage, who arrived at the top of the stairs leading to Detroit Avenue just as he rushed into Dr. Scully's office. Moreover, neither Wood nor anyone else in the vicinity had heard the firing of the two.32 caliber shots that took Scully's life. Frank Heil, a bookkeeper on the second floor, admitted to hearing vague sounds of a scuffle nearby. So did Elizabeth King and Katherine Burke, who lived just above Scully's quarters. But their evidence was as useless as that of Lawrence Maxwell, a druggist working just below Scully's office. Yes, he'd heard a "loud rumbling" at about 7:25 P.M.

But he thought no more of it after the sound died away, especially as he heard "no voices and no shooting."

As the first critical hours after the murder passed, more sensational but equally unhelpful witnesses came forward. One was a 13-year-old boy, who said that a suspicious stranger on Mulberry Street—within a five-minute walk of the murder scene—had asked him directions to the New York Central train station. Another was Vera Fields, who told of a young man oozing blood from a head wound, who came into her West Side restaurant just minutes after Scully's body was found and demanded she call him a cab. An hour before Scully was murdered, Charles Fergus, a cashier working in the bank below Scully's suite, had seen a large man wearing a gray coat and brown fedora leaving the second-floor hallway. A taxi driver told of two excited men who jumped into his cab outside the Forest City building and told him to drive "like hell." More irrelevant still was the tale told by an unidentified matron. Three days after the murder she told police she had seen a "well-dressed man with a sallow complexion" lurking furtively at the entrance of the Forest City building on the murder day—but at 1 P.M., not 7:30.

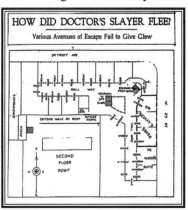

HOW DID DOCTOR'S SLAYER FLEE?
Various Avenues of Escape Fail to Give Clew

Floor plan for the Scully murder, Forest City building, West 25th and Detroit Avenue. *Cleveland Press*, March 5, 1930.

The police had a number of plausible theories but no solid clues. The evidence of his wounds showed that Scully had been beaten severely on the head with a pistol, and then shot once in the side as he continued to grapple with his assailant. The killer had fired the second, mortal shot as Scully lay on the floor and then fled as Scully uttered the series of cries that brought Dr. Wood to his side. Cleveland police detectives surmised—much later—that the unseen killer had evaded capture and even detection by hiding in one of the empty rooms adjacent to Scully's suite. Then, after the hue and cry had abated, the wily murderer slipped out of the building and disappeared—for good.

The police were even more at sea as to likely motivations for the murder. Their initial hypothesis that Scully was the victim of a robber collapsed when they found money in his pockets and his flashy diamond ring secreted away in a drawer. The second theory, that the physician had been the target of a dope addict who acted out of drug lust, had little more credibility than the robber theory: there were no drugs missing and no evidence that Scully's office had been ransacked. Which left the inevitable third theory: *cherchez la femme*. Someone jealous of Scully's attentions to a female, police reasoned, had killed the courtly doctor in a classic murder of elimination.

Scully's friends initially poured scorn on the idea that Scully's murder had been a crime of passion. Hugh Duffy, his best friend, laughed at the notion: "I only saw him with a woman once in my life. He wasn't that kind." The Baroness Amanda Von Senten, an old acquaintance, echoed the sentiment: "He liked women collectively and enjoyed their company at a party. But he had no love affairs." Their skepticism that Scully had fallen victim to affairs of the heart was echoed and reinforced by the comment of George Breslin, a criminal lawyer who accompanied Scully's brother Jeremiah while the latter made his brother's funeral arrangements: "His life was what it seemed to be on the surface, that of a quiet, middle-aged man."

That unromantic assessment of Dr. Alfred P. Scully soon began to unravel. The day before his funeral, Estelle Sogola, Scully's former secretary, told investigators that Scully had received frequent telephone calls from a woman whose identity he hid from her. And Sogola further recalled an ugly scene several months earlier, when a female visitor had barged into the office and begun screaming at Scully about "another woman." The final gothic touch to this more interesting, albeit lurid, profile of Scully was added by a young girl who tried to break into Scully's office the night after his murder to retrieve some personal souvenirs of their "friendship." Arrested as she wept beside his casket at the McGorray Brothers Funeral Home on Lorain Avenue, the 21-year-old female was soon released by the police.

Things really began to get interesting after Scully's safety deposit box was opened. Although his estate totaled only about $22,000, the announcement that the 62-year-old Scully had not left a valid will triggered the most entertaining developments of the Scully mystery. Just as the Cuyahoga County Probate Court was about to appoint Hugh Duffy as administrator of the tangled estate, a thirtyish woman calling herself the wife of Dr. Alfred P. Scully appeared in Cleveland. Better yet, she brought with her an adolescent boy purporting to be Scully's son and a story worthy of the tabloid talents of Cleveland newspaperdom.

Tells of Secret Wedding

She called herself "Eunice Rockwell." She claimed that she had first met the esteemed doctor when she was but a lisping sprite in pigtails in Mount Vernon, Ohio. By the time she matured into a Baldwin-Wallace undergraduate in 1915, however, Dr. Scully's interest had begun to change from the avuncular to the conjugal. As the beguiling Ms. Rockwell related to entranced Cleveland lawmen and reporters between bouts of noisy weeping, she had kept her youthful marriage a secret to avoid alienating her family. Later, after their son Paul was born in 1917, she continued to mask her relations with Dr. Scully for fear of stirring up the anger of a mysterious "other woman" who would appear from time to time, threatening harm to both Eunice and Dr. Scully. And so the years passed, Eunice retained her bashful anonymity, and she and the discreet doctor maintained long-distance relations until that fateful day when she picked up a Florida newspaper to read of her husband's shocking demise.

Cleveland News,
May 14, 1930.

It was great copy, and grateful reporters gave Eunice her due, as she dutifully sobbed at every fresh remembrance of her murdered husband and spouted cryptic—and utterly useless—hints as to the identity of the "mysterious woman" who, Eunice loudly supposed, had finally made good on her maledictions on poor, martyred Alfred.

Unfortunately for Eunice, her sighs and tears proved to have better currency with newspapermen than with the unsentimental officials of the Cuyahoga County Probate Court. When they had the nerve to insist that she provide proof of her marriage, she got huffy and announced that she would never have asked for Scully's estate if she had anticipated "how much publicity and unpleasantness there would be." But plucky lass that she was, she was determined to "see it through" for the sake of her fatherless child. So it was back to Florida in search of the elusive license, which, unsurprisingly, never turned up.

What did turn up were three siblings of Ms. Rockwell, who knew her better as their long-lost sister Eunice Mitchart of Mount Vernon. While they did corroborate her story about at least knowing Dr. Scully, they could not help in authenticating her alleged marriage. Indeed, they only further muddied her claims with their disclosure that she had been declared legally dead in 1926. Eunice was last seen in Cleveland six months later, still vainly trying to convince officials that she deserved the dower portion of Scully's estate.

No one has thrown any further illumination on the Scully murder to this day. As one policeman put it only 24 hours after the murder, "Whoever killed Dr. Scully was either extremely lucky or a perfect engineer of escapes."

There was a brief flurry of excitement in late 1930 when Ross Valore fleetingly emerged as a suspect. Valore had already been convicted of the 1930 murder of R. Miller Wilkinson, a senseless killing in which Valore and his confederates tried to rob guests at a party on Glengary Road in Shaker Heights. It turned out that Valore's wife Cecilia, a rather disturbed woman and hardened career criminal herself, was a sister of Scully's erstwhile secretary, Estelle Sogola, and the distraught Cecilia now accused her prison-bound hubby of several murders, including Scully's. Despite heroic efforts, however, and despite the account of an alleged eyewitness who had seen a couple resembling Ross and Cecilia in a car at the scene on the murder night, the Cleveland police could not pin the Scully rap on Valore.

Perhaps Scully just lived on a bad corner. It was across the street in March 1975 that Alex "Shondor" Birns, Cleveland's most notorious 20th-century gangster, was blown to pieces by an explosive thoughtfully placed under his automobile seat. And if you look out Scully's window (third from the corner on the West 25th side, second floor), you can see the site that in 1870 housed the office and living quarters of the equally unlucky Dr. William Jones (murdered by Dr. Jay Galentine, as chronicled in the pages of *They Died Crawling*.)

Chapter 9

A MOST UNQUIET GRAVE

The Sarah Victor Scandal (1868)

This story is dedicated to Victoria ("Vixen") Richards, a kindred connoisseur of homicidal craft and behavioral perversity.
She did not inspire it, but she is certainly worthy of it.

— *The Author*

When arsenic was alleged to have been found in my brother's
stomach, no person could possibly have been more astonished
than I was.

— Sarah Maria Victor, *The Life Story of Sarah M. Victor For Sixty
Years: Convicted of Murdering Her Brother, Sentenced to be Hung,
Had Sentence Commuted, Passed Nineteen Years in Prison, Yet is
Innocent, Told By Herself*

No matter what one believes about the William Parquet murder
mystery, this much is certain: after 135 years the known facts and
puzzling ambiguities of his dreadful death still provoke shudders in
even the most seasoned connoisseur of Cleveland crime. Did Sarah
Maria Victor methodically poison her own brother with arsenic
after first forging his will, his power of attorney, and two insurance
policies on his young life? Did she nurse him tenderly in his
sickbed during his weeklong death struggle, seeing to his every
comfort and striving with all the resources at her command to keep
him from the grasp of the Grim Reaper? Or was that deathbed vigil
a contrived charade to facilitate and mask further administrations
of fatal white powder to her helpless, trusting sibling? Was Sarah
Victor really the cold-blooded and calculating murderess whom
the Cleveland newspapers joyfully vilified and 12 Cuyahoga
County jurors voted to send to a hangman's scaffold? Or was she—
as her own memoirs and her many friends insisted—simply the

Poisoner and prey: Sarah Victor and her brother William Parquet. *Cleveland Leader*, June 24, 1868.

most traduced, betrayed, and unlucky female ever to be brought
unjustly before the bar of Forest City justice? Therein hangs one of
the juiciest tales of Cleveland Gilded Age depravity . . .

As she was an habitual, even congenital liar, it is difficult to
chronicle the early years and antecedents of Sarah Victor with
exactitude. Born in Pickway, Ohio, she was the sixth of nine children born to a Frenchman named Parquet and his first, American-
born wife. Sarah persistently cultivated the impression that her
father was a man of means when she was born on May 5, 1827, yet
there is little except her dubious assertion to support this notion.
Sometime in the early 1830s, Sarah's mother came to Cleveland
with her children—husbandless and with little more than the
clothes on their backs. Sarah's story, retailed almost three score
years later, was that her father had become insane when his
endorsement of a friend's bad loan forced him into utter bankruptcy. Whatever the reason, Parquet was often absent from home
during Sarah's childhood. The most likely explanation from the
available evidence is that he was simply a hardened, improvident
sot. Mid-century Clevelanders would remember him as a quaint,
somewhat comical figure, who sold apples on the street with his
children, a jack-of-all-trades whom little boys mocked with shouts
of "Old Pockets," their disrespectful corruption of his surname.
Said to be violent toward his family when in drink, he had a crazed

temper reputedly equaled on such not-infrequent occasions by the pugnacious demeanor of his wife. In any case, "Old Pockets" could not keep his family from penury. In the late 1830s his daughter Sarah was "taken" by a family named Wemple in Collamer, a small rural village in what is now East Cleveland. Such informal adoptions were quite common at that time, and there is evidence that some of Sarah's siblings were also adopted by childless couples who felt sorry for the perpetually indigent and quarrelsome Parquet family.

Many such extralegal adoptions worked out; Sarah Parquet's did not. Completely uneducated when she came to the Wemples, she was soon withdrawn from the local public school after her schoolmates teased her for her ignorance and adoptive status. But Sarah was nothing if not intelligent, and after a term at a private school, she returned to confront her erstwhile tormentors with unrivaled academic superiority. As she entered adolescence in the late 1830s, however, things took an irreversible downward domestic turn. Sarah's subsequent story was that her relations with the Wemples deteriorated when she was unjustly blamed for petty thefts committed by their adopted son and because she abandoned their Presbyterian affiliation to worship at the local Disciples church. The story told later by others— and repeated publicly in newspapers— was that Sarah became incorrigibly defiant and disobedient. The gossip in

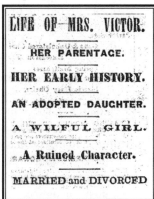

LIFE OF MRS. VICTOR.

HER PARENTAGE.

HER EARLY HISTORY.

AN ADOPTED DAUGHTER.

A WILFUL GIRL.

A Ruined Character.

MARRIED and DIVORCED

Cleveland Leader, June 24, 1868.

Collamer was that she refused to do any housework, stayed out until all hours, and was often discovered with members of the opposite sex in unsanctioned circumstances. By the early 1840s, the Wemples had given up on her. Sarah eventually returned to the domestic irregularities of her father's household. In her absence, Sarah's mother had died, but "Old Pockets" had hastily acquired a new spouse, a widow named Austin, who gave him three more children and died forthwith. The two children most important to our narrative were William, born in 1839, and Libbie, born in 1842.

Dependent on her own resources at a young age, Sarah tried domestic service in the households of several of Cleveland's most respectable families, including those of Seth Abbey and Dr. Horace Ackley. (Members of the Cleveland renowned Rowfant Club on Prospect Avenue might well be shocked to learn that their home, Dr. Ackey's former residence, was once the workplace of Sarah Victor.) Somehow, things just never worked out. Sarah's version of her various fallings-out with employers consisted of a litany of excuses, all hinging on innocent misunderstandings, domestic accidents, and unforeseen emergencies. But persistent rumor had it that a résumé of bad behavior and missing personal property followed young Sarah Parquet as she flitted from household to household in Cleveland during the early 1840s. Finally, in 1842, the town became too hot for her, and she "lit out for the territory" to make a new life.

The territory (rural Wisconsin) was new enough, but the patterns of Sarah's old life followed her there. Married in 1843 at the age of 15 to a young farmer named Charles Smith, Sarah found herself the mother of three children by 1850. Alas, domestic felicity eluded her. According to the lachrymose account in her ghostwritten autobiography, Charles Smith was a no-good, alcoholic, philandering scoundrel and lazy bum. Despite her finer instincts, however—or perhaps because of them—Sarah stayed with him, notwithstanding his numerous extramarital affairs and even after he brought a prostitute into their home as a "boarder."

Things hit rock bottom for Sarah Parquet Smith about 1850. By that time she had returned to Cleveland and was desperately trying to make ends meet by running a rooming house on Ohio Street. According to Sarah's later story, Charlie did nothing to support her and the children, although Cleveland journalists would eventually make uncharitable references to a certain "Buckeye Insurance Co.," a fraudulent concern with which he was closely associated in his Cleveland years. Finally, by about 1854, Sarah had endured enough. After a fight in which Charlie threatened her with a pistol, she fled their hovel, divorced him, and sought anonymity by changing her dwelling and her name. Her new surname, "Victor" (never legally assumed), was taken from the brand name of a patent stove she purchased, although unkind journalists would later suggest that she chose it as a token of her triumph over Charles Smith.

Little is known of Sarah's next decade and a half except one fact and a plethora of lurid rumors. The fact is that starting in 1859 she became the kept mistress of one Christopher Columbus Carleton, an insurance broker who pursued his vocation with his son-in-law

James in the firm of Carleton & Lee. Carleton's wife had died in 1858; Sarah, by her own admission, was financially destitute. It was probably just a matter of time before the worldly Carleton slipped into an irregular relationship with the attractive divorcee who looked far younger than her thirty-two years. Within several years Carleton gave Sarah a life tenure in his two-story, medium-sized white frame house at 18 Webster Street. There is ample evidence that they lived together for the next decade in what a future prosecuting attorney would characterize as "concubinage."

As for the rumors, well, *nothing* was too awful to say about Sarah Victor once she had been publicly pilloried as the poisoner of her own brother. Ill report of her ranged from the infamous to the just plain weird. Vilified as a prostitute and brothel keeper in the public prints after her murder indictment, it was asserted that she had run a notorious house of ill fame in Fremont, Ohio, before transferring her trade in female flesh and debauched misery to Cleveland. Or, as the *Cleveland Leader,* Sarah's most censorious critic, put it in florid dudgeon:

> About this time she was kept as a mistress by a certain man [Christopher Carleton], but is thought to have been public property to a considerable extent. She did not confine herself, either, to prostituting her own virtue, but was the means of robbing many a hearthstone of its most cherished gem. Never, till the great day of accounts will it be known how many homes she has blighted, how many hearts she has caused to be broken, how many wives she has ruined, how many maidens she has led astray. She seems to have made a business of securing victims to the hellish passions of wicked men. Many a heart rending story could be told of her accomplishments in this direction. But the mind revolts from such unnamed crimes.

Not content with such undocumented imputations of her vileness, the Cleveland newspapers also competed with each other in cataloging Sarah's alleged oddities during the decade before her extreme notoriety. It was said that she wore green goggles and a Shaker bonnet for several years, in a vain effort to disguise her identity, presumably from the bibulous Charles Smith and the minions of the law. It was asserted that she assiduously practiced her poison craft on her neighbors' cats, dogs, and chickens so regularly that the wary soon learned to keep domestic pets away from the vicinity of 18 Webster Street. It was rumored that she had murdered her father and her son Charles—*and shed not a tear in pub-lic for them!* None of the rumors was ever proven at her murder trail or later, except for the admitted fact that Sarah had lived "in sin" with Christopher Columbus Carleton for ten years.

Sarah herself was keenly aware of how badly the stain of her acknowledged unchasteness colored public perceptions of her. In her autobiography she would ruefully admit that she had erred most imprudently in transferring her affections from the abusive Smith to the evasive Carleton: "I did not, until it was too late, real-ize that I was shunning the rock only to fall in the whirlpool, or *vice versa.*" As for the green goggles and bonnet, they were probably assumed to temporarily hide the serious burns that Mrs. Victor received in a house fire caused by her son Charlie, who was play-ing with matches.

By 1865, Sarah Victor was doing pretty well, considering her 38 years of hard knocks. Although Carleton refused to make good on his ancient promise to marry her, their relations were constant and convivial, and he delivered on his promise of a life interest in the house on Webster Street. Sarah was a member in good standing of the Trinity Episcopal Church on Scovill Avenue and much involved in its charitable activities. Working as a skilled seamstress over the years, Sarah had acquired a small store of capital and had begun to speculate modestly in real estate, buying and selling small lots. She had enough funds to afford the domestic services of two women, Annie Miller and Anna Morehouse, and there was also the rent contributed by her younger half-sister, Elizabeth (Libbie) Gray.

Libbie was 15 years younger than Sarah and had already com-piled an unfortunate domestic history. She had been unhappily married several times, most recently to a "Dr." Gray, who had become notorious for vending a patent medicine known as "Golden Pain Searcher" on the streets of Cleveland. Working in a millinery shop, Libbie, together with her young son, lived on and off with Mrs. Victor in imperfect amicability for most of the mid-1860s. It was clear to everyone who knew the two sisters that they didn't get along; it was equally clear that Sarah dominated every-one in the house and ruled their lives with an iron hand and unfor-giving discipline. Then, about the end of 1865, William Parquet came to live at 18 Webster Street.

William, Sarah's half-brother by her father's second wife, was

26. He was five feet, five inches tall with a light complexion, dark hair, and gray eyes. Although illiterate, he was considered of average intelligence by those who knew him, and his health was generally good, as evidenced by his three years of military service during the Civil War, which included involvement in most of the battles of General Grant's 1864 Virginia campaign. Sarah would later claim that she was close to William while he was in the army and would cite the many letters she wrote to him at that time. Naturally, however, she was not able to prove exactly when she wrote her alleged letters (to an illiterate!). The epistles in reply from the unlettered William to his beloved sister Sarah were suspiciously undated and improbably well-written missives from a completely unlettered man. There were, however, two other alleged documents that William was kind enough to send his sister during that long, cruel war: a power of attorney (giving her complete financial control of his assets) and his will (leaving everything to Sarah Maria Victor). But more of that later . . .

William came home from his three-year stint in the 12th U.S. Infantry in the fall of 1865. Although his discharge was quite honorable, Sarah said he came to her house completely broke, having nothing more to show for his long military service than a letter of praise from his commanding officer. Well, not *just* that: William also returned with a distinct case of syphilis, for which Sarah soon referred him to a Cleveland physician, Dr. Levi Sapp, for the usual heroic mercury treatment.

About this time, Sarah also took out an insurance policy for $2,300 on William's life. Sarah would later claim that it was William's idea and that he had insisted it be done while he was in the army, when violent death seemed imminent every day and all of his fellow soldiers were doing the same. The blunt fact, however, is that the application for the insurance was dated September 5, 1865—five months after the end of the war. Moreover, it was clear in retrospect that William, ever illiterate, did not fill out or sign the application himself. Cynical souls will delight in the disclosure that the insurance policy, No.218,555 with the Connecticut Life Insurance Company, was taken out through insurance broker Christopher Columbus Carleton. The premium was $51.50, with $29 paid in cash by Mrs. Victor and the remainder loaned on a note incurred by the same Sarah M. Victor. Neither Carleton nor his partner, Lee, could remember even seeing William Parquet about the insurance, remembering only that Sarah seemed to have complete charge of the matter. Dr. S. R. Beckwith, who examined William on behalf of the Connecticut Life Insurance Company, pronounced him a good risk, despite his bout with venereal disease, and the insurance policy went into effect in the fall of 1865.

William stayed at Sarah's house until the spring of 1866. His life there could not have been too dramatic, as Sarah did not allow him to have visitors at the house and she insisted on accompanying him on those rare occasions he ventured out. He then took a job as a hostler at a tavern run by E. M. Fenner in Euclid Township. And on March 16, 1866, he made application to the firm of Carleton and Lee for $1,500 in accidental death insurance. Mrs. Victor would initially claim, at William's inquest, that she knew nothing about the accidental death policy. She later changed her story at the trial, recalling vividly that William had insisted on the policy, as he was fearful of working around Mr. Fenner's horses. Once again, someone other than William Parquet signed his name to the policy, and Mrs. Victor, once again, paid the premium. No one seems to have thought it odd that an ex-soldier who had spent four years around horses was now afraid to be in their presence.

Two months later, William had an accident in Fenner's barn, falling into a hayrack and painfully injuring his side. He was treated by Dr. Sapp and everyone believed (and ultimately testified in court) that he made a full recovery from the injury. Everyone, that is, except Mrs. Victor, who insisted only after his death that William had been much troubled by his injuries during the last nine months of his life. Whatever the truth, it is a matter of record that William returned to his usual work at Fenner's within several weeks of his injury, and none of his fellow workers nor his employer noticed any decline in his health.

In January 1867, William quit his job at Fenner's and again took up residence at Sarah's house on Webster Street. The likely reason was an unrequited romantic attachment that he had formed to Ann Fenner, one of his employer's daughters. Sarah would later insist that William was driven away by Ann's parents, who wanted someone with better prospects in life than an illiterate handyman for their daughter's intended. But there was never any evidence that Ann returned William's affections, and she herself testified to the contrary at Sarah's trial. It is true that William died and was buried wearing a ring locket with her picture in it—but he had stealthily acquired the picture from one of Ann's sisters.

William's last public appearance was on December 23, 1866. Attending a Christmas party at the Fenner house, he was seen there by Carrie Libenthal and Martha Burns, both of whom would recall that he seemed in good spirits, danced up a storm, and was "real lively."

Just when William Parquet began to sicken unto death will never be known. His sister Sarah would always claim that his decline began on the evening of Saturday, January 26, when he slipped off the front steps of her house and hurt himself. Sarah's thought was that he had aggravated his old hayrack injury. She immediately put him to bed with a mustard poultice and a dose of ginger tea. William was better the next morning, Sarah would recall, but still rather low. Yet not low enough, apparently, for Sarah to call in a doctor, or low enough for anyone else in the house to even notice that William was not himself.

There was no ambiguity about the next phase of William's illness. Sometime during the night of Monday, January 28, he became ill in his bedroom. Wracked by stomach pains and paroxysms of vomiting, and uttering painful groans, he became so ill that Sarah took him into her own bedroom. William was no better on Tuesday, shrieking in agony, retching uncontrollably, complaining of stomach pains, and crying ceaselessly for water and alcohol. Either that day or the next—no one could ever remember which— Sarah called in Dr. Sapp. Although somewhat puzzled by his patient's symptoms, Sapp made a tentative diagnosis of dysentery and prescribed the usual regimen of aconite and bryonia. He specifically cautioned against giving William any alcohol and asked that he be called again if William's condition worsened. Before he left, Mrs. Victor expressed her belief that William was going to die. Nonsense, retorted Dr. Sapp, there was no reason to think Sarah's brother was in any danger of death. But Sarah told Dr. Sapp that William had already told her that he thought he was going to die. There was no doubt in her mind he was right: she told Dr. Sapp that she had already seen one sister and one of her own children die *right after they had experienced similar premonitions of death.*

William Parquet never left his sister's bedroom alive. Over the following week, he continued to suffer terrible stomach pains, continual vomiting, persistent thirst, and strained and bloody stools. Throughout his prolonged agony, Sarah was at his side, giving him most of his medicine and nourishment and maintaining a practically ceaseless bedside vigil that was the admiration of all who witnessed her apparent sisterly devotion. Some of William's many visitors during his seven-day agony were puzzled—especially in retrospect—that Sarah frequently administered various kinds of alcohol and heavy doses of chloroform to her suffering patient. But Sarah would brook no interference or advice with her nursing. Everyone, especially her sister Libbie, knew better than to contradict the imperious Sarah. Nothing was done to or for William without her say-so.

For six days, William Parquet lingered in pain, never getting much better or much worse. On Sunday night, February 2, there was a noticeable decline in his condition. Just after Sarah gave him some whiskey, William went into a screaming fit and someone volunteered to go for Dr. Sapp. "No," said Sarah, reiterating her comment that William was going to die anyway, and adding that Dr. Sapp didn't want to be bothered in the middle of the night. In any case, Dr. Sapp showed up the next morning and, after examining his patient, pronounced him in no danger of death.

Dr. Sapp was in for a big surprise. Shortly after 5 A.M. the next morning, William roused himself from his near-coma and said to Sarah, "Goodbye, Sister." A short time later, he muttered, "I'm going home" loud enough to be heard by several of those in the sickroom. At 6 A.M. he expired and Dr. Sapp was called in.

Dr. Sapp, a competent homeopathic physician, was, to say the least, greatly puzzled by William's death. His observations had not led him to expect anything like this outcome. He immediately asked Sarah to let him perform an autopsy to determine the cause of death. Sarah adamantly refused, even after Libbie and various neighbors and friends added their support to Dr. Sapp's entreaty. It was William's last request, she tearfully told Dr. Sapp, that she not allow the doctors to cut up his dead body. According to Sarah, William had been traumatized as a young boy by Cleveland medical students, who had gruesomely paraded a "resurrected" corpse through the streets and forced the impressionable William to watch their grotesque procession. It was simply out of the question, insisted Sarah, especially as she knew that medical students often stole parts of autopsied corpses as grotesque trophies for their private revels.

Eventually, Sarah tentatively agreed to allow just Dr. Sapp and Dr. Beckwith to examine William's corpse, but it is a fact that no autopsy was performed before William was buried in the family plot at Woodland Cemetery on February 6, 1867. Later—much later—Sarah would change her story and insist that she had forbade the postmortem because she feared exposure of William's "private disease" through some physical evidence that he had suffered from syphilis. But Dr. Sapp testified that there was no such evidence on William's body, and Sarah, in her 1887 autobiography, ultimately denied ever mentioning William's venereal disease to Sapp or anyone else.

William Parquet's body was not to rest in peace. Several hours after the funeral, Sarah, apparently concerned that the doctors might still insist on an autopsy, returned to Woodland Cemetery. There she mentioned her concern to cemetery foreman Patrick Barry and asked him to bury a box containing the bones of two of her children on top of William's casket. This was done and the dirt was shoveled back over the grave. Sarah remained apprehensive that someone would disturb her brother's grave and returned there periodically to mark it with twigs, so that she would know if anyone had tampered with it. And she told her servant, Anna Miller, that she was going to have someone watch the grave to prevent any disturbance. (At the same time, Sarah saw to it that William would at least be able to see whoever might come for his body: his casket had a glass window inserted in the top, just over his face.)

William Parquet's death was a matter of considerable speculation to all who knew him—and his sister Sarah had a different answer for just about everyone who asked her about it. Under "Cause of Death" in the Woodland Cemetery register, she wrote, "Inflammation [infection] of the Lungs." Several weeks after William's death, at the time she filed for payment of the $1,500 accidental death policy, she told James Lee that he had died from the effects of his hayrack accident at Fenner's. She told her servant Anna Morehouse that William had died from the effects of the "private disease" he had contracted while in the army. She told her neighbor, Hannah Newell of 21 Webster Street, that William had died of an "inflammation of the stomach" caused by his hayrack accident. She told her neighbor Miss Ida Weile of 16 Webster Street that William had died of heart disease. And she told Dr. Sapp that she thought William's death was caused by his eating a frozen turnover or pie that he had consumed on the Monday night he was taken sick . . . but more of that later.

Sarah's statements to her relatives and neighbors about William's insurance and personal property were of like diversity.

She told Libbie that William had left no insurance but had bequeathed all of his real and personal property solely to her, including several property lots and his watch. After Libbie prodded her further, Sarah eventually produced a handwritten will to that effect, allegedly sent to her by William while he was in the army—but which she would not allow Libbie to read. Sarah told her friend Eliza Welch after William died that he had left no insurance whatsoever. She told E. M. Fenner (at the time she successfully dunned him for some of William's back pay) that William's insurance policies had lapsed before his death. Sarah told Anna Morehouse that she had tried to obtain the army bounty due William but had been unsuccessful—which was a lie. She also asked Anna to tell everyone that she had not gotten any insurance from William's estate. And Sarah told her neighbor Jared Newell that she had received no insurance at all.

Sarah Victor suffered no such confusion in securing the insurance money. Several weeks after William's death she showed up at the offices of Carleton & Lee to file papers for payment of both William's life and accident policies. James Lee told her plainly that there was no question of filing for the accident policy, as William's death had clearly not been accidental. Sarah tried to insist that William had died from the after-effects of his hayrack fall but did not pursue the matter emphatically, perhaps fearing that an autopsy might ensue if she persisted. In due time, a check for $2,300, issued by Carleton & Lee, was promptly cashed and turned back to the firm for piecemeal disbursement as required by Mrs. Victor. During the following year, Lee and Carleton paid out various sums to her; there was only about $500 left when she was arrested in February 1868. Sarah also filed for, and collected, William's back pay from E. M. Fenner and the remainder due from his army bounty, neither of which she shared with Libbie or anyone else.

Somehow, some way, various disquieting rumors about William Parquet's death began festering throughout Cleveland in the months that followed his demise. Maybe it was the multiple, conflicting stories told by Sarah to her friends, relatives, and neighbors. Maybe it had something to do, as Sarah believed, with her sister Libbie's anger about not getting any of William's estate. Maybe it was Sarah's continual apprehension about someone digging up her brother's body, a fear that seemed suspicious to those curious about the manner of William's demise. Maybe it was even, as Sarah claimed in her autobiography, a bizarre plot by her neighbor Jared Newell to blackmail her and to divert attention away from Newell's own murderous past.

By the late fall of 1867 there was a general rumor that William might have been poisoned. Indeed, Sarah herself eventually brought the matter up with E. M. Fenner, sweetly inquiring whether someone in his family just might have poisoned William to keep him away from Fenner's daughter Ann. Not surprisingly, Fenner was shocked and offended by the question, but when he demanded to know where Sarah had heard such a story, she confessed she couldn't quite remember the name of the woman who had told her such a horrid tale.

Matters took a more ominous and concrete form when Sarah's sister Libbie became involved. Still living at 18 Webster Street, Libbie was incensed at Sarah's getting everything; she didn't believe that William had left no insurance. When she found out about the property lots, the army bounty, and the personal effects, she began making inquiries. Eventually, a merchant on Erie Street tipped her off about the insurance. She went to the offices of Carleton & Lee on December 17th or 18th of 1867. Mr. Lee candidly admitted to her that her sister had received the $2,300 insurance payment, and Libbie forthwith paid a call on probate judge Daniel Tilden. Tilden was aroused enough by her suspicions to send her to Cuyahoga County sheriff Felix Nicola, who began making discreet inquiries of his own. His investigation culminated in a journey to Woodland Cemetery on January 28, 1868, and the exhumation there of William Parquet's body in the presence of Deputy Sheriff George Ridgeway, Dr. Proctor Thayer, Professor J. L. Cassels, and a cemetery work crew.

Meanwhile, Sarah was busy. She had become aware of the suspicions swirling about her and during the last weeks before William's exhumation labored mightily to prepare the minds of her friends and neighbors for what might come. About the time William was being hauled out of the earth, she recalled to Annie Miller that William had become ill after he ate a frozen turnover brought into the house by Libbie. Sarah also confided that the turnover might have been originally shoplifted by William that evening at a local grocery, the point of her confidence to Annie Miller seeming to be that the turnover had not been of *her* making or provision and that it was Libbie who brought it into the house.

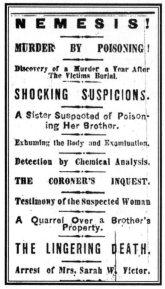

N E M E S I S !

MURDER BY POISONING !

Discovery of a Murder a Year After
The Victims Burial.

SHOCKING SUSPICIONS.

A Sister Suspected of Poisoning Her Brother.

Exhuming the Body and Examination.

Detection by Chemical Analysis,

THE CORONER'S INQUEST.

Testimony of the Suspected Woman

A Quarrel Over a Brother's
Property.

THE LINGERING DEATH.

Arrest of Mrs. Sarah W. Victor.

Cleveland Herald,
February 6, 1868.

At this time Sarah also mentioned William's "private disease" as the reason she had opposed an autopsy and told Annie further that she herself had once suffered from syphilis, shamefully inflicted upon her, she implied, by her no-good, long-gone husband. Sometime during those same few weeks before the arrest, she told the same insinuating story about the turnover to Sheriff Nicola.

Sarah had gone to see Nicola because she was concerned about the ugly rumors that were circulating; she asked Nicola to stop Libbie from telling libelous stories about her. She also tried to enlist Dr. Sapp as an intermediary, hinting in a letter to him that Libbie and others were attempting to blackmail her for things she hadn't done. Dr. Sapp refused to become involved, as did Cleveland's U.S. postal authorities when Sarah asked them to assist her in tracing what she said was a threatening letter.

The storm finally broke over Sarah Victor's head on February 5, 1868. After receiving a report from Chemical Professor J. L. Cassels on his analysis of William Parquet's internal organs, Cuyahoga County coroner J. C. Schenck swore out an inquest panel composed of citizens H. H. Little, Moses Hill, S. H. Fox, William Bowler, N. A. Gray, and Charles Whitaker. After a visit to Woodland Cemetery to view William's body, they returned to Sheriff Nicola's office and began taking testimony from the first witness called, Sarah Maria Victor.

Sarah would later maintain that she was caught completely by surprise when Deputy Sheriff Ridgeway called on her and asked her to come downtown with him that afternoon. But come she did, without protest, and at 3:30 P.M. she took the stand and told her version of her brother's death in a flood of tears. Producing his alleged will and power of attorney, she stated that he had died from injuries sustained in his hayrack mishap and that his final illness had seemingly been triggered by eating a piece of pie or turnover. She admitted giving William brandy, whiskey, wine, milk, lemonade, gruel, coffee, and tea during her weeklong sickbed vigil. She insisted she did not know that Dr. Sapp had forbade the consumption of any alcohol. She also denied giving William any chloroform during his final illness. She admitted that she kept arsenic in the house to kill rats, storing it under a rug in her sister Libbie's bedroom As soon as Sarah finished her testimony, she was arrested by Sheriff Nicola on a charge of murder and removed to the county jail.

Why Sarah had been so quickly charged became clear with the next day's testimony. Dr. Sapp, the first witness, testified about the symptoms of William's death struggle and his shock at the unexpected death of his patient. He recounted Sarah's fervent opposition to an autopsy, recalled Sarah's morbid emphasis on William's alleged premonitions of death, and mentioned his surprise at discovering that William had been given frequent alcoholic drinks contrary to his expressed orders. He also produced the letter he had received from Sarah three weeks before, seeking his aid against Libbie's supposed machinations against her. The undated missive made it clear that Sarah was more than willing to play the character assassination game herself:

> I thought I had better let you know doctor, the son of the man that we were speaking about [probably Jared Newell, Sarah's neighbor, whom she claimed was mixed up in the plot to blackmail her] saw me at your office, and will probably tell her [Libbie] they saw me there and she may not call on you. If she don't wont [*sic*] you call on her as soon as you can, I will pay you for your trouble. You might say I heard what she had reported and called on you and said if there are any doubts or suspicions that anything was wrong on my part that all should be investigated for the satisfaction of respectable people but not for such low creatures as those who wrote those low letters. Tell her please that as she has circulated bad things that I had done, that to prove me guilty she must prove herself innocent and truthful and by so doing she must bring those that has known her from a child and through life and that I must do the same; tell her friends of a few weeks won't answer, for it is a serious case and if you take it in hand it must be a thorough thing. Then ask her what reference she can give, ask her what places she lived in before she came here, and what names she can give you to write to, and what was her name when she lived there, and what church was she a member of, the clergyman's name, the occupation of her husband and such other questions as you think of, and if she don't answer sat-

isfactorily and freely, tell her you are not quite satisfied, and that she must bring forward all those that have made themselves interested. Doctor, you can do and say more than I and I leave it all to you as my friend and physician. (Signed) S. M. Victor

Dr. Proctor Thayer testified next. The widely respected Cleveland physician and frequent expert witness in criminal trials described William's exhumation and stressed the corpse's unusually good state of preservation, a condition often correlated with the presence of arsenic in the body. Indeed, William's corpse had been so well preserved, Thayer marveled, that the lungs were still inflatable and Deputy Sheriff George Ridgeway had immediately recognized the deceased, whom he had known casually. Thayer told further of how he had taken tissue samples from William's vital organs, placed them in sealed vessels, and given them to Professor John L. Cassels.

Cassels now took the stand, and it was his testimony, more than that of any other witness or any item of circumstantial evidence, that propelled Sarah Victor toward a hangman's noose. Cassels was one of the founders of the Cleveland Medical College, a widely respected scientist, and a frequent expert witness whose word carried great weight with jurists and juries. He testified that he had run five different tests over the course of a week for the presence of arsenic in the stomach, liver, kidney, and heart of William Parquet. He had found none in the kidney, spleen, or heart, and only a small trace in the liver. But he had found two or three grains in the stomach and suspected that several more grains had been lost in the testing process. Cassels told the inquest panel that the deceased could only have lived from five to seven days after ingesting such a quantity of arsenic, and that the absence of significant amounts of arsenic in organs other than the stomach indicated that a large dose of arsenic had been ingested shortly before death, most likely within the final 24 hours. Noting that the symptoms of arsenical poisoning were "pain and heat in the region of the stomach, thirst, sometimes vomiting, sometimes diarrhea, green and bloody stools . . . dysentery, great prostration, death preceded sometimes by convulsions"—all symptoms exhibited by the deceased—Cassels concluded, "there is no doubt in my mind that the person died from the effects of arsenic."

Other witnesses followed Cassels, but it was clear what the ver-

dict would be when he had finished his testimony. If William Parquet had died of a fatal dose of arsenic administered within the last
24 hours of his life, there was only one logical suspect. At the end
of the second day's testimony, the inquest panel deliberated for just
ten minutes before issuing its verdict that "William Parquet came
to his death from the effects of arsenical poison administered, as
we believe, by Mrs. Sarah Maria Victor." Unable to make bail,
Sarah remained ensconced in one of the more genteel suites of the
county jail, with her meals sent in from the nearby Richards &
Company restaurant.

Sarah soon secured the counsel of one of Cleveland's leading
defense attorneys, Marshal S. Castle, well-known to crime con-
noisseurs for his ferocious, if unsuccessful, 1865 defense of Dr.
John Hughes, the poetaster murderer of Tamsen Parsons. Although
assisted by local legal lights R. P. Ranney, C. W. Palmer, and James
M. Coffinberry, Castle handled virtually all of the trial burden. In
her 1887 autobiography, Sarah bitterly attacked Castle's handling
of her case, from the moment he waived her preliminary examination before Justice of the Peace G. A. Kolbe on February 10. She
also claimed that Castle took on her case only because he wanted
the fee, and that he forced her to sign over to him all of her remaining assets. In addition, she declared (19 years after the fact) that
Castle was "almost constantly under the effects of liquor" during
her two-week trial. Whatever the truth of her unlikely accusations,
it was the perception of most trial observers that Castle had an
unruly, irrational client who constantly badgered him with her own
legal tactics, most of which were concerned with the counterpro-
ductive character assassination of prosecution witnesses.

Sarah's trial on a first-degree murder charge opened before
Common Pleas Judge Horace Foote on Wednesday, June 10, 1868.
She sat at the defense table, attired in black, listless and silent
except when prompting M. S. Castle to harry her enemies with
innuendo. The 36 men in the venire were quickly whittled down to
an acceptable jury of 12 men, all of them from the western side of
Cuyahoga County. Those few excluded were challenged on the
usual grounds of having already formed an opinion as to Sarah's
guilt or innocence or because they opposed capital punishment.
And then, after a break for lunch, prosecutor J. M. Jones opened for
the state with a lucid, uncomplicated charge that Sarah had murdered her brother for his insurance money. Citing the evidence of

Mrs. Victor engaged in useful toil in prison.

Thayer and Cassels that William had died of arsenic administered within 24 hours of his death, Jones outlined Sarah's ceaseless attendance at his sickbed and the strong improbability that anyone else could have had the opportunity to administer the fatal dose. Declining to make an opening defense statement, Castle merely offered the usual caution to the jury that his client deserved the presumption of innocence. Then the first of 39 witnesses was called.

Thayer and Cassels repeated their inquest testimony, dwelling in detail on the large amount of arsenic in William Parquet's stomach and the absence of any organic disease. Thayer particularly stressed the fact that chloroform could be used to mask the symptoms of arsenic poisoning. Then prosecutor Jones began to weave the web of circumstantial evidence tying Sarah to the arsenic with a parade of witnesses to her conduct in William's sickroom. Servant Annie Miller swore under oath that Sarah insisted on doing all of the cooking for William herself and that she had administered most of his medicine and liquids while he was bedridden. She recalled Sarah's suggestive remarks about the famous turnover just a week before her arrest and noted that Sarah had concluded that conversation by giving Annie a present of two chains and a bracelet—something the stingy Sarah had never done before. At this point, prosecutor Jones abruptly halted Annie's testimony, objecting that Sarah was telegraphing signs to the witness on how to answer his questions. M. S. Castle vehemently denied the charge, but it may have influenced the jury, as they had already heard Annie emphasize how domineering Sarah was in her domestic circle.

The testimony of various witnesses about William Parquet's alleged will and power of attorney was muddled and inconclusive, particularly as to the handwriting and the validity of the witnessing signatures. But it was clear, even after some of the testimony was excluded, that the illiterate William could not have written or signed either of the documents. Which meant that Sarah Victor was at least likely to be a forger, if not necessarily a cold-blooded poisoner. And the testimony of other witnesses as to Sarah's administration of her brother's assets before his death further cemented her image as a scheming, grasping conniver. Several Cuyahoga County officials offered detailed accounts of how Sarah had transferred much of William's real estate into her own hands even while he was alive. They were followed by a parade of Sarah's neighbors, all of whom testified as to her iron control of the sickroom and her passionate aversion to an autopsy.

Sarah's already bleak prospects took a decisive turn for the worse on the fourth trial day, June 13, with the appearance of her half-sister Libbie Gray on the stand. Demolishing Sarah's after-the-fact story about the mysterious turnover, she recalled that it was of Sarah's making and re-created the context of William's Monday-night snack in damning detail:

> [He] complained of being hungry and went to the cupboard and ate a piece of pie; I asked him for a piece and he told me to go and get a piece for myself. I said nothing to Annie Miller about eating that pie. After he told me to go and get a piece he offered me a piece; I said if I can't have the whole I don't want any.

Libbie, who made a good impression on the jury and spectators, further tightened the looming noose around her sister's neck by recalling that Sarah had administered multiple doses of chloroform to William throughout his illness and ordered others to dose him with the same, despite Dr. Sapp's orders to the contrary. Libbie also remembered Sarah giving William a small quantity of a white powder, probably morphine, on the end of a knife blade. She denied spreading rumors about her brother being poisoned and insisted that she had never discussed the matter publicly until it was all over the newspapers in February.

Marshal Castle didn't help his client with his nasty cross-examination of Libbie Gray. Rather than confuting any of the damning details of her testimony, he chose instead to blacken her character by demanding to know whether she had been married to a succession of men, including a Mr. Bayless, a Mr. Robinson, a Mr. Gibson, and a Mr. Karther. His tactic, clearly prompted by whispered conferences with Sarah, backfired miserably, exciting sympathy for Libbie, who, at Judge Foote's sympathetic prompting, declined to answer Castle's insinuating interrogatories. A little while later, Castle tried the same tactic on Anna Morehouse as she left the stand, audibly baiting her with the taunt, "You haven't seen your husband since you were here, have you?" "No," said the imperturbable Morehouse, "I haven't and I don't want to and it is a pity there ain't more women that do as I do!"

Four days later, after a forced recess due Mrs. Victor's deteriorating health, prosecutor Jones avenged Libbie Gray's ordeal with his brutal cross-examination of Christopher Columbus Carleton. Carleton's testimony about both the insurance and the details of William's sickroom was redundant, but Jones had decided to use him to destroy Sarah's character for the edification of the jury. After establishing that Sarah had paid virtually no rent on her Webster Street house for 10 years, Jones asked Carleton outright whether Sarah had not, in point of fact, been his "kept mistress" for the last 10 years. Judge Foote immediately cautioned Carleton that he need not incriminate himself by answering, and Carleton remained silent. Not dismayed, Jones hammered back, demanding to know whether Carleton had paid Sarah "a stipulated price per week for her concubinage" during her decade's residence at 18 Webster Street. Carleton again refused to answer, but the damage had been done: Jones had established that Sarah was a kept woman with no other apparent means of support than the petty earnings from her needlework. The implication was clear that her precarious financial security might well have made the possibility of William Parquet's insurance a tempting opportunity.

All this was but a prelude to the main event, Sarah's direct testimony on Thursday morning. The courtroom was packed, with many women present, as Sarah, dressed entirely in funereal black and sporting a black veil, was helped to the witness chair. She testified well into the afternoon, repeating much of her inquest testimony and adding new details. She remembered much more about the famous turnover, asserting that she had begged William not to eat it because it was "frozen" and it might make him sick. She denied spreading conflicting stories about his cause of death, insisting that she had always thought he died from the effects of his hayrack fall in Fenner's barn. She admitted giving Billy a little whiskey once during his last illness but denied dosing him with

divers kinds of alcohol or even knowing that Dr. Sapp had prohibited the same. And she denied repeatedly dosing William with
chloroform during his sickbed ordeal, admitting that she had only
done it once or twice and then thrown it out the window.

Late that afternoon, prosecutor Jones caught Sarah in a carefully
laid trap. They were discussing Sarah's sly query to E. M. Fenner
as to whether some of his family had poisoned William to keep him
away from Ann Fenner. Sarah repeated her story that the notion
had been suggested to her by an unidentified woman but admitted
that the woman had not actually used the word "poison." Jones
pounced: Why, if that was the case, had Sarah used the word
"poison" in her subsequent colloquy with Fenner? Sarah tried to
evade a direct answer but eventually muttered that she had only
"inferred" poison from the woman's conversation. A similar embarrassment ensued when Sarah disputed Anna Morehouse's story
about her having had syphilis. Sarah vehemently denied having
such a conversation but refused to reply when asked if she had ever,
in fact, had syphilis.

A few minutes later, after the last witnesses had testified, M. S.
Castle informed Judge Foote that the defense had concluded its
presentation. As he finished, Sarah suddenly rose to her feet, began
gesticulating in a wild manner, and commenced a delirious rant
against her adversaries, especially Libbie Gray. It was apparent to
everyone that Sarah still thought she was in her jail cell as she
raved on in the crowded courtroom:

> She [Libbie] has gone by my window four times—why will she
> do so? She makes me feel so badly—are they going to sell my
> life for her friendship? What am I here for? Four months in jail?
> I did not think she would let me stay here so long—ain't this too
> bad. Mrs. Hatch [Sarah's jail attendant], she will repent it. I
> know she will. I never want to see her till she comes here and
> tells me she is sorry—then I'll forgive her. She don't know how
> bad she makes me feel. I do believe she will come forward
> before the trial comes on and say that I am innocent. She throws
> her head, poor girl, girl! The Lord forgive her. I've suffered, I've
> suffered. Tis hard, ain't it, Mrs. Hatch? Now I'll go and lay down
> and think no more about it. I don't want to see her, poor girl.
> Poor boy—I wonder if she's gone to put flowers on his grave
> today—the papers say they are going. I must live a little longer.
> Give me medicine. Give me strength. The most glorious day of
> my life will be when I go into the Court House. I will see Mr.

Jones and tell him all about it. After this is over I don't care to
live any longer, after I have proved myself innocent. That miserable Newell. He wanted the land. I wouldn't sell it to him. He is
the cause of all this—that miserable man. Why won't they tell
me the whole truth? Did I ever think I should come to this? Why
does she go to the City Hotel to board—to put poison in my
food? Poor boy. She knew she hadn't a dollar in this world. I got
that land for him that he might have a way to save his money.
Mr. Castle said they would kill me. Poor girl—why don't she
come to see me? She knows. That miserable man, that miserable
Newell. I've suffered so much in my life . . .

Seemingly oblivious to where she was and what she was doing,
Sarah mumbled on in this fashion for some time, as her attorneys
and Dr. Beckwith tried to calm and quiet her. Removed to a settee,
she finally subsided after Beckwith gave her some wine and a powerful sedative; she was taken back to jail. By 6 P.M. she was
reported to be herself again, and the next day's *Plain Dealer*
expressed the skepticism of many who thought Sarah was laying
the groundwork for the old insanity dodge: "Those who have
known her for years state that she has often had these fits when
excited, and they need cause no alarm for her safety."

Sarah returned to Court on Friday and, after the appearance of
the 39th and last witness, Homer B. DeWolfe began the closing
arguments for the state. The case, he said, was a simple structure of
five propositions: (1) William Parquet had died of arsenic poisoning; (2) Sarah had a strong economic motive for administering the
poison; (3) Sarah had both the means and opportunity to administer the arsenic; (4) the case against Sarah was based on the general
principles of circumstantial evidence; and (5) all circumstantial
evidence in the case pointed without exception to Sarah Maria Victor. DeWolfe then reviewed the symptoms of arsenic poisoning for
the jury and recapitulated the testimony of witnesses about
William's sufferings. He stressed Sarah's need for money and
dwelt upon her successful machinations to obtain William's personal property, his bounty money, and his insurance—her claims to
which were supported by an improperly witnessed and highly suspicious will. He noted that Sarah had admitted having arsenic in
the house and that she, by the testimony of many witnesses, was in
William's sickroom almost constantly. And DeWolfe particularly
stressed Sarah's refusal to allow an autopsy on her dead brother as
evidence of her guilt.

DeWolfe devoted much of his final peroration to the question of circumstantial evidence. Aware of the popular prejudice against it, DeWolfe remarked:

> In cases of suspected poisoning, the evidence must of necessity be circumstantial, for no one who poisons another ever calls a jury of twelve men to witness the act. Poison is peculiarly a woman's weapon, and especially the weapon of abandoned women.

DeWolfe ended his powerful presentation with a plethora of citations from legal authorities to the effect that circumstantial evidence was as strong in some cases as direct evidence.

C. W. Palmer's opening argument for the defense acutely zeroed in on the most glaring weakness in the state's case. Palmer stressed that there was only the testimony of one man—Professor Cassels—to support the claim that William Parquet had died of arsenic poisoning. William might well, Palmer insisted, have died of some internal inflammation, as his sorrowing sister Sarah believed in good faith. Cassels was an expert—and experts had been known to be wrong. And Cassels's belief that the fatal dose had been administered only 24 hours before death was inconsistent with the testimony of many witnesses that William's symptoms had been the same throughout his weeklong illness. Ergo, if Sarah had been giving William all that chloroform to mask the effects of her arsenic—as claimed by the state—why had she bothered with it, since she didn't give the fatal dose until almost a week had passed? Summarizing his objections to the seemingly damning evidence, Palmer pleaded that all of the circumstances pointing to Sarah's guilt were equally supportive of her innocence.

M. S. Castle began his final argument on Saturday afternoon, June 20, by reviewing his own authorities on the strength and meaning of circumstantial evidence. But he didn't get very far before adjournment. The trial was further delayed until Monday afternoon by Sarah's continuing psychological deterioration. But after Castle finished on Monday, prosecutor Jones rose to his feet and unleashed the flood of his scalding commonsense logic on Palmer and Castle's alleged sophistries. Jones noted that their "pretense" that William had died from "some kind of inflammation" was a common ploy in poisoning cases like this one. Indeed, he scornfully declared, the state had thoroughly proved that William had died of arsenic poisoning and "if it had not been proved, the crime might as well be struck off the statutes." The defense, to be sure, had disparaged the accuracy of Professor Cassels's chemical tests—but why had they not produced even one expert witness to challenge his evidence? Only Sarah Victor had profited financially from the death of her brother, and there was ample evidence that she had labored mightily and stealthily to that end. Her story about keeping arsenic under the rug of her sister Libbie's bedroom to kill rats was an obvious attempt to throw suspicion on Libbie, especially as Sarah had kept a cat for six years. And the various stories Sarah had told about the famous frozen turnover—or was it a pie?—were transparently clumsy attempts to prepare an alibi.

Jones resumed his attack on Sarah on Tuesday morning, but he didn't get very far. Sarah had become more and more agitated as he continued his argument, and she had another outburst when Jones mentioned her attempts to throw suspicion on the Fenner family and others with her 11th-hour talk of poison. Raising up her head, which had been buried in her handkerchief for much of the trial, Sarah looked at Jones and shouted, "Don't tell them any more that ain't true—don't, I beg of you!" She was immediately given another sedative by a sheriff's deputy and soon calmed down. But as Jones ended his argument by noting that there was not a single living witness to confirm Sarah's statements about what had happened in the sickroom, Sarah suddenly raised her right hand and said to Jones, "Yes, there's a God! There's a God who knows!" C. W. Palmer managed to hush her up and Jones concluded his argument, pleading with the jury not to be blinded by "mawkish sentimentality." Actually, Jones had already shrewdly allowed for that possibility, tempering his demand for a death verdict with a suggestion to the jury that "if they found anything in her conduct or life to warrant it, they might commend her to the clemency of the Governor for commutation of sentence."

Judge Foote's charge to the jury was a careful one, stressing the laws covering circumstantial evidence and the necessity to allow only such evidence as seemed true "beyond a reasonable doubt." It is possible, however, that Judge Foote subtly tipped his hand in his final comment to the jury, solemnly warning those 12 West Side men: "A reasonable doubt of Mrs. Victor's guilt acquits her; but it would be at the peril of your own souls to acquit her if you believed the crime to be proved, and had not reasonable doubt." The jury went out at 12:15 P.M. on Tuesday, June 23, 1868.

Apparently, Sarah's jury elected not to imperil their souls overmuch, as they returned with a verdict of "guilty of murder in the first degree" after little more than four hours of deliberation. After foreman Charles H. Babcock read the verdict, Castle had the jury polled and they all firmly repeated, "Guilty." Sarah, weak and pale, sat slumped in her chair with her head buried in her arms. She showed no reaction whatsoever until she returned to the jail, where she fainted and lapsed into a stupor. The next morning, lawyers for the Connecticut Mutual Life Insurance Company filed suit to recover the $2,300 they had paid Sarah on the policy covering William Parquet.

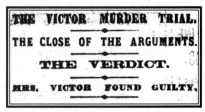

THE VICTOR MURDER TRIAL.

THE CLOSE OF THE ARGUMENTS.

THE VERDICT.

MRS. VICTOR FOUND GUILTY.

The *Plain Dealer*, June 24, 1868.

Sarah's physical and mental condition continued to decline during the 10 days between the verdict and her sentencing. By the time she appeared before Judge Foote again on July 3, she had lost more than half of her original 130-pound weight and appeared to be a distracted, mumbling wreck of her once imperious self. Carried by deputies to a table, she sat before Judge Foote, playing with a fan and an orange with a string around it and staring vacantly at nothing. Occasionally, she could be heard muttering, "I don't want to hear Mr. Jones talk so hard against me any more." By the time Jones asked Foote to pronounce sentence, Sarah had launched into the verses of "There Is Rest for the Weary," audibly singing:

> In the Christian's home in glory,
> There remains a land of rest.

Sarah showed no reaction to the sentence, except for a slight startled jerk of her body as Judge Foote uttered the words "To be hung by the neck until dead." It was later reported in the newspapers that he added the traditional sweetener, "And may God have mercy on your soul"—but some present would later insist that he pointedly omitted the phrase.

Sarah's scheduled execution date was August 20, 1868, but it is probable that few thought she would ever mount a scaffold in downtown Cleveland. It was believed that no woman had ever been executed in Ohio, and a growing chorus of voices pleaded that Sarah's life be spared because of her insane condition and her physical frailty. Some still thought she was faking it, and their point of view was expressed by the *Cleveland Leader* the morning after she was sentenced, its correspondent editorializing: "It may seem to some a little hard that a woman in such condition should be thus sentenced, but the court and prosecution had medical advice to the effect that all her insanity is assumed." Within 10 days, however, the *Leader* had altered its opinion to align with its traditional opposition to capital punishment. Sardonically jeering at those who wanted Mrs. Victor's life spared merely because of her physical condition, the *Leader* wondered:

> We now learn that Mrs. Victor is acting in the most disgusting manner. She does not seem disposed to die game. From a woman of a hundred and thirty pounds she has run down to about sixty, and is so weak that the sheriff had to carry her into the court room, and she could not stand up to receive sentence. At this rate unless execution is hurried, there will not be weight enough in her body to hang . . . . If it is shameful to sentence sixty pounds of flesh to the gallows, how is it helped by making it a hundred and thirty? Does the shame decrease as the flesh increases?

The *Leader* further noted that Mrs. Victor was *not* the first woman to be hanged in Ohio: some years before a black woman had been hanged for killing a fellow convict in Columbus, and no "mawkish sentimentality" had been mustered to prevent *her* execution.

Sheriff Felix Nicola, no mawkish sentimentalist himself, became convinced within a few days after Judge Foote's sentence that his prisoner was insane, and he wrote a letter to Ohio governor Rutherford B. Hayes to that effect. Nicola's opinion was backed by the medical advice of Drs. Beckwith, Schneider, Verdi, and Peck. This was exactly what Hayes, probably unaware of the previous Columbus hanging, wanted to hear, not wishing to be the first Ohio governor to permit the hanging of a female. And so, on July 15, Hayes postponed Sarah's sentence until November 20, 1868, and ordered Nicola to take her to the Northern Ohio Insane Asylum in Newburg until her reason was restored. Although Sarah gained most of her weight back during the three months she spent there, she was judged to be still insane in October and Governor Hayes commuted her sentence to life imprisonment. She was bundled off to the Women's Ward of the Ohio Penitentiary in Columbus. One of the conditions of her commutation was that she be held in solitary confinement for the rest of her life.

Seven years went by. Sarah's physical health soon recovered its wonted robustness, and by 1875 it was apparent that her reason, if ever truly absent, was fully restored. Living in a cell especially constructed for her, she almost never left its walls, received few visitors, and devoted herself to making quilts and clothing for various orphanages throughout Ohio. Perhaps as a token of her revived mental health, Sarah also began legal efforts in 1875 to get herself out of prison. These bore first fruits in 1877, when Judge Bingham of the Franklin County Common Pleas Court, after 18 months of consideration, shocked Ohio jurists on June 28, 1877, with a ruling that Sarah Victor be returned to Cuyahoga County to be hanged. Bingham's tortured legal reasoning was that, as Sarah had never legally consented to the commutation of her death sentence, it was still in effect; her legal status was that of an escaped prisoner still under sentence. No one expected Bingham's drastic ruling to stand, and Sarah remained in prison until it was duly struck down by the Ohio Supreme Court. But the case was a good index of Sarah's desperation to get out of prison and did much to remotivate both her partisans and enemies in the crusade to spring her from prison.

More years went by. Ohio governors came and went, Ohio Penitentiary wardens arrived and departed—and Sarah Victor stayed in her private cell, sewing and appealing, appealing and sewing as the years went by. Eventually, the mandate of solitary confinement was relaxed, and Sarah was permitted to give newspaper interviews, in which she excoriated her enemies and proclaimed her complete innocence. Finally, on Christmas Day, 1886, Governor Joseph B. Foraker granted her a pardon after she had served 18 years of her life sentence. Just after she walked through the gates of the Penitentiary, she told a *Plain Dealer* reporter:

> Yes, I am free at last; free from further punishment of a crime I never committed. I have a number of friends in Cleveland, who never believed me guilty of the crime, and with whom I shall make my home in the future . . . I shall face the world as an innocent person wrongfully punished should do; but it may be some little time before I am able to comprehend the great change in my life that has been so suddenly and unexpectedly brought

about. I have lived all these years in the hope that justice would
at last be done and though it has been long delayed, I will try to
begin life where I left it twenty years ago.

Perhaps not surprisingly, Sarah Victor soon realized she could
not resume her wonted Cleveland life. Although she had amassed
a small sum from her fine needlework during all those years in
prison, all of her Cleveland property was gone. Judge Foote, Marshal Castle, and C. W. Palmer were now dead. Christopher Columbus Carleton, although still to be found in the Forest City, was distinctly averse to rekindling their erstwhile ties when apprised of
her impending return. "I know nothing whatever of Mrs. Victor,"
he told a *Plain Dealer* scribe, "don't know where to direct you to,
and in fact I haven't thought anything about it." Soon conscious of
her isolation and continuing notoriety, Sarah elected to stay in
Columbus, where she had found a home with Mrs. James Taylor
and been befriended by several females active in the Women's
Christian Temperance Union. Eventually, she made her home in
Corry, Pennsylvania, with the family of Dr. Gray, her sister Libbie's ex-husband and sometime purveyor of the "Golden Pain
Searcher."

Of Sarah Victor's further fate we know little, except that the
Connecticut Mutual Insurance Company never got its $2,300 back
from her and that in 1890 she successfully disputed the legal suit
of one Henry Bowen, who claimed that she still owed him $118 for
medical treatment while she was in jail awaiting trial in the spring
of 1868. Sheriff Nicola was called as a witness in Bowen's suit, and
he testified that only Dr. Beckwith had attended Sarah in jail and
that Bowen was known to him only as a horse doctor and seller of
lightning rods. The case was dismissed, and Sarah Victor returned
to the obscurity that had blessed her before February 1868.

Sarah did leave one further testimonial to posterity, a lengthy,
tearful autobiography ghostwritten by one Harriet L. Adams and
published the year after Sarah got out of prison. Adams, it seems,
had been approached by representatives of the WCTU to help
Sarah, and her aid took the form of translating Sarah's anguished,
self-serving, and melodramatic recollections into publishable
form. Ungracefully entitled *The Life Story of Sarah M. Victor For
Sixty Years: Convicted of Murdering Her Brother, Sentenced to be*

Hung, Had Sentence Commuted, Passed Nineteen Years in Prison, Yet is Innocent, Told by Herself, Adams's tome was a 431-page rant filled with self-pity and unsubstantiated character assassination. Claiming she was innocent of any guilt in her brother's death, Sarah held that the charges against her had been contrived by her neighbor Jared Newell. It seems that Newell—who was now conveniently dead—had been connected with the 1853 murder of a Cleveland prostitute named Christiana Sigsby. Newell suspected, Mrs. Victor now stated, that she knew of his involvement in the Sigsby murder and capitalized on Libbie's known resentment about her brother's will to falsely incriminate Sarah and deflect attention from his own guilty past. Moreover, she now claimed that William Parquet had likely been a suicide; indeed, Sarah now recalled several occasions on which she had prevented him from taking his life. The revisionist tales now told by Sarah were preposterous, as were her attempts to refute the testimony of the dozens of prosecution witnesses at her trial. Replete with affidavits of her good character from those who had known her in prison and her new chums in the WCTU., *The Life Story of Sarah M. Victor* remains an obscure but amusing classic of cloying, mendacious self-pity.

So, did Sarah Victor really kill her brother for the insurance money? All of the evidence against her, as in the case of Sam Sheppard, was circumstantial. Some distinguished jurists had doubts about convicting her on that basis at the time, and the strictly circumstantial nature of the case was a factor in her eventual pardon. Indeed, in a similar case 50 years later—the Kaber arsenic *cum* murder-for-hire affair in Lakewood—virtually identical criminal counts of arsenic poisoning were withdrawn by the prosecution as being too weak to prove in court. And for all of its 39 witnesses, the state could not produce one who could say that he or she had seen Sarah give her brother arsenic in his sickroom during the week of his last illness. But, as in the case of Sam Sheppard, what *other* conclusion could a rational human being draw from the circumstances? There was no other person with an apparent motive for William's death—unless Sarah's weird story about Jared Newell was true. (The Christiana Sigsby murder was never solved, and there is nothing to connect Newell to it except Sarah's unsupported accusation.) It was apparent that Sarah lied about everything connected with her brother's death—unless one is willing to believe that *all* of the witnesses against her, including the respected Drs. Sapp and Beckwith, perjured themselves. Moreover, Sarah *acted* like a guilty person from start to finish, from the moment she informed Dr. Sapp of her premonitions of William's death, through her hysterical opposition to an autopsy, and on to her clumsy attempts to conceal her inheritance and manufacture alibis about pies. And her own version of the events, like Sam Sheppard's fable about the "bushy-haired intruder," was simply unbelievable from start to finish. Virtually nothing in the skein of events that led to William Parquet's death could be explained without assuming that Sarah had plotted to poison him with arsenic from the start.

It is perhaps fitting that no one knows where Sarah Victor sleeps today, untroubled by the accusers who pursued her in life. William Parquet also rests undisturbed in an unmarked grave in Woodland Cemetery, presumably with the bones of Sarah Victor's two children still in a box on top of his casket. Perhaps, too, that window in the top of his casket is yet intact, affording a convenient view should his errant sister decide to look in on him just one more time.

Chapter 10

PADDLE WHEEL DEATHTRAP

The 1850 *G. P. Griffith* Disaster

Considering its scope, it's a wonder that the 1850 *G. P. Griffith* disaster isn't better known to denizens of Northern Ohio. After all, it remains the worst Lake Erie disaster ever, with an unrivaled body count. No competitor even comes close: in just a few minutes, at least 140 and possibly as many as 250 helpless men, women, and children were killed, their pitiful corpses littered across a Lake County beach. Some have speculated that its relative obscurity is due to the fact that the *Griffith* carried no cargo of treasure, unlike more illustrious shipwrecks. But if sheer horror could be transmuted into gold, the *Griffith* story would be worth millions.

Built in 1847 in a Maumee shipyard, the 587-ton *Griffith* was one of many similar vessels constructed to transport the surge of immigrants that came through Buffalo en route to points west during the glory years of the Erie Canal. Measuring 193 feet in length, with a state-of-the-art cross-head steam engine, twin 31-foot paddle wheels, and two smokestacks, the solidly built craft was carefully designed by *Griffith* engineer D. Stebbins to avoid fire hazards that had destroyed previous Great Lakes carriers with great loss of life. Noting that many fires originated in the smokestack area, Stebbins placed "water jackets" around the *Griffith* stacks and allowed for an additional air space between them. With a one-eighth interest of his own in the boat, he, like *Griffith* captain Charles Roby, was determined to avoid a fiery catastrophe. Travel proceeded smoothly for the first three years, and the *Griffith* transported thousands safely from Buffalo up to Detroit and many points in between.

The *Griffith* left Buffalo on its final voyage on June 16, 1850. No one will ever know exactly how many persons were on it as it

steamed west into the setting sun, its paddles churning at a satis-
factory 10 miles per hour. Most accounts allow for as many as 320
people onboard: a crew of 25, about 40 cabin passengers, and
approximately 255 deck fares, who found what open space they
could for the lake voyage. Virtually all of the deck passengers were
westbound immigrants, a majority of them Germans from Baden,
as well as some Irish, some Scandinavians, and a group of 34 Eng-
lishmen bound for Medina via Cleveland. Most of them could not
speak English, most of them had their life savings on their persons
(money belts for the men, skirts with coins sewn into the hems for
women), and most of them couldn't swim. Only fire and darkness
were wanting for a first-class disaster, and those came shortly after
the *Griffith* left Fairport at 2:30 A.M., June 17.

Able seaman Richard Mann was on duty in the wheelhouse
when he saw the first sparks near the smokestacks about 3:30 A.M.
He alerted Second Mate Samuel McCoit, who hurled a bucket of
water at the sparks and sounded the alarm. But it was too late:
within seconds, flames were climbing the stacks and the fire was
already out of control. Someone may have shouted the command
to Mann, but he knew what to do and was already turning the *Griffith* south toward shore as the raging flames began to burn toward
the frantic human cargo aft of the wheelhouse. By now Captain
Roby was awake and on deck; it was his intention to beach his vessel as quickly as possible. The *Griffith* was only about two and a
half miles out, not far from the Chagrin River mouth, and headed
toward the Willoughbeach shore (now in Willowick, just north of
East 305th and Lakeshore Boulevard). But the fire was gaining
rapidly, the lifeboats could not be launched for fear of their being
swamped, and Captain Roby could not be sure how long his engine
could push the steamer before it was immobilized by the fire.

In the end, the engine made no difference. Just as it lost almost
all pressure, there came a shock, as the *Griffith* shuddered into a
submerged sandbar about two hundred yards from the unseen Lake
County shore. The sandbar was only eight feet down, but it was just
high enough to stop the *Griffith* dead in the water. Simultaneously,
the cessation of motion allowed the flames, which had been pushed
aft by the boat's movement, to reverse direction as the prevailing
wind took charge.

Most of the passengers died quickly. Those trapped aft as the
Griffith was struggling toward shore either died where they stood

or jumped into the water. One of them was seaman Richard Mann, who bravely stood his post at the wheel until the flames cooked him to a crisp. And those who jumped into the water didn't last much longer than Mann. Many of them, unable to swim and weighted down by valuables on their bodies, sank like stones to the bottom and didn't come up. Among these dead were Captain Roby, his wife, his daughter, and his mother-in-law. He stayed with the doomed ship as long as possible before throwing himself and his family into the water. Virtually all of the drowned perished in only eight feet or less of water.

In all, perhaps 40 persons managed to make it to shore from the sandbar. One of them was Dr. William Maronchy, a cabin passenger who had embarked at Erie. An indifferent swimmer, he soon tired of his exertions and was terrified of his companions in the water, some of whom grabbed on to anyone they could in their struggle to stay afloat. Another was John Rhodes, a five-year-old English boy. Pulled out of the lake by a fisherman, he was believed dead when laid out on the beach. But a local resident, Captain Kennedy, picked him up by the feet and shook the water out of him vigorously until he sputtered back to life. He later picked out his parents from the dead lining the beach. A more typical experience was that of a girl of 18 who grabbed on to a wooden boom and floated to shore. What was untypical was her sex: she was the only female on board the *Griffith* to survive the tragedy.

It took the local residents some time to fish whatever corpses they could find out of the water. (As many as one hundred may never have been accounted for; it is believed that badly burned corpses, unlike merely drowned ones, remain underwater because they will not hold the gases that otherwise inflate dead bodies.) Some were so thickly distributed that hooks thrust into the waves brought up half a dozen bodies at once, still clinging to each other by the hand. Others were merely charred skeletons heaped upon the burned hulk of the *Griffith*. Most of them could not be identified, but a substantial number were removed by boat for burial in Cleveland. That left 96 corpses to deal with, and as the severe June heat rose throughout the day, local residents decided something had to be done about them—soon. So they hastily dug a pit, not far from the beach, on the Mosher farm. It was 30 feet long, 6 feet wide, and 8 feet deep. They stacked the corpses in it like firewood and covered them over with leaves and dirt. There were 24 women,

47 men, and 25 children. In the list compiled of the dead they were cursorily identified only by such phrases as "a child of six months," "Mr. Hopper, a large genteel man," "a woman with gold earrings," and the like.

The inquest into the *Griffith* fire did not answer any of the anguished questions about the unprecedented disaster. There were rumors, still circulating on the Internet to this day, that First Mate William Evens was drunk (like Captain Roby, he was in fact asleep) that fatal night and spurned all fire warnings with the oath that he would "run his boat to Cleveland or run it to hell." Modern researchers have focused on engineer Stebbins's partiality to a newfangled engine lubricating oil he acquired before leaving Buffalo: subsequent tests proved that the oil burned with dangerous ferocity. Stebbins, who survived to testify at the inquest, emphasized his suspicions that a clandestine cargo of matches in the freight hold was responsible for the sudden conflagration. (Any such cargo would have invalidated the *Griffith*'s $27,000 insurance coverage.) Still other investigators favored that perennial favorite, "oily rags," as the cause.

There is little remembrance or trace of the *Griffith* tragedy today. Although it burned to the waterline, the hulk of the *Griffith* was eventually towed to shore, stripped, and sunk, probably just east of the Chagrin River mouth. Two Wickliffe divers recovered its bell in 1974.

The *Griffith* dead buried on the knoll by the lake did not rest in peace for long. Only two days after the mass internment, the corpses were brought up and buried in individual graves with crosses. Over subsequent decades, the *Griffith* burial plot became neglected and forgotten. As late as 1913, curious boys would occasionally unearth skeletons from the Mosher farm plot, but that ground has long since been claimed by Lake Erie erosion, the 96 corpses joining those never reclaimed from the lake. So much for the inaccurate concluding prophecy of one Kate Waver, woefully retailed in her 1850 poem, "Loss of the Steamer *Griffith*":

> But no—kind strangers bury them Beneath the daisied turf.
> On Erie's green banks, sleepingly by
> The solemn-sounding surf.
> There, with its music for their dirge,
> Together let them lay,

Till the trump sounds on sea and land,
The resurrection day!

During the early 1920s, the Willoughbeach Amusement Park briefly flourished where Lake County folk of the previous century had gawked at exhausted survivors and plotted schemes to scavenge valuables from the wreck. (There were persistent rumors that the corpses were stripped of rings by ghouls drawn to the scene, but there is no hard evidence.) Today it is simply a residential area in the heart of a bedroom suburb, across from the bustling Shoregate shopping center.

A welcome, and hopefully initial, token of the long overdue recognition due the *Griffith* tragedy finally came two years ago. After lengthy agitation and lobbying, Willowick resident and *Griffith* enthusiast Frank McCarty persuaded the Lake County Historical Society and the Lake Metroparks to place a memorial to the disaster in the Lakefront Lodge Park in Willowick. The 42-by-30-inch marker is part of the Ohio Bicentennial Commission's program to place historical markers throughout the state.

Chapter 11

WHEN MONSTERS WALK

Mary Jane Brady and the Collins Twins (1943)

Child murders are the worst. In an age of disintegrating families and throwaway progeny, every day seems to bring more tidings of mothers drowning tykes or toddlers being hit with drive-by gunfire. The truth, of course, is that children have never been safe from insane predators—inside or outside the family—and Cleveland has had its odious share of slaughtered innocents. It's an ugly chapter, from the hammer murder of Maggie Thompson in 1887 (chronicled in *The Corpse in the Cellar*) to the 1989 killing of Amy Mihaljevic. But any perusal of Cleveland's child butcheries over the years must still end with the conclusion that 1943 was the worst of the worst: the year of Mary Jane Brady and the Collins twins.

Edward Ralph could have been a poster boy for any number of social and psychological pathologies. Born to a violent, alcoholic father, Edward grew up in an unstable household made memorable by the frequent paternal beatings he endured. A precocious delinquent, Edward was only seven years old when convicted of robbery and sentenced to a year at Hudson Boys' School in 1918. There he learned divers sexual perversions and, after taking to drink at age 14, became a full-blown alcoholic. By 1926 he had progressed to car theft, earning himself another stint in the Boys' Industrial School at Lancaster. Then, following some minor scrapes with the law, he made the front pages of Cleveland newspapers in late 1930 as "The Fiend." Several dozen assaults on young women on the streets of Cleveland climaxed in December 1930 with the unprovoked shootings of Beatrice Gallagher, Mary Pshock, and Janet Blood. Pshock and Gallagher survived but Janet Blood did not, provoking the most intense police dragnet in Cleveland history.

Edward Ralph, killer of Mary Jane Brady . . . and Janet Blood?

Edward Ralph was arrested on January 26, identified by both Pshock and Gallagher as "The Fiend," and soon packed off to Mansfield Reformatory. He escaped in 1932 but was soon captured and returned to jail. The years went by. For all the Cleveland police knew, Edward Ralph had been swallowed by oblivion.

He had not. In January 1941 he was released on parole from Mansfield and returned to Cleveland. By day he worked as a driver for a pie company and by night drank himself into bellicose stupefaction. His temper had not improved with age, and he was beginning to suffer from blackouts. By now he was married to a 19-year-old girl named Rita, and she was pregnant with their first child. But that didn't stop the abusive Eddie from shacking up with Bernice Radloff, the wife of an absent serviceman, in early May. The day he moved into her first-floor apartment at 757 East 82nd Street, just south of Gordon Park, proved the beginning of the end for Mary Jane Brady.

Mary Jane was just five years old: blond, blue-eyed, and winsome. She had lost her father to a traffic accident, but she was doted upon by her mother, widow Dorothy Brady, her sister Barbara, age three, and her teachers and classmates at Stanard School. It was a happy, extended family, and there was no reason for Dorothy to hesitate about visiting her aunt Mabel Martoff that Thursday evening of June 3, 1943. A card game was in progress when she, Mary Jane, Barbara, and Dorothy's sister dropped in about 8 P.M. There were plenty of adults in the building, and there was little Jimmie Radloff, age six, to play with Mary Jane and Barbara. So what difference could it make if Dorothy and her sister slipped off to the movies? They would be back by eleven, and Jimmie and the card players would keep an eye on Mary Jane . . .

When Dorothy and her sister returned about 11 P.M., they found Barbara asleep on the Martoff couch. But there was no sign of

Mary Jane or, for that matter, Jimmie Radloff or his mother Bernice. After a fruitless search of the neighborhood, Mrs. Brady called the police, and they began combing the area at about 1:30 A.M.

It didn't take long to find Mary Jane. She was only 100 feet away from the rear of the apartment, about a third of the way down a wooded slope. She was lying face down under a tree, still clad in her gingham dress and quite dead. She was badly bruised and covered with blood, and patrolmen Thomas Osborne and Thomas Ellis could clearly see finger marks from a man's large hands around her throat.

The search for suspects soon led them to Bernice Radloff's door. When no one answered, Cleveland police lieutenant George Smythe entered through a window. There he found Bernice, passed out drunk on the floor. Edward Ralph was bending over her, trying to rouse her, and when Smythe asked him who he was Ralph attacked him. After he was subdued, police saw the blood on his shirt, on the rug, and at several other locations in the flat. Thirty minutes later Ralph was undergoing the third degree at Central Police Station. At first he said he couldn't remember anything except drinking at 15 bars in a row before waking up on Bernice's floor. Seven hours later, Edward Ralph cracked and confessed. It wasn't the 420 minutes of policemen shouting in his face or the lie detector test that he

A slaughtered innocent: Mary Jane Brady. *Cleveland News*, June 4, 1943.

failed. It wasn't even Mary Jane's blond hair and blood that they found on his clothes. It was when they brought in little Jimmie Radloff. In a halting voice, the six-year-old told of how Eddie had taken Mary Jane to the front room of the Radloff apartment, told Jimmie to go to sleep, and shut the door behind him. Then Jimmie told of hearing Mary Jane's cries, a terrible noise that he tried to block by pulling the covers over his head until he fell asleep. When Jimmie finished his awful story, Edward Ralph signed a formal confession that he had raped and murdered Mary Jane Brady. As he himself later put it: "The evidence was so damnable and a 6-year-old child who wouldn't lie accused me. I was forced to admit that I killed the child."

Witness to evil: Jimmie Radloff, 6, testifies against Edward Ralph, June 21, 1943. *Cleveland News.*

Ralph's indictment, trial, and execution may have set a judicial speed record for Cuyahoga County justice. He murdered Mary Jane on June 3, and his trial opened on June 21, after two out of three court-appointed psychiatrists had testified that he was sane. After Eddie's lawyers waived a jury trial, a three-judge panel consisting of Samuel Silbert, Frank Day, and Stanley Orr heard his case. But even his court-appointed lawyers, Alfred C. Jones and Nathan Bachner, scarcely had their hearts in the case. None of the witnesses for the prosecution was cross-examined, and the defense understandably waived identification of Mary Jane's bloody undergarments. Ralph himself remained in a semi-stupor while witnesses testified against him, burying his face in his hands and sobbing audibly. During his own appearance on the witness stand, he lost his temper and screamed at Assistant County Prosecutor John A. Mahon, "I know I'm going to the chair! Why waste any more time?"

Despite his written confession already in evidence, he doggedly maintained that he didn't remember killing Mary Jane and insisted, "This whole city is prejudiced. This trial is just a farce." The three-judge panel delivered its expected death verdict at 11:30 A.M., June 22, just 19 days after the murder. Speaking for the court, Judge Day called Ralph a "menace to society" and characterized his crime as "the most atrocious ever committed in this county." He then sentenced him to die in the electric chair on October 4. Three hours later, Ralph's wife Rita won an uncontested divorce from her doomed husband.

Ralph kept his date with death punctually, but not before the usual public blubbering by his anguished relatives. Ex-wife Rita lobbied for a life sentence instead of death, tearfully admitting that

Eddie had the mentality of a demonic 12-year-old and couldn't stay away from booze. "But," she insisted, "he's my man and I love him." Rita's emotional plea was supplemented by a formal clemency application made by her stepfather, Loyal Calkins, who argued against the finality of electrocution. Loyal's wife went even further, lilting to reporters: "Eddie should be paroled to our care. I'd like to have him around the house again. He's a good boy."

Justice may have been satisfied by Ralph's electrocution at 8:01 P.M. on October 4. (Curiosity as to whether he was Janet Blood's killer was not satisfied: he refused even

Send Child Slayer to Electric Chair

Cleveland Press, June 22, 1943.

to discuss her murder the day before he was executed.) But the social problem exposed by his bestial crime—the presence in Cleveland of large numbers of untreated mentally ill criminals, as well as official indifference—was not going to go away In an editorial published the day after Mary Jane Brady's murder, entitled "MUST IT HAPPEN AGAIN?" a shocked *Cleveland Press* writer concluded bleakly, "But it will happen again." Just how soon, he surely could not have guessed.

The nasty prologue to the Collins tragedy began just before noon on Wednesday, August 11, just nine weeks after the Brady murder. John Buchanan, the nine-year-old son of city food inspector Enos B. Buchanan, thought the man in the blue Chevy who picked him up on a corner near his parents' home was a family friend. He was not: he was 17-year-old Henry William Hagert of Lakewood, and he was a younger and even more malevolent version of Edward Ralph.

Henry, like Ralph, had started going bad at the age of seven. According to his mother, Ida Hagert, it was from the after-effects of "brain fever" and double pneumonia. But whatever it was, Henry became unstable and prone to angry, aggressive behavior from that time on. He managed to make it to Emerson Junior High, but his education ceased abruptly in January 1942 with his arrest by the Lakewood police on multiple auto theft charges (Henry was going 60 miles per hour when they shot out his tires). At least his formal education ended—for, like Edward Ralph, Henry could claim a graduate degree in sexual perversion after his 11-month stint in the Boys' Industrial School at Lancaster. Despite two escape attempts, however, Henry was paroled in January 1943 and thereafter lived with his parents at their home at 15915 Clifton Boulevard. But his irascible behavior did not improve, and finally, after months of mounting abuse, his mother Ida had him committed to the psycho ward of Cleveland City Hospital in early July.

Just why Henry Hagert walked out of that hospital on August 9 has never been satisfactorily explained. Ida Hagert later claimed that she begged chief staff physician Louis Karnosh to keep Henry incarcerated. But, in the aftermath of the Collins tragedy, Karnosh contradicted Ida's version of events, stating that it was she who had repeatedly insisted on the release of her son. In any event, according to hospital records Henry was diagnosed as having a "psychopathic personality," but his condition could not legally justify his being held against his will. Which is why Henry Hagert was waiting in his blue Chevy sedan when John Buchanan stepped out in front of the Beach Cliff Theater on Detroit Road.

Find City Aide's Son Injured In Wood;Kidnaped, Boy Says

The first victim: John Buchanan. *Cleveland News*, Aug. 12, 1943.

Henry's initial plan was to murder John after sexually assaulting him, but his purpose wavered as they drove aimlessly around Cleveland that afternoon and into the night. Henry later claimed that he grew to like John so much and was so moved by his tearful pleas for his life that he decided not to kill him. That didn't stop Henry from torturing and sexually abusing the terrified child, but it did save John's life. After the two slept in Henry's car behind a Rocky River grocery chain store overnight, Henry decided to release John to his parents. Henry didn't want to get caught, so he drove John to a remote patch of woods, just 100 feet west of Clague Road and about 600 feet south of the Nickel Plate Railroad tracks. There, he tied a T-shirt around John's head and sexually assaulted him again. He then drove to a pay phone and placed a series of calls to John's frantic parents. Refusing to identify himself, he gave a series of garbled clues as to where their son could be found. The police found John Buchanan about noon, under the fallen tree where Henry had left him. He was dazed, bleeding, and thoroughly traumatized by his 24-hour ordeal. But before detectives took him to St. John's Hospital, he managed to tell them that the man who had abducted him drove a "blue car." It wasn't much of a clue, but—coupled with his incredible complicity in his own capture—it proved to be a fatal one for Henry.

He had more mischief to commit after he abandoned John Buchanan, but 2 P.M. the following afternoon found him back at the site where he had left the boy. By that time, *Plain Dealer* reporter Todd Simon and staff photographer Andrew Kraffert were also there, setting up to photograph the scene. The odd-looking fellow who ambled up and inquired, "Is this where they found that boy, like it says in the papers?" immediately intrigued Simon and Kraffert. As Henry wandered around the area, asking more questions, Simon was suddenly reminded of the clichéd notion of the criminal returning to the scene of his crime. Simon knew it was a "one-in-a-million" shot, but he was quite unnerved by the surly stranger. As Henry engaged Kraffert in conversation, Simon covertly scribbled a description of the creepy young man: short, slight, stoop-shouldered, chin jutting out, slit-eyed, pimply-faced, and wearing a blue shirt, a gray felt hat, and gray pants. More importantly, Simon also wrote down the license plate number—Q8-53—of the blue Chevy. What neither Simon nor Kraffert knew was what Hagert later admitted to the police: he was so miffed at Kraffert's wary manner that he would have shot him on the spot if he'd found him alone.

John Buchanan's clue about the car and Simon's notes proved to be Hagert's undoing. Later that afternoon, Cleveland police detective Inspector Frank W. Story mentioned the "blue car" to Simon and the reporter turned over his notes. Within minutes, Cleveland and Lakewood police were looking for Henry at his home. When they learned he had been absent from it the night of Buchanan's abduction, they began methodically cruising the West Side in search of Henry. Cleveland police detective Paul Robinson and Lakewood detective Sergeant Myron Shattuck soon found him, sitting on a coping in front of the Lakewood Public Library at Detroit and Arthur Avenues. Although he still had a gun hidden under his shirt, he surrendered peacefully. A half hour later Cleveland and

Lakewood police began questioning Henry about the abduction of John Buchanan. The interrogation didn't evolve as officials had planned. After two hours of fruitless questioning, Cleveland police superintendent of ballistics David Cowles began preparing Henry for a lie-detector test. As he began removing Henry's shirt, a

loaded. 32 caliber pistol and a bill-fold with a slip of paper sticking out fell on the floor. The slip of paper had John Buchanan's name on it, and even as Cowles stooped to pick up the pistol, Henry tonelessly said, "The gun you have in your hand is the one I shot the other two with."

The *other* two? The Cleveland police already knew that James and Charles Collins, the 13-year-old twin sons of George and Penelope Collins of 3043 West 111th Street, were missing. They had vanished about noon on Thursday while on their way to their jobs as caddies at the Lakewood Country Club in Westlake. Last seen standing on Warren Road near Detroit Avenue, they had been the objects of a search even more frantic than the dragnet for John Buchanan. As the police and Hagert now journeyed to the death scene, Henry blithely confessed, "I killed them just for the heck of it."

Henry William Hagert, killer of the Collins twins. *Cleveland Press*, August 14, 1943.

They found James and Charles just where Henry said they would, in the woods at the dead end of Saddler Road in Bay Village. The bodies were about 300 feet apart and both shot at the base of the skull. There at the grisly scene, Henry explained without any apparent emotion or remorse how he had seen the twins the previous morning as they tried to thumb a ride on Warren Road. He had already passed them once but then decided to return and pick them up. Henry had probably already decided to kill them, much as he had originally intended to kill John Buchanan. But the fate of the twins was sealed when he asked them where they wanted to go and

'I Just Felt Like Killing Them, So I Did,' Says Twins' Slayer

"*Yes, I killed them*"   "*They think I'm nuts*"   "*I feel dizzy*"   "*Just like a dream*"

Cleveland News, August 14, 1943.

one of them said, "Okay Jeeves, onward to the west." Hagert was "burned" by this "smart-aleck" remark, and his blue Chevy soon arrived at the end of Saddler Road in the Bay Village woods. Telling Charles he would kill James if he heard him get out of the car, Hagert marched James several hundred feet into the woods before shooting him in the back of the head at close range. Then he returned to the car for Charles, whom he dispatched in identical fashion, about 300 feet further into the woods. He had one bad moment, when he was accosted by West Side residents Mildred Bucha and Margaret Wilson, who were berry picking in the area. They actually saw him with the twins and conversed with at least one of them and Hagert. But the boys were too terrified to reveal their peril, and the women had no idea of Henry's real purpose in the woods. So they thought it was just someone "shooting at targets" when they heard two gunshots a bit later and then saw Henry's blue Chevy roar back up Saddler Road.

If Clevelanders had been shocked by Edward Ralph's cold-blooded indifference, they were even more appalled by Henry Hagert's flip bravado about his horrible crimes. Over the next week, reporters for the *Plain Dealer*, *Cleveland Press,* and *Cleveland News* furnished their readers with shocking samples of his psychopathic, affectless personality:

It's pretty serious, you know. I kidnapped one kid and killed two
others . . . I just felt like killing them, so I killed them. Now it all
seems like a bad dream . . . I had the urge to kill before but I
always managed to suppress it by running. I'd run down the
street because I felt I had too much energy. The Collins boys
were just victims of circumstance. I would have killed anyone at
that time. It just happened to be them . . . I'm not especially sorry
for any of those folks I have hurt . . . the whole thing is just like
a smashed fender . . . when it's done, it's done—that's all.

The machinery of justice did a sloppier, if necessary, job on
Henry Hagert than it had on Edward Ralph. Since Henry was only
17, the first move against him was a delinquency charge of first-
degree murder in juvenile court. There, after a panel of psychiatrists (many of whom had already evaluated Edward Ralph) looked
him over, Judge Harry L. Albright declared that Hagert "is now
insane and probably has been for some time," and ordered him held
for the Cuyahoga County grand jury. This put the prosecutor's
office in a bind, for as Assistant Prosecutor John Mahon noted,
Henry now had the option of asking either for a legal hearing on his
sanity or pleading insanity at his trial. If he were judged insane at
the hearing, he would go to Lima State until he recovered his sanity enough to be tried for murder. But if he were found not guilty,
the state would have to let him go for good, unless they could hold
him on another charge.

This clearly would not do, and on October 5, 1943, a second
panel of psychiatrists reported to Common Pleas judge Charles J.
McNamee on Henry's sanity. They judged him sane, and he was
immediately bound over to the grand jury. The formal sanity hearing on October 25 ratified the panel's sanity verdict, with five psychiatrists voting down the three who affirmed Henry's insanity.
The hearing was highlighted by Henry's own antics and the
pathetic testimony of his mother Ida. She told the court that Henry
had told her of often seeing little midgets on the fender of his automobile, mocking him. And when Dr. Harry A. Lipson described his
interview with the accused, Henry jumped up and screamed, "No,
you didn't, you didn't talk to me!"

The trial, which began on November 22, turned, as expected, on
the voluminous psychiatric testimony. With Judge McNamee presiding, court-appointed lawyers Edward E. Lurie and Roy C.
Green defended Henry, while John A. Mahon and Frank T. Culli-

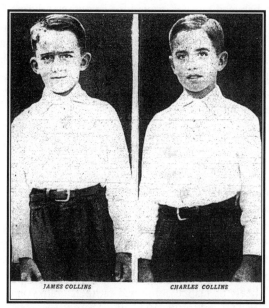

JAMES COLLINS   CHARLES COLLINS

The Collins Twins, James & Charles.

tan prosecuted for the state. Five psychiatrists testified that Henry was sane, including the venerable H. H. Drysdale (a name familiar to readers of these chronicles), who termed Henry "a petulant, cruel, ruthless, determined, egotistical young man with no respect for God, man or the Devil." Several psychiatrists tried to support the defense claim that Henry was crazy, but their testimony was fatally undermined by Detective Paul Robinson, who retailed his conversation with Henry just before his second sanity hearing:

> Hagert: I'll bet you a dime they say I'm insane.
> Robinson: What makes you think that?
> Hagert: Well, I fooled 'em once, and I'll fool 'em again.
> Robinson: Are you insane?
> Hagert: Naw.

Robinson's dramatic disclosure followed the testimony of Dr. Richard E. Stout, who told the jury that Hagert had told him the first thing he would do if he were set free "would be to kill Todd Simon."

The defense, prudently, did not put Henry on the stand, believing that it would be inconsistent with his insanity plea. Henry, for his part, behaved himself, except for an outburst during Cullitan's final peroration. When Cullitan suggested that Henry only picked on young boys because he was a coward, Henry rose up and screamed, "Shut up, you _____!" But for the most part he looked down at the floor during the proceedings, especially during the harrowing testimony of Penelope Collins, mother of the murdered twins, and John Buchanan.

To no one's surprise, the jury took only a little over two hours to reach its verdict of "guilty of first-degree murder—without a recommendation of mercy." The first ballot was 11 to 1, with one holdout for mercy; the second, unanimous vote quickly followed. Most of the jurors, one suspects, thought Henry was insane by any imaginable standard of common sense, but they knew not what else to do with such an incorrigible monster. Henry himself took the verdict with typical aplomb. Laughing back in his jail cell for the benefit of reporters, he jeered, "I killed two. The state can only kill one. Me, I put one over on them. I guess I didn't act crazy enough."

The wheels of justice continued on their cranky and eccentric course. On December 28, 1944, the Ohio Supreme Court overturned the trial verdict. They ruled that the introduction of evidence from his pretrial sanity hearing at his criminal trial was "probably prejudicial" and ordered a new trial. It came in March 1945, and this time his lawyers waived a jury trial in favor of a three-judge panel consisting of Judges Samuel H. Silbert, Arthur H. Day, and Julius Kovachy. The same witnesses and experts were all trotted out to repeat their lines—and the same death verdict was returned on March 9, 1945. The irrepressible Henry spit at the three judges as they announced their decision.

Henry kept his second date with the electric chair on October 3, 1945. When they came for him, he stopped playing "It's Roundup Time in Texas" on the phonograph in his cell and went quietly. As they strapped the electrodes on, he quipped, "Do a good job of it now. Give me a good dose—it's good for what ails me." The first jolt hit him at 7:03 P.M. and he was pronounced dead at 7:08. By his request, the corneas of his eyes were immediately removed for transplant to a living patient. Henry was particularly insistent that they go to a sightless World War II veteran.

There's no edifying moral to the tragedies of Mary Jane Brady and the Collins twins. These murders stirred up much public agitation for reform in society's methods of dealing with psychopaths like Ralph and Hagert. Much newspaper ink was wasted in recounting the promises of state and local politicians to prevent and control such monsters. Yet four years later, a killer with a resume virtually identical to those of Ralph and Hagert was waiting on a rainy East Side street for Sheila Ann Tuley. Three years later, another pervert found Beverly Potts at Halloran Park. Beverly Jarosz, Tiffany Papesh, Amy Mihaljevic . . . the list goes on and on. So let's give the last word to William F. McDermott, famed *Plain Dealer* scribe, who wondered eloquently at society's mismanagement of sickos like Henry Hagert:

> Another public failure the Hagert murders bring sickeningly to mind concerns our penal institutions. For a year, Hagert was a scholar at the Boys' Industrial School in Lancaster. Formerly such institutions were called reform schools. They do not seem particularly successful in forming their inmates. Hagert is a shining example of their failure in that respect. What he confesses learning about in the Boys' Industrial School is sexual perversion . . . A future and more enlightened age may regard it as strange and barbaric that we should try and reform people of criminal tendencies by clapping them behind walls where they are obliged to associate for years with other weak, maladjusted and vicious prisoners, learning all the evil they know, giving and taking contamination from their kind.

We have learned little since Edward Ralph and Henry Hagert roamed Cleveland streets, and McDermott's strictures will still be valid and available the next time we need them.

Chapter 12

THE KILLER
IN THE ATTIC

The 1903 Reichlin Murder

For sheer improbability, it is hard to beat the Reichlin murder. Consider the victim: Agatha Reichlin, a devout Catholic housekeeper with no known enemies and a saintly reputation. Consider the place: a small-town Catholic rectory, where Agatha kept house for her brothers, a priest and a publisher. Best of all, consider the accused: another staid, middle-aged Catholic priest, charged with a brutal midnight murder. Lorain County has had its share of shocking events—the Meach Brothers Massacre (see *The Corpse in the Cellar*) and the 1924 Lorain Tornado come to mind—but its superlative mystery remains the unsolved Reichlin murder.

By all accounts, life in the church parsonage at the southwest corner of Reid Avenue and 8th Street unfolded like one grand, sweet song in the spring of 1903. Presiding over the household was the Reverend Charles W. Reichlin, 40, founding pastor of nearby St. Joseph's Roman Catholic Church. His brother Casimir Reichlin, 42, the respectable publisher of the German-language *Lorain Post*, lived with him, as did their younger, unmarried sister Agatha, 34, who kept house for the two bachelors. Charles had come to the U.S. for his seminary training several decades before at the instigation of his uncle, the Reverend Casimir Reichlin of St. Stephen's Church, Cleveland; his siblings had emigrated together from Switzerland in 1895. They had moved to Lorain in 1896 and after seven years the threesome was respected and even cherished by Lorain townsfolk, especially Agatha, who supplemented her arduous domestic duties with charitable work among her brother's flock. The genial tenor of their evenings together was oft enlivened by family singing, moderate beer consumption, and the frequent presence of another brother, Martin, who lived nearby. No one

Cleveland Press, May 1, 1903.

could have predicted this family idyll would end in a few seconds of nocturnal violence.

Thursday, April 30, the night of Agatha's murder, began innocuously enough. The Reverend Charles was away, substituting for a vacationing priest on Kelleys Island. But his place was happily filled by a substitute of his own, 51-year-old Reverand Ferdinand Walser, a priest of the Precious Blood Fathers and pastor of Sacred Heart Church in Toledo. Martin Reichlin dropped by for the evening, which was pleasantly passed with conversation, German songs, and a bottle of beer apiece for the men. These frivolities ended promptly at 10 P.M., when Martin departed and Casimir, Agatha, and Walser retired to bed. All of them slept on the second floor, Walser in a room adjacent to Agatha's and Casimir across from both of them. The only unusual circumstance later recalled by Casimir was the sound of someone going down the stairs to the first floor and returning somewhat later. He assumed it was Agatha and recurred to his own morbid thoughts. They were sufficient distraction, as he later recalled for the coroner's inquest:

> I lay awake for perhaps half an hour, although I usually sleep soundly on going to bed. Something seemed to worry me that something was going to be wrong. I never had that feeling before. I felt there was going to be trouble in the family.

Casimir was right about that. The Reverend Walser had gone to sleep immediately after 10 P.M., but sometime after midnight he was awakened by what he thought was a pistol shot. He lay still, decided he was mistaken, and dozed off again. A few minutes later he was reawakened by the sounds of sobbing and moaning coming from Agatha's room, only a dozen feet from his bed. Walser knew she was an uneasy sleeper, and he propped his head on his elbow and waited for her to awaken.

Agatha didn't awaken. The next thing Walser heard was the sound of a match being struck, and he looked up to find the door to Agatha's room ajar. In the doorway, he caught a glimpse of a man wearing a slouch hat and sporting a mustache, looking at him and carrying what appeared to be a dark lantern in his hand. Surmising the stranger was a burglar, Walser shouted, "Here, what do you want here, get out!" The mustachioed man turned and fled through Agatha's room and into the adjacent attic, an unfinished space accessed through Agatha's closet. Walser ran to Casimir's room and roused him. Casimir went into the attic and found it empty, a tell-tale ladder propped up outside leading to its only window from a

"The Murderer's Victim," *Cleveland Press*, May 1, 1903.

flowerbed below. He then turned to rouse Agatha, but it was no use. By the time he struck his second match in the darkened room he could already tell she was dead.

Captain Stephen Ketchum's squad of Lorain police got to the rectory just after 1 A.M., about 20 minutes after Casimir's grim telephone call. Their initial researches added little to what Casimir and Walser already knew. The apparent killer had fled, presumably down the ladder, and Walser's glimpse of the mustachioed man was too vague to proceed upon further. Agatha had been brutally murdered, her face smashed and her skull splintered by some heavy object. Whether she was sexually assaulted was never determined, nor was it clear whether she had been strangled to stifle her cries before she was killed. The ladder was still propped up outside, its rungs covered with mud, presumably from the shoes of the murderous intruder. (It would be days before the bumbling police learned that the ladder had been stolen from a nearby neighbor's lot.) A few feet away from the ladder the police found a five-pound stone, smeared with Agatha's blood and hair. (It was never proven whether the stone was brought into the house or even if it was the actual murder weapon.) As they had no other clues to go on,

The setting. *Cleveland Press*, May 1, 1903.

Ketchum's squad occupied themselves largely with consoling the shaken Walser and Casimir as best they could. Acting on Ketchum's advice, the traumatized Casimir immediately sent to Armstrong's Hotel for a gallon of whiskey, which he and Walser shared to the satisfaction of everyone there. If the whiskey did not actually impede the investigation, it certainly furnished subsequent, delicious gossip for Lorain townsfolk and damaged the reputation of all concerned.

The mystery of Agatha's death only deepened the following day, intensified by sensational newspaper publicity. It seemed inconceivable to most criminologists, amateur or professional, that the slaying had been committed by a Reichlin family foe or even a burglar bent on acquiring swag. Agatha was a benevolent virgin and her brothers had led blameless lives. There was no reason to believe that the rectory contained any valuables (excepting the sacred vessels in a safe), and nothing had been taken by the homicidal intruder, including rings and watches on a shelf by Agatha's bed. Given these perplexing facts, it was inevitable that sleuths started thinking of an "inside job," thinking spurred by two additional considerations. One was the absence of blood on the ladder, despite its copious presence at the slaying scene and on the supposed murder rock. The other consideration was the household presence of a pugnacious (some said "vicious") St. Bernard with

PRIEST CHARGED WITH
MISS REICHLIN'S MURDER

REV. FERDINAND WALSER.

Priest or predator? The Reverand Ferdinand Walser.
Cleveland Leader, May 2, 1903.

full run of the premises at night. Why had this notoriously bel-
ligerent and noisy dog not barked during the intruder's ascent of
the ladder—despite its proximity to the dog's usual lair? By Friday
afternoon, ugly suspicions were festering in Lorain town. They
inevitably centered on the most alien element in the puzzle: the
Reverend Ferdinand Walser. On Saturday morning, after consulting with Mayor F. J. King, Lorain County sheriff G. P. Braman, and
deputy coroner S. S. Cox, who had conducted Agatha's autopsy,
Lorain County prosecutor Lee Stroup formally charged Father
Walser with "maliciously, unlawfully, purposely and with premeditation killing Agatha Reichlin with a rock."

Stroup would later defend Walser's arrest as motivated by concern for his safety—ugly hints of mob violence were said to be
bruited—but it seems likely that baffled Lorain lawmen didn't
know what else to do. An additional justification cited was the

behavior of the pack of bloodhounds that Lorain County authorities had managed to recruit from Fort Wayne, Indiana, after a fruitless canvas of Ohio. The dogs, which were brought in to disrupt the shaken Reichlin home at 1:00 A.M. Saturday morning, distinguished themselves by simply running back and forth between Walser's bed and a bed in Agatha Reichlin's room. Sober souls would eventually point out that the latter was not the murder bed, but by that time Walser was already in jail.

The remainder of the Reichlin murder drama played out as a sloppy, albeit macabre, Keystone Cops comedy. The Reverend Charles Reichlin returned home in time to see Walser arrested and to join Casimir and many others in championing the complete innocence of the stunned, befuddled priest. Casimir, whose dark hair reportedly turned white overnight, went so far as to state: "If Father Walser is guilty, then I am guilty. If he should hang, then they ought to hang me." After Coroner French's inquest rehashed the meager physical evidence and heard witnesses from three nearby homes tell of sighting burglars in the neighborhood on the murder night, French closed the proceedings on Tuesday, May 5, with a verdict of "murder by an unknown hand." Four hours later, Mayor King piously reiterated his lofty motives in arresting Father Walser and then discharged him from jail. The good Precious Blood father, whose pious dignity had never wavered throughout his ordeal, addressed his erstwhile accusers with tears in his eyes:

> You cannot say a word against me. You have hurt me a great deal. Agatha Reichlin is the last person I would have killed and I would not have killed anybody . . . I could not kill a chicken. I wish to express my heartfelt thanks for liberation from the dreadful charge that has hung over me.

Father Walser was mobbed by a crew of well-wishers as he left the court in quiet triumph.

Walser's legal exoneration did not satisfy some interested parties, particularly after the arrest of an itinerant criminal, Frank Kennedy, proved valueless to the stalled investigation. While Lorain lawmen focused on the possibility that an unknown "maniac" tramp was the killer (possibly a member of a rumored criminal hobo freemasonry known as the "Lake Shore" gang), outside sleuths, particularly Cleveland's Jake Mintz, maintained that they could easily solve the mystery if given a free hand. Egged on by Mintz—and perhaps encouraged by the $5,000 reward posted for the killer—Prosecutor Stroup agreed to the exhumation of Agatha Reichlin's corpse. This was accomplished to little purpose on the morning of May 14, despite the vociferous opposition of her brothers. Both Coroner French and Jake Mintz professed to see hitherto undisclosed "marks of violence" on the decaying corpse, but in fact their grisly reexamination added nothing to the case. Probably the best evaluation of the exhumation was the Reverend Reichlin's, who termed it "strange and unnatural"—but that didn't stop Mintz et al. from soon baying for a second exhumation and some additional third-degree sessions for Father Walser.

Lorain folk had seen enough, however. Reichlin family friends were particularly appalled by the exhumation and soon deluged Mayor King with anonymous letters bearing the warnings: "Prepare to meet your God" and "An avenging nemesis is on your track." When the Lorain Council balked at further underwriting the murder probe, Mayor King relented. But the case dragged on into September, when Prosecutor Stroup and a grand jury sifted through the evidence one more time before abandoning the probe. This final effort provided such sights as Walser and Reichlin acting out the murder night in pantomime and a curious juror climbing the famous ladder to the attic window.

The Reichlin murder remains unsolved to this day. There is the remote possibility that Jake Mintz took the solution of the mystery to his grave in 1947, but don't hold your breath. His last words on the subject, uttered on May 22, 1903, are still replete with tantalizing, if empty braggadocio:

> To my mind there is but one solution to the mystery, and I have that solution figured out to such a nicety that any jury in the country would return an indictment. We have perfected a chain of evidence that is complete in every feature, circumstantially. All that is necessary is to establish a few points upon which we are working.

Chapter 13

SOONER OR LATER...

The 1949 Thompson Trophy Tragedy

In hindsight, it now seems like the inevitable accident. On September 5, 1949, during the annual National Air Races held at Cleveland Airport, a modified F-51 Mustang air racer crashed into a Berea home, killing the plane's pilot, a young mother, and her infant son. Even the *Plain Dealer*, which had never ventured a discouraging word about the Labor Day weekend event, opined solemnly, "What was bound to happen sooner or later in the National Air Races happened late Labor Day afternoon." Behind that phrase lies the untold tale of an accident that never should have happened.

The National Air Races were started in 1920 and lured to Cleveland in 1929 by the city's power elite (Alva Bradley, M. J. Van Sweringen, et al.). They soon became an annual ritual and emblem of Cleveland's pretensions to premier urban status. Held at Cleveland Airport, the races attracted enormous crowds, featured such aviation celebrities as Charles Lindbergh, James Doolittle, and Wiley Post, and garnered Cleveland coveted media attention throughout the world. Among the events were such crowd-pleasers as the cross-country Bendix Trophy race (a long-distance marathon from Los Angeles to Cleveland) and the daredevil Thompson Trophy contest (a closed-course, high-speed race around pylons), ensuring that the National Air Races became a fixed institution in Northeast Ohio—despite their real dangers to both pilots and civilians. Dangers that increased every year, as the aircraft got faster, the crowds waxed greater, and—in retrospect the most obviously ignored element—the once exurban region surrounding the Cleveland Airport became suburbanized, with ever-growing housing subdivisions. By the late 1930s, indeed, it is fair to say that it was not a question of whether a terrible tragedy was going to occur, but when.

The death toll began at the very first races held here in 1929. Five pilots were killed in cross-country flying accidents away from the Cleveland area. Locally, pilot Thomas Reid was killed on August 31 when his big green Emsco aircraft crashed in the woods near West 226th Street and Westwood Road, just three hours after he set a new world record for solo endurance flight. Other lowlights of the 1929 event were the crash of Lady Mary Heath's Great Lakes Trainer through the roof of the Mills Company at 965 Wayside Drive, and the near death of parachutist Norma Stevens when her chute failed to open properly in an abrupt descent on Grayton Road.

The mayhem resumed on September 3, 1934, when Douglas Davis, the winner of that year's Bendix race, lost control of his plane during the eighth lap of the Thompson Trophy race, a high-speed course with tight turns plotted at low altitudes over the suburbs ringing Cleveland Airport. Just as Davis negotiated the number two pylon, his black-and-white monoplane shot straight up into the air—and then straight down at a speed of at least 350 miles per hour. Seconds later, the plane smashed into a field in North Olmsted Village near Lorain and Gessner Roads. Efforts to extricate Davis's pulverized corpse were hampered by thousands of Clevelanders who thronged the scene trying to scavenge souvenirs from the grisly wreckage.

The next fatality came at 6:50 P.M. on September 2, 1937, when the wings of pilot Lee Miles's Miles-Atwood Special disintegrated during speed trials at the airport. Miles was killed instantly when his fuselage slammed into some woods on the property of John C. Fischer at 4950 Grayton Road. The tragedy was almost repeated the next day when Count Otto von Hagenburg of Germany, a celebrated stunt flyer, crashed while performing a routine that put his plane upside down at an altitude of one foot—while doing 150 miles per hour.

Amazingly, Hagenburg walked jauntily away from his broken plane with only a slight head wound and a wave to the stunned crowd.

The deadly pace of these airborne disasters accelerated in 1938. During a qualifying trial on August 31, the engine of Russell G. Chambers's plane exploded at an altitude of 150 feet. Crashing into Will Thomson's pear orchard between Wagar and Clague Roads in Rocky River, Chambers died several days later from a fractured skull. Three days after his crash, a connecting rod in George Dory's fleet Bushy-McGrew racer broke while he was flying in the Greve Trophy Race. The courageous Dory managed to maneuver his plummeting plane through a crowded residential area before it crashed into the dead end of West 227th Street, about one-third of a mile north of Lorain. The badly injured Dory was pulled from his smashed craft by an eight-year-old boy and his father. Everyone marveled at how "lucky" it was that his plane had not hit someone's home.

The 1939 races, the last held before the end of the coming war, brought more of the same. On September 3, some 65,000 spectators saw Leland Williams's red Brown Racer spin out of control and smash into a field on the farm of Charles Nock between Rocky River Drive and Grayton Road. Williams was killed instantly, but the mess was soon cleaned up and the usual lack of thought given to the potential carnage to come.

If success is measured by attendance, the 1947 races were the best ever, with several hundred thousand spectators jamming the three-day event. But there was no letup in the violence, which began even before the formal events commenced. On August 25 pilot James C. DeSanto bailed out of his Curtiss P-60E aircraft after watching his elevator and tail fall off the plane during a test sprint. He landed safely, suffering only minor bruises, but his plane crashed into a corn patch owned by Fred Techmyer on Hummel Road in Brook Park. The following day pilot Claude Smith also parachuted to safety after something in the left wing of his Falcon Special snapped and he careened toward the ground. He landed in a field off Eastland Road some seconds after his plane slammed into a lot on Eastland, just 150 feet from the home of W. A. Waddups. Four days later James C. Ruble, an entrant in the cross-country Bendix race, bailed out of his burning P-38 Lightning fighter over the Arizona desert after his engine caught fire. No one was hurt in that mishap either, but the worst was yet to come.

It came during the Thompson Trophy race on September 1, aptly described by the *Plain Dealer* as "the wildest, fastest 30 minutes of air racing in history." While 75,000 spectators goggled, Clevelander Anthony R. Jannazo lost control of his navy surplus Corsair and plunged into a field on Royalton Road, near Marks Road in Strongsville. As his plane exploded, hurling Jannazo's decapitated body clear, the Corsair's engine skipped across Royalton Road, narrowly missing a car with four persons in it, knocked down three apple trees, and buried itself in the ground. Minutes later, J. L. Ziegler bailed out of his P-40 fighter after his engine failed, landing in a patch of swamp off Brookpark Road and breaking his right leg. His plane continued on, a wing slicing off the top of a boxcar in the New York Central yard near West 150th Street and the fuselage crashing into an adjacent mesh of railroad tracks. About the same moment, Mrs. Melvin Patrick was hit and injured by Ziegler's Plexiglas cockpit cover, which landed on her while she was watching the air races from a chair in her yard at 5100 West 148th Street.

And there was still more destruction before the end of the 1947 races. Woodrow Edmondson was just rounding pylon number three when the engine of his P-51 Mustang exploded. Instead of bailing out, he tried landing it on the farm of H. M. Jacobs near Albion and Webster Roads. Edmondson was badly injured when his plane skidded into a grove of trees and caught fire. Meanwhile, another Thompson racer, Jack B. Hardwick, walked away from the crash landing of his P-51 with only a bruised elbow. After his engine failed early in the race he succeeded in bringing his plane down in an empty field off Rocky River Drive in Brook Park. The races were getting bloodier by the year, and no one seemed to be counting the cost.

The year 1948 may have lured National Air Races officials into a false sense of security. There was but one fatality, and it could have been much worse. Midget plane racer Paul A. DeBlois was piloting his Bee Gee Baby Sportster through tests for the next day's Goodyear elimination race when his tiny plane literally began falling to pieces in the air over Cleveland Airport. Seconds later DeBlois was killed when his plane crashed into a gravel beach in the Rocky River Reservation of the Metropolitan Park, several hundred feet north of the Brookpark Road bridge in Parkview Village. But that was mere anticlimax to the carnage of '47, so the debris were once again scraped up and preparations made for the 1949 races.

William P. Odum was a seemingly experienced, popular flier. Flying thousands of hours for the Royal Canadian Air Force during World War II, he quickly became a star on the competitive air race circuit after the war. Then, in 1947, he vaulted to worldwide fame by breaking Howard Hughes's 1938 record for round-the-world flight. An affable, charming 29-year-old, Odum was a

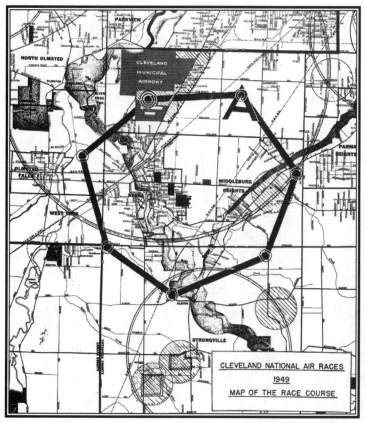

Map of the Thompson Trophy Race, National Air Races, 1949.

favorite with fans of the National Air Races, both for his aeronautic feats and his personable manner. But after the tragedy that took his life and the lives of a Berea mother and her son, his piloting peers agreed that he should never have been at the controls of the death plane, a souped-up F-51 Mustang fighter.

To begin with, Odum had no experience in the *Beguine,* the plane loaned to him by celebrity flier Jacqueline Cochran. Secondly, he had never flown in any closed-course pylon competition, much less the Thompson Trophy race. Thirdly, the *Beguine* was designed to fly on a four-pylon course, not the seven-pylon Thompson. Cook Cleland, famed Cleveland flier who competed with Odum in the fatal race, put it this way after the tragedy:

[I] don't think he should have been in the Thompson Trophy
race at all. Not only I but some of the other pilots will tell you
the same thing. He was a Bendix (the cross-country speed dash)
pilot, not a closed course speed pilot. It takes two different kinds
of temperament. Odum made an excellent cross-country flyer
but I guess the ship he flew today was just too much for him.

It seems that Odum himself agreed with his peers, although he
was quoted too late to spare himself and his victims. He told one of
his fellow pilots, "I don't belong in this thing—I'm used to flying
high off the ground." But none of these misgivings was publicly

Jeanne Laird, killed in her
house.

articulated by anyone as Odum
arrived in Cleveland to compete in
the 1949 races, much less after he
won the closed-course Sohio race
with a record speed on Saturday,
September 5.

With nine other Thompson con-
testants, Odum took off in his dark
green racer at exactly 4:45 P.M. The
end of the high-speed race's first lap,
following a course laid out around
seven pylons, found Odum in third
place. Rounding the number one
pylon near the airport, he headed
southwest at a speed in excess of
400 miles per hour.

It happened as he passed the number two pylon, situated at Lewis and
No Bottom Roads in Olmsted Township. Perhaps attempting to over-
compensate for a wide turn, Odum
turned his plane 60 degrees, instead of the expected 35 or 40. Then,
as he tried to bank the plane back on course, the F-51 flipped over
on its back and sped directly toward a brand-new residential neighborhood at West and Beeler Roads in Berea.

As Bradley Laird later put it, his "whole world ended" in just
seconds of fire. At exactly 4:48 P.M. he was standing outside the
$16,000 ranch house at 429 West Street that he and his wife Jeanne

had just moved into on August 31. The 36-year-old stationery salesman was washing the outside windows of the house and having a playful water fight with his five-year-old son Bradley David. In the front yard was his father-in-law Benjamin Hoffman, 56, who was watching Laird's 13-month-old son Craig cavort in an adjacent playpen. It was a happy domestic scene, completed by the presence of Jeanne Laird, 24, who was watching her family and keeping half an eye on the air races through the bathroom window.

Odom Crash Hero Haunted by Failure to Save "Babies"

September 9, 1949.

C. V. Talbot, one of the Lairds' neighbors, saw the crash. He was watching the planes in the air when he heard someone say, "Look, there's one of the planes off its course. It's coming right here." A second later, Talbot saw a streak of silver light, as the plane careened over his house top. Another second later, he heard a soft "ploosh" as the plane hit the Lairds' attached garage and the nearly full gas tanks inside ignited.

Odum's F-51 Mustang hit the Laird house so hard and fast that it bored through the concrete foundation and buried its nose six feet into the earth underneath. Odum was killed instantly and incinerated so completely that rescuers found little more than his watch when they finally found his remains four feet down. Jeanne Laird probably also perished fairly quickly. She was trapped in the bathroom as the house was enveloped in the gas-fed flames and could not have survived long.

The hero of the disaster was Benjamin Hoffman. Stunned by the impact of the plane and the ensuing fire, he turned to see his 13-month-old grandson Craig in flames in his playpen. Grabbing the child, he ran into the street, frantically tearing the burning clothes off the baby and screaming "Save the children! Save the children!" to neighbors as they rushed to give aid. Even after he was put in an ambulance, Ben Hoffman broke away three times to try to save his daughter from the blazing house.

It was too late. Bradley Laird had already tried to rescue his trapped wife several times but had been driven away by the flames. He was lucky to save his son Bradley David, who escaped unhurt. There was little for Berea firemen to do when they arrived at the site except to put out the fire and help the neighbors carry furniture out of the house and onto the lawn. Ben Hoffman survived his ordeal with burns on his head and hands. Baby Craig was not so lucky, dying at Berea Community Hospital three hours after the fire from burns over 80 percent of his tiny body.

The aftermath of the disaster was what Clevelanders had come to expect from such affairs. Bradley Laird took his family back to Minneapolis. Insurance companies, including Lloyd's of London, paid off the accident claims against Odum's estate and the National Air Races. Led by anguished and outraged Berea citizens, a number of affected suburbs quickly passed ordinances banning closed-course air racing in their civic air space.

And the National Races disappeared from Cleveland until 1964, when they were reborn at Burke Lakefront Airport in the much tamer, safer format in which they continue to the present. Few people, especially those civic officials and elite citizens who had brought the races to Cleveland, ever admitted that what had occurred was bound to happen, given the careless negligence with which they had conducted the prestigious event.

Chapter 14

JAZZ AGE HIT-SKIP

The Alice Leonard Story (1928)

As discerning readers of these woeful chronicles know, there is no corner of Cuyahoga County so obscure as to lack its own horrific story. Consider the case of Mayfield Heights. Today the stretch of SOM Center Road that runs south from Ridgebury to Mayfield is just another suburban thoroughfare of upscale houses and mind-numbing shopping plazas. Three-quarters of a century ago it was but a bland rural route dotted with homes, farms, and the occasional public building. It may look prosaic, as it did then—but it is not. For this is the place where Alice Leonard went missing in 1928, only to reappear as the forlorn victim of one of Ohio's most craven cowards.

As is often the case, this victim of a remarkable fate was generally unremarkable herself. Attractive but not beautiful, intelligent but not brilliant, 15-year-old Alice Leonard was an enthusiastic and popular member of her Mayfield Central High class. With blue eyes, dark-red hair, and a freckled face, vivacious Alice was a good student of generally high spirits who mixed well with her classmates. The daughter of laborer Martin Leonard and his wife Margaret, Alice loved games and sports and had not yet become a "boy crazy" adolescent. All in all, she was a perfectly normal girl, and as 1928 rolled around there was no reason to doubt that she would continue her happy existence in the Leonards' two-story frame house on Woodrow Road.

Saturday, January 28, was a cold, snowy day. The forecast called for worse to come, but Alice insisted on going to the basketball game that night at Central High (today the Mayfield Heights Middle School on SOM Center south of Ridgebury Boulevard). She had borrowed a red dress, a blue coat, and a hat from her neighbor, Mrs. McMahon, and all she needed now was a quarter to get into the game. Margaret Leonard didn't have the money, but she told her daughter Alice to go to the village butcher, Anthony DeCillo, and borrow the money "on account." Margaret Leonard tried walking down SOM Center with Alice to get the money, but she was on crutches from a recent injury and it was very cold. She soon turned back and Alice continued up the road. It was the last time her mother saw her alive.

Alice Leonard sketch. *Cleveland News*, April 3, 1928.

Alice got the money and made it back to Central High in time for the game. She was seen there, talking to a short, fat girl, by her schoolmate Anthony Penza and two of his chums. They did not, however, see her go into the gymnasium, and no one else at the school remembered seeing her at the game. No one knows exactly when, but at sometime around 9 P.M. she must have left the school grounds and started walking down SOM Center toward her home on Woodrow. It was dark, and snow was falling steadily on the lonely road as she trudged south.

When Alice failed to return home by 12:30 A.M., Margaret Leonard braved the cold—it was now only four degrees above zero—and her crutches to go looking for her daughter on the highway. She found no trace of Alice that night or the next day, when several of her neighbors joined her search. For reasons never explained, however, she did not notify Mayfield marshal Nick G. Wright of her daughter's disappearance until Monday afternoon, January 30. Not that it would have made a difference, but Margaret's reluctance to notify the law would be cited against her later when she bitterly criticized the police search for her missing daughter.

During the two months that followed, Mayfield Heights lawmen, assisted by Cuyahoga County deputy sheriff Gideon A. Rabshaw, had no more luck than Margaret Leonard. With no physical trace or eyewitness report of Alice's movements after 9 P.M., they occupied themselves mainly with articulating plausible theories as to what had happened to her. One theory popular with the villagers themselves was the "gas hawk" hypothesis: the fearful notion that one of the young men often seen motoring the village roads and "getting fresh" with the local girls had lured Alice into his roadster. Subsequently, the theory went, when she resisted his disgusting overtures, the "gas hawk" had hurled her out of the still-moving car—or she had jumped in panic while protecting her virtue—and her smashed body lay hidden somewhere in the woods or an unseen ditch. Several of the high school girls were said to have spoken of seeing Alice get into a sinister two-tone yellow-and-black Chevrolet that night, but no one was able to quite pin the story down.

Veteran sleuth Gideon Rabshaw had no patience with the "gas hawk" theory, nor did he take any stock in a hysterical Margaret Leonard's theory that her daughter had been deliberately murdered. He thought that Alice had simply been the victim of a hit-skip motorist, who had then hidden her corpse. But no one listened to him, and the gothic spectacle of Mrs. Leonard's daily highway searches dominated the case during the weeks following Alice's disappearance. Although she ceaselessly pursued her daily pilgrimage, Margaret herself gradually came to believe that Alice was dead. After exhausting every other possibility, she went to a fortune-teller, who gave her the bleak but oddly comforting news that her Alice would turn up right in Mayfield Village . . . in the end.

The end came unexpectedly on Monday, April 2, 1928. The spring thaw had done its work, and Coach Harvey Sheetz was warming up the Mayfield Heights team on its secondary practice field off SOM Center. Bernard Pirk, a 17-year-old right fielder, was shagging flies in the tall weeds there, about 100 yards from the highway and 150 yards north of the school. As Pirk chased a fly ball into the grass, he thought he saw what looked like a football tackling dummy in the foot-high weeds. He took a closer look and realized it wasn't a dummy: it was Alice Leonard, lying face up and dead in the soggy residue of the winter snow. Pirk ran stammering to Sheetz with his story; shortly thereafter Gideon Rabshaw and his men were on the scene. It was obvious to all of them that Alice had been there since the night she vanished.

Many persons would later take credit for solving the Alice Leonard mystery, but the major credit must go to Rabshaw, Cuyahoga County coroner A. J. Pearse, Mayfield Heights Central High janitor Gerald Kasper, and *Cleveland News* photographer Perry Cragg. It was Pearse whose expert autopsy quickly disclosed two important facts supporting Rabshaw's hit-skip thesis. One was that

Where the body was found.
Cleveland News, April 3, 1928.

Alice had died of a fractured skull. The other was that, though her blue coat was missing, she had not been sexually assaulted, which further discredited the still-popular "gas hawk" hypothesis. Now, Rabshaw reasoned, it was time to look for someone with memories of an automobile accident on the night of January 28.

Only two hours after Alice's corpse was found, Rabshaw found the man he was seeking in the high school janitor, Gerald Kasper. Kasper now recalled that just before midnight on January 28 he had encountered local resident Roy Grootegoed near the school gymnasium. Roy, 20, had told Kasper that his automobile was stuck in a ditch and that he was waiting for his friends to help push it out. An hour later, chums Harley Williams and Ed Shultz had shown up, and the four of them had pushed Roy's roadster out of a muddy ditch. Kasper remembered that the automobile had a broken headlight and a smashed windshield. He also recalled that Roy Grootegoed had a black eye and a bruised face.

Rabshaw and his men caught up with Roy as he was digging a cellar for a neighbor on SOM Center. They took him to his house to question him, and while Rabshaw grilled the handsome, soft-spoken Roy, *Cleveland News* photographer Perry Cragg wandered out to the barn to look for Roy's automobile. He found it—and he also found, just behind the oil barrel where Roy had hidden it, Alice Leonard's missing blue coat. The rest was child's play for Rabshaw. After listening to more of Roy's stone-faced denials of any guilty knowledge, he suddenly brought out the blue overcoat from underneath his own jacket and brandished it in Roy's face. Roy immediately broke down and told the shameful story of the night of January 28.

It was a dark, snowy night, he recalled, and he was doing about 30 miles an hour down SOM Center when an oncoming Peerless touring car suddenly veered over the center line. Attempting to avoid a collision, Roy skidded to the side and hit the unseen Alice Leonard dead center. Owing to the snowy road conditions, he dragged her body two hundred feet before he could bring his auto to a stop in a muddy ditch. When he finally shuddered into the ditch, he discovered Alice's body on the front of his car and her blue coat caught up in its wheels.

Roy told Rabshaw that he sat there on the running board for a long time in the cold, just sobbing and holding Alice's body in his arms. "I didn't know what the heck to do," he confessed. But his imagination didn't fail him for long. Initially he told Rabshaw that the three men in the Peerless helped him hide the body in the nearby snow of the Mayfield school field. Eventually, he confessed that he did the craven deed alone. After hiding the body, he went to his friends with an invented story about a minor auto accident and just hoped for the best. He and his family were as well

As Roy Faces Court; Pastor Visitor
CLERGYMAN PROVIDES ATTORNEY AFTER FATHER'S REFUSAL TO AID

Hit-skipper Roy Grootegoed faces the music. *Cleveland News*, April 4, 1928.

known as the Leonards in the close community of Mayfield Heights—his father Semon had once run for marshal—and his terror of discovery during the next two months was constantly exacerbated by reminders of the ongoing search for Alice.

It didn't end the way anyone involved expected. Although community sentiment favored indicting Roy for second-degree murder, Cuyahoga County prosecutor Edward Stanton advised that manslaughter was the only feasible charge. And when Roy's case came up before Justice of the Peace William Zoul on Friday, April 6, Zoul was forced to dismiss the charge entirely. Although castigating Roy as the most contemptible of cowards, Zoul noted that there was no evidence of criminality in the accident that had caused Alice Leonard's death. Moreover, as there was no law in Ohio at the time mandating that a motorist either report an accident or render aid to an automobile accident victim, no charge whatsoever could be brought against Roy Grootegoed.

This verdict, of course, satisfied no one except Roy and his lawyer, George Gurney. Alice's mother, who fainted several times during Zoul's hearing, stated that she would never forgive Roy for leaving her little girl to die in the snow. (There was some suspicion, never proven and implausible, that Alice was still alive and had frozen to death in the school field.) Prosecutor Stanton tried to have the charge taken up by a Cuyahoga County grand jury, but it refused his request on April 11. The sour feelings of most folks were best expressed by Gideon Rabshaw at the end of Zoul's hearing. As Zoul's decision freeing Roy was announced, the boy's supporters began to cheer and applaud. Rising to his feet, Gideon Rabshaw thundered, "Applaud? Applaud the mother whose daughter was killed and thrown into a field!" There was a shamed silence, and then the voices of some of the Leonard family friends could be heard murmuring, "That's right, that's right."

There is little visible trace of the Alice Leonard tragedy left today. Alice still sleeps in a Calvary Cemetery grave, joined by her grieving mother in 1944. Roy's stern Dutch father Semon ("I don't want any fancy lawyers to keep my boy from being punished if he deserves it") passed on in 1951, followed by Roy himself in 1968. But this terrible story did leave a valuable legacy. It was specifically because of the Alice Leonard tragedy that the Cleveland Automobile Club successfully lobbied the Ohio legislature to close the loopholes that let Roy Grootegoed walk away scot-free from his craven deed. That's something to think about the next time you motor down SOM Center Road or ride by the scene of an automobile accident.

Chapter 15

"I AM SETTLING FOR ALL PAST WRONGS..."

William Adin's 1875 Cross-Town Bloodbath

The narrative of each of the nine Cuyahoga County public executions held between 1812 and 1879 reveals features, motives, and personalities unique to each murderer and the circumstances of his judicially mandated killing.

John O'Mic was the youngest executed, and his snuffing out in 1812 was the most lugubriously macabre. (See George Condon's hilarious account in *Cleveland: The Best-Kept Secret*.)

James Parks's crime, a murder by decapitation in 1853, was one of exceptional brutality, and his extended sojourn on the death rows of both Summit and Cuyahoga counties was by far the longest, thanks to legal technicalities that would make F. Lee Bailey proud.

The 1865 crime of Dr. John Hughes (chronicled in *The Corpse in the Cellar*) was Cuyahoga County's first capital atrocity committed in the name of "love," by a villain of singular and almost demonic vanity.

The 1866 hanging of Alexander McConnell was certainly, if unintentionally, the most painful execution, and all the more regrettable because he may have been the only one of the nine condemned who truly repented of his black deed.

The civic cesspool exposed by the denouement of the Skinner murder case in 1868 and the execution of Lewis Davis was, from first to last, an unprecedented public morality play that soiled everyone involved in it on both sides of the law.

John Cooper's spectacular violence against James Swing in 1871 was an early instance of "black-on-black" Cleveland crime and was also remarkable for resulting in the shortest capital trial ever held in Cleveland.

Stephen Hood's cold-blooded slaughter of his stepson in 1873 set new standards for stony-heartedness and unrelenting mendacity. And Charlie McGill, the last of the nine men executed, gave the good Dr. Hughes stiff competition in the category of the ultra-stylish *crime passionel.*

But for sheer cussedness, mayhem, and gore galore, there is nothing to beat William Adin's triple-murder bloodbath on December 4, 1875.

Bill Adin's last day as a free man began in typical, even mundane fashion. Rising at 4 A.M. in his bedroom in his house on the "Heights" (as the Tremont neighborhood was then called), the 56-year-old expressman (he made his living delivering packages for Cleveland firms) dressed quietly, went downstairs to the kitchen, and lit a fire. Thinking it too early to wake his wife, Barbara, the short-statured, bewhiskered Yorkshireman walked 75 feet down the street to Engine House No. 8 of the Cleveland Fire Department. There he chatted for about an hour with fireman Otto Schuardt. Schuardt had talked many times with Adin of late, and he knew the direction the conversation would take the moment Adin walked in the door. It started out with an innocuous remark about a recent fire but almost immediately veered to Adin's favorite topic: his family troubles. This was a whiny monologue Schuardt had heard before—as had everyone who knew the sociable, talkative Adin. Indeed, his alleged family troubles were well known all over Cleveland.

No one knows when they started and to what extent they were real or imagined. But it was no secret that William Adin was a deeply unhappy man at the end of 1875, and he poured out the familiar litany of his woes over the next hour. His wife was stealing from him, he told Schuardt, and his stepdaughter Hattie was robbing him too. He'd caught them both, and it was all Hattie's fault for poisoning her mother's mind against him and getting her to steal the money for her own benefit. Now the two of them were trying to get him to sign his property over to them: the house/grocery store structure where he lived and ran his business at the southeast corner of Scranton and Starkweather. They'd been stealing from him for years, he thundered to Schuardt, and now he didn't even have the money to pay the interest on his bank loan or his county tax bill.

And now that streetwalker Hattie was living with that no-good friend of hers, Mrs. George Benton, in that house of ill fame on Forest Street (East 37th Street, near Central Avenue). He'd put up with it for years, Bill Adin shouted, and he wasn't going to stand for it anymore. He was going to have a "settlement for all past wrongs," by God, and he "might just as well settle first as last." He believed, in fact, that "he would settle with her right now—this morning!"

Adin ranted on for over an hour in this fashion about his wife and stepdaughter. Then, hearing the station clock strike, he asked fireman Peter Cary what time it was. Told it was 6 A.M., he departed for home. Schuardt thought no more about the conversation after Adin left. He and everyone who knew Adin had heard it all before, and he supposed that Adin was talking about a financial "settlement."

Just how good-natured, industrious, thrifty William Adin had come to such a pass will never really be known. Born in Barnsley Commons, Yorkshire, on February 17, 1819, Adin had grown up in a family of modest means with eight children. Leaving home at age six, he had enjoyed but three days of schooling and from the age of 16 walked with a limp after being kicked by a horse. That accident didn't seem to affect his disposition or work ethic, however, and he labored at various manual occupations around Yorkshire before emigrating to Cleveland in 1852. During the next few years he pursued various careers, including farming, coal mining, and a stint as a steward on a Great Lakes ship. In 1858, he married Barbara McKay, a widow his own age, and they worked together for some years at a downtown peanut stand on Superior Avenue, along with Barbara's daughter by her first marriage, Hattie McKay. In the early 1860s, Adin began working as an expressman with his own horse and wagon. Over the next few years he built up a solid and lucrative business, developing a reputation as a reliable, industrious worker and doing delivery work for such reputable Cleveland firms as Cobb, Andrews & Company, and Brooks, Schinkel & Company. By the late 1860s, Adin had prospered enough to build a house on the "Heights," with a room for Barbara to run as a neighborhood grocery with Hattie helping out behind the counter.

William Adin.

Everything seemed grand: Bill Adin's property was worth an impressive $6,000, and he doted on Hattie enough to yield to her plea to send her to a good commercial college.

Somehow it all went wrong in the early 1870s. Maybe it was mental illness, maybe it was a midlife crisis, maybe it was, as the old murder indictments used to read, "at the instigation of the devil." But at about the same period that his stepdaughter Hattie McKay turned into a beautiful and personable young woman, affable Bill Adin's disposition soured. There is no evidence to support his fanatical conviction, repeated until he fell through the hangman's drop, that his wife and Hattie had orchestrated a plot to steal everything he had and dispossess him of his property. But there is no question that he believed it by 1874, and by that time he was roaring and ranting his wild accusations against his wife and stepdaughter throughout the length and breadth of Cleveland.

There may have been something darker, too, involved in William Adin's change of attitude toward his 23-year-old stepdaughter: Hattie McKay told at least one person that he had unsuccessfully tried to "ruin" her several times. He also didn't like her independence: he tried to get her fired from her sales job at the J. R. Shipherd millinery store, telling Shipherd that his stepdaughter was a prostitute and common thief and demanding that Shipherd fire her. Meanwhile, he stepped up his abuse of Barbara, threatening her with physical harm and telling everyone he met that she stole money out of his pants while he was asleep at night. By the autumn of 1874, both Hattie and her mother had taken enough abuse. On the night of December 3, after a violent quarrel that climaxed when Adin smashed down the ill and bedridden Barbara's bedroom door with an ax and threatened to kill them, Barbara and Hattie fled the house with two trunks of their belongings. Taken into the Forest Avenue (East 37th Street) home of one of Hattie's sympathetic friends, a Mrs. Elizabeth Benton, Hattie commenced a completely independent life and Barbara filed for divorce on December 14.

Alas, it was not to be. Barbara was granted temporary alimony and eventually won a supplementary lawsuit for recovery of her possessions from the house. But in the end, it was the familiar, sad domestic story: William the husband cried, William the spouse pleaded, and William Adin the contrite helpmate promised he would turn over a new leaf and be good, if only sweet Barbara would come back to him and drop her divorce suit. Which she did, in the spring of 1875, returning alone to face his eventual and inevitable wrath, as her more sensible daughter refused to leave Mrs. Benton's welcoming refuge. Shortly after her return, Adin ran into Justice of the Peace E. W. Goddard, who had presided over the disposition of their domestic legal troubles. When Goddard congratulated Adin on his reconciliation with Barbara, Adin launched into a passionate repetition of his grievances and swore that he would "pay her back for it."

William Adin returned home from his firehouse colloquy shortly after 6 A.M. on December 4. Barbara had prepared breakfast and the food was on the table when they resumed a quarrel waged the night before. It followed the usual text: William asked her for money to pay the taxes, Barbara said she had none, and he launched into his usual litany of threats and accusations. Things got nastier and nastier until finally he said, "Barbara, ain't you ashamed of yourself for taking and concealing the money; the taxes must be paid and there must be money somewhere and now let me have it to pay the taxes!" Retorted Barbara, "You lie, you mean scamp!" Those were her last recorded words on earth. Picking up an ax and a clawhammer in a corner of the kitchen, Adin furiously and methodically beat and bloodily smashed her to death with powerful blows of the deadly implements. It couldn't have lasted long: no one in the neighborhood heard any noise, and Dr. H. W. Kitchen's careful autopsy

Barbara Adin.

that afternoon disclosed two wounds capable of causing instant death. In addition, Barbara Adin's scalp was pounded to splinters, her ear badly slashed with the ax, and a large ax-shaped wedge of her brain knocked out. William Adin did not do anything by half measures. Then, dragging her bloody body behind the grocery and screening it off with a partition, Adin took his mare out of the stable, hitched up his delivery wagon, threw his bloody hammer into it, and started out for the east side of Cleveland.

Adin left his home shortly after 6:15 in the morning. He was in no hurry, apparently, as he drove to a downtown market, picked up a parcel of meat at the Central Market (intersection of Ontario,

Woodland, and Broadway), and delivered it to one of his regular customers on Garden Street (Central Avenue). One of his acquaintances, a Mr. Busch, saw him on Garden Street and hailed him, whereupon Adin asked him the time, was told it was almost 7 A.M., and continued on his way in his rig. Seconds later he turned south onto Forest Avenue.

A few doors north of Mrs. Elizabeth Benton's home at 900 Forest, Adin tethered his mare to a telegraph pole. Michael Burke, who lived near the Benton home on Forest Avenue, watched him do it and also noted the affectionate care with which he carefully draped a horse blanket around the winded and chilled horse. A short time later, Kasander Sabb, a black man, saw Adin put something into his coat as he opened the gate at the side path to the Bentons' back kitchen entrance. Neither man thought anything of it—William Adin and his express wagon were a familiar sight in Cleveland at all hours, and anyone who had lived there for any length of time had at least a nodding acquaintance with the burly expressman.

Elizabeth Benton, a pleasant 30-year-old housewife, was on the side porch adjacent to the path as Adin passed by. Her husband George had just left for work downtown, and she was shaking out the tablecloth crumbs from the breakfast she had just finished eating with her houseguest, Hattie McKay, when Adin brusquely asked, "Where is Hattie? "In the kitchen," replied Elizabeth Benton, no doubt wondering what new mischief her friend's stepfather was about.

She soon found out. Climbing the back stairs, Adin entered the kitchen and slammed the door behind him. Accosting Hattie, he demanded she return home with him. She refused, and, without another word, Adin pulled out his bloody clawhammer and began hitting her in the head. Neighbors who heard but did not see the mayhem later described the noise as sounding like "someone breaking coal on the floor." Hattie never had a chance: the first blow knocked her to her knees, and her stepfather continued his work until her skull was a splintered wreck with her brains actually oozing out. Adin seems to have been aiming strictly for the top of her head; Hattie's other injuries,

Hattie McKay.

including a broken jaw and facial injuries, were incurred as she desperately tried to turn away from his relentless hammer.

No one remembered hearing Hattie scream, but Elizabeth Benton somehow became aware of the trouble in her kitchen. Forcing open the door, she confronted Adin as his encrimsoned hammer rose and fell. As he later resentfully recalled, she "flew at me like a cat," desperately trying to halt his assault on Hattie. Turning his back on the prostrate and unconscious Hattie, he snarled, "*You* are the cause of all this!" and proceeded to hit Elizabeth again and again . . . and again with his heavy hammer. When she stopped moving or making any noise, he returned to hammering Hattie. A few seconds later, Mrs. Benton revived and tried to crawl out the door, only to be dragged back into the kitchen and beaten some more by the methodical Adin.

Elizabeth Benton.

The entire lethal scene probably only lasted a minute or two. No one except Adin himself witnessed the entire sequence of events, but bits and pieces of it were glimpsed by various witnesses. Although beaten almost as badly as Hattie, Elizabeth Benton actually survived long enough to describe seeing Adin from the porch and recount what happened when she entered the kitchen. Lizzie Arnold, a 14-year-old girl who was living at Maggie Corrin's house next door, saw Mrs. Benton shaking the tablecloth, saw Adin enter the back door, and then watched through the window as he repeatedly hit a kneeling figure with a hammer. And Mrs. Corrin and her houseguest Emma Tarbet both saw Adin as he left the back door, walked "leisurely" down the side path, through the gate, and to his wagon. As he passed through the gate by the sidewalk, Mrs. Corrin heard him say, "I am ready to go now," and then both she and Emma watched him throw his hammer into his wagon and drive off.

Realizing that something was amiss, Maggie Corrin ran from her house and into the Benton kitchen. The scene she found there was almost indescribably grisly. There was blood everywhere, on the walls, ceiling, door, and kitchen utensils. Hattie was lying in a pool of her own blood, her head a pulpy, smithereened ruin. Mrs.

Benton was on her hands and knees, blinded by her own blood, moaning, "Hattie! Oh, Hattie! Oh, Hattie!" As Mrs. Corrin watched in paralyzed terror, Elizabeth pushed the door open, crawled outside on her hands and knees, and tried to climb the side fence. Pulling herself together, Maggie Corrin managed to carry her back to a sofa in the kitchen, and then she sent for medical aid and the police.

Shortly after 7 A.M., Adin arrived home, after exchanging the usual mundane greetings with acquaintances he met along the way. As was his habit, he opened up his grocery for business, pulling the shutters down and preparing for the day's customers. Christian Boest, a neighbor with his own store across the street, had been waiting for Adin to open his store—like many neighbors he practically set his clock by Adin's regular habits—and he entered Adin's grocery about 7:30 A.M. "What's up?" he said to Adin. "Oh, nothing," replied Adin, who must have been only 12 feet away from his wife's bloody body behind the partition when he made his casual reply. The two men traded commonplace pleasantries for a moment, and then, as Boest no doubt expected, William Adin brought up the subject of his family troubles. Recounting his early morning argument with Barbara, he complained with intense anger that she had called him a liar and that she had said she didn't care what happened to him. Boest, who had heard this kind of talk many times before, remarked that he had thought they had become reconciled of late. "Well," responded Adin, "that was her cunningness. After she tried the law on me, she thought she had better keep still and get [away with] it in that way. I married her for pity's sake, thinking she was a nice woman." Recalling again that she had called him a liar, Adin said, "I saw that things were bad and I might as well have the worst. I am now having a settlement for all past wrongs." Thinking he meant a financial settlement, Boest asked when it was going to take place. Adin's cryptic reply made little impression on Boest, who was probably not even listening to Adin's all-too-familiar litany: "Well, it will all be out, and in a few moments you will know all, anyhow." Boest did ask where Barbara was, and after saying she'd been sick, her husband added, "I don't think she'll be around here no more." No one seems to have ever asked Christian Boest whether he thought it strange—or even noticed—that his neighbor William Adin was thoroughly bespattered with the fresh blood of his recent victims.

Boest left the store about 8 A.M.; 15 minutes later Sergeant

Henry Hoehn and another Cleveland policeman drove their buggy into Adin's yard. Adin had made no attempt to disguise himself or conceal his actions on Forest Street, and Hoehn had started in hot pursuit of the hammer killer within 30 minutes of his ghastly rampage. (Little more than 11 years later, Sergeant Hoehn himself would be very nearly killed with an iron coupling pin, wielded by a ruthless "Blinky" Morgan rescuing one of his confederates from police custody on a train stopped in Ravenna.) Jumping from his rig, Hoehn went up to Adin, who was pumping water for his mare, and said, "Are you Adin?" "Yes," said the expressman, "and I know what you want."

What Adin wanted, naturally, turned out to be something a little different from what Hoehn had in mind. Telling Hoehn he needed to get a dog chain from his house, he tried to close the door behind him but made no effort to resist when Hoehn pushed by him into the store. Walking to the end of the counter, Hoehn espied the bloody body of Barbara Adin. "My God!" shouted Hoeh. "What is this?" "Well," said the entirely unflustered Adin, "as you are here, you might as well know the whole of it." Pointing dramatically at the body, he said, "There lies the cause of all my troubles. Now here's the whole business: I killed her this morning." Then, picking up his bloody hammer and ax, he handed them to Hoehn, saying about the ax, "This is what I killed the old woman with." Hoehn would often subsequently recall the hideous detail of Barbara Adin's false teeth lying on the floor, scant inches away from her smashed and disfigured head.

Hoehn had seen more than enough and wanted to put Adin in a secure cell as soon as possible—there had been angry talk of lynching him within minutes of the affray on Forest Street. But Adin refused to leave just yet, insisting on arranging for the care of his dog and mare before he was taken away. When the impatient Hoehn grabbed him by the collar, Adin eyed him icily and warned, "Now you want to keep cool and don't handle me that way." And so it was that Hoehn fretfully trailed Adin as he methodically made his arrangements, trudging back and forth several times from his own house to those of several of his neighbors. His chores finished, he graciously allowed Hoehn to take him into custody and on to the Central Police Station on Champlain Street. His parting words to Christian Boest as they drove out of the yard were "Take good care of the mare."

At the beginning, at least, Adin made no attempt to conceal

either his long-germinating motives or his bloody acts. Conversing cheerfully and calmly with Sergeant Hoehn on his journey to jail, he repeated the well-worn rosary of his family woes and showed no concern for his victims or even any apprehension of the likely consequences he was going to face. Bragging of the speed with which he had traveled from his store to Forest Street on his fatal morning errand, he ingenuously boasted, "But my mare can travel very fast when I let her out." Well did that very afternoon's *Plain Dealer* account of the tragedy opine that "the demeanor of the prisoner during the interview conveyed the impression that he either did not realize the enormity of the crime or was lost to all sense of feeling." When informed, to his surprise, that Hattie and Mrs. Benton were still living, he expressed his disappointment freely, both to Hoehn and many others throughout that terrible day: "I wanted to put an end to all the damned whelps. They drove me to it. I'm sorry—I meant to make a clean sweep and fix the crowd." He also expressed regret that he had not been allowed the opportunity to kill his beloved mare, worrying that she might be mistreated by another owner. When asked if he cared more for his horse than for his late wife, Adin replied, "Certainly I do!"

Even as he uttered and breezily repeated such inhuman sentiments, Cleveland's medical, police, and legal institutions began to grapple with the consequences of Adin's bloody work. Three witnesses were heard at Coroner T. Clarke Miller's inquest, and by 4 P.M. of the murder day, a verdict of willful murder was returned. William Adin forthwith engaged the legal counsel of attorneys Carlos B. Stone and Henry McKinney. Barbara Adin's funeral took place the following Wednesday at the Congregational church on the "Heights," and it was said that to the eyes of the crowd that filed past her *open* casket there was "scarcely anything about the head to be seen that would indicate the terrible death. It was turned enough to the left to conceal the frightful wound just beneath the jaw and in front of the left ear, while the fearful wound on top of the head was carefully covered with hair." Following the obsequies, Barbara's coffin was taken to Woodland Cemetery for burial.

Despite her appalling injuries, Hattie McKay lingered until the morning of Friday, December 10. Fortunately, she was unconscious for most of her last hours, although it was reported that the occasional "moans she uttered were heart rending." Her funeral took place the next day at the Memorial Presbyterian Church at the corner of Cedar and Case Avenue (East 40th Street). "Tastefully dressed in white and placed in a beautiful coffin," her corpse too, "had been so treated after death as to retain scarcely any indication of the deadly assault, while the wounds on the head were so dressed as to be hardly perceivable." Reverend Horton, who preached her funeral sermon, insisted that she had forgiven her stepfather before she died, but given her persistent coma, that might have been piously wishful thinking on the Reverend's part. Then it was off to Woodland Cemetery to join her mother. Mrs. Benton, sad to relate, somehow survived for five weeks after Adin's assault, finally succumbing to her horrible wounds on Saturday, January 8. Whether she forgave her murderer is unknown but unlikely, as she was often conscious enough to suffer audibly from the effects of her injuries.

Considering the state of public feeling in Cleveland against William Adin, he received a reasonably fair trial. From the moment that his crimes became known, there was open talk in Cleveland streets of vigilante justice, and on several occasions, as he was being taken to and from court, cries of "Hang him to a lamppost!" and "Someone get a rope!" came from the angry crowds watching him cross Public Square. The sole indictment against him was the murder of Hattie McKay. This prosecutorial strategy was no doubt chosen because of the three murders, premeditation and deliberate malice could most easily be proven for hers. Potential indictments for the murder of his wife and Mrs. Benton were held in reserve, just in case he escaped hanging for Hattie's murder.

Although he still expressed no remorse for his bloody deeds, Adin's demeanor and potential defense began to shift subtly as his February court date approached. While still adamant that his victims had deserved death for their wrongs against him, he soon began to insist that he could not remember anything from the moment he picked up the ax in his kitchen until he drove his rig back to the "Heights" two hours later. And as early as Monday, December 6, only two days after the murder, he began to complain that he had been suffering from severe headaches for the past two years. As a cynical *Plain Dealer* writer noted, "This gives rise to the suspicion that he intends to try the insanity dodge, though no one who has yet seen him believes that he is at all deranged, mentally." Not that Adin really thought that such an excuse was necessary, mind you. As he told his many visitors over the 10-week prelude to his trial, he fully expected to be acquitted, convinced that the expected disclosure in court of his family problems would exonerate him: "But I mean that everything about our troubles will come out then, and the people will understand it."

The people, at least those 12 good and true men on his jury, got their chance to understand this peculiar man on Monday, February 21, 1876, when his trial opened before Judge Edwin T. Hamilton in Cuyahoga County Common Pleas Court. Defended by McKinney and Stone, Adin was prosecuted by the redoubtable Samuel Eddy and William Mitchell. But it took quite some time to winnow out those 12 men as, over the next week, 163 out of the 200 men called in four venires were closely interrogated to discover whether they had preconceived opinions on the case or a disqualifying antipathy to capital punishment. Anyone who had read about the case in the newspapers was particularly suspect, and the *Plain Dealer* displayed considerable mirth in its extended commentary on the ironies and contradictions of the jury selection process:

> The Adin case illustrates how stupid a man must be to serve as a juror . . . In some cases [of juror examination] it was astounding how some candidates had read all reports of the triple murder and yet had formed no opinion as to the guilt or innocence of the accused . . . So far almost every examined has either read a newspaper account or has formed an opinion. Among the accepted jurors so far is an ex-member of the board of education but he will probably be peremptorily challenged—on the grounds of intelligence, perhaps . . . One was examined yesterday who said he had no conscientious scruples against hanging and when questioned further said he had no conscience. Thus the work goes bravely on, men who read the newspaper and form opinions being rejected.

Eventually, the *Plain Dealer* scribe so despaired of the jury process that he suggested that Summit County undertake Adin's prosecution, as a payback for Cuyahoga County's service in the matter of James Parks.

Adin's trial lasted until Saturday, March 4, 1876. The defense's concern about newspaper coverage proved irrelevant, as virtually all of the testimony offered had already appeared in news accounts of the three inquests and printed interviews with the incessantly chatty Adin. Otto Schuardt and Christian Boest recounted their conversations with Adin on the murder morning. Maggie Corrin, Emma Tarbet, and Lizzie Arnold testified to what they had seen at 900 Forest Street on December 4. Lizzie, articulate beyond her years, was an especially persuasive witness and the only living person who had actually seen Adin wielding his deadly hammer. Henry Hoehn, ex–Cuyahoga County sheriff Felix Nicola, and several others recounted Adin's many admissions of guilt on the murder day and afterward. Justice of the Peace Goddard and Sergeant S. J. Burlison of the Cleveland Police Department were deposed to offer evidence of Adin's preexisting malice toward Hattie McKay. Burlison's testimony was particularly devastating, concentrating on a hostile encounter he'd had with Adin shortly after Hattie and her mother fled the house in December 1874. Burlison, at Hattie's request, had gone to Adin's house to retrieve some books she needed for her job. When he told Adin of his errand, the expressman became enraged, picked up a hatchet, and began screaming at Burlison that he was surprised that such a respectable man was running around with a streetwalker like his daughter. When Burlison asked him why he had the hatchet, Adin said, "For protection," and Burlison ultimately departed without the books.

Burlison's testimony triggered the only real moment of excitement in the trial. As he spoke, Adin, who hitherto had sat slumped over the table with his face in his arms, raised his head and shouted, "Oh, you liar, as you be!" His married sister, Esther Hague, a Cleveland resident who stuck by her brother to the end, immediately ran to his side and calmed him into silence while he smirked as if he had said something funny and winked at a nearby reporter. Adin, of course, had his own self-serving version of his confrontation with Burlison, which he had offered to a *Cleveland Herald* reporter two days after the murder:

> Sergeant Burlison strutted in then and I said to him, "Burlison, you are out of your place, if you arrest me I'll jerk you like everything." I said further, "If you take those buttons off and stand up fair for me, I'll soon see which is the better one."

As in the case of Stephen Hood, the evidence brought by the defense to support its insanity defense was pretty insubstantial. Several acquaintances of Adin testified as to his exemplary character before the triple murders, but Messrs. Stone and McKinney doubtless knew that such testimonials were legally irrelevant—as Prosecutor Eddy would point out in his closing argument. Adin's sister Esther Hague, who lived on Sterling Avenue (East 30th Street), swore that their paternal grandfather, known as "Crazy Jonas," had been insane and confined to a locked room during his last years. George Aleberry, who had emigrated to Cleveland with Adin in 1852, corroborated Esther's story about Jonas, but his dramatic tale of Jonas chasing him with a knife was deflated by his admission that George and his friends had been tormenting Jonas and trespassing on his land at the time. Esther also claimed that while she was living with her brother just after his wife and step-daughter left in December 1874 he had exhibited considerable absentmindedness, insomnia, and depression. But her obser-vations were undercut by Adin's own per-sonal physician, Dr. G. C. E. Weber, who admitted under cross-examination by Eddy that nothing in Adin's behavior led him "to suspect that there was any mental alteration." Weber had noted that Adin was unusually obsessive in talking about his family problems during their last meeting, but that didn't count for much. And Dr. Proctor Thayer, perhaps the most respected physician in Cleveland, was called by the prosecu-tion as an expert witness to state that he had found no evidence of insanity during his 30-minute examination of Adin in jail.

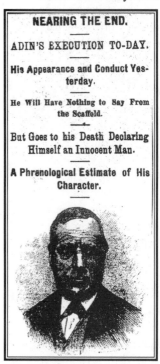

NEARING THE END.

ADIN'S EXECUTION TO-DAY.

His Appearance and Conduct Yes-terday.

He Will Have Nothing to Say From the Scaffold.

But Goes to his Death Declaring Himself an Innocent Man.

A Phrenological Estimate of His Character.

Cleveland Leader,
June 22, 1876.

The final scenes of the trial played out as expected. While Adin sat at the defense table, indifferent, with his head buried in his arms, William Mitchell opened the final arguments, strongly mocking "the insanity dodge" as altogether "the last resort of those who have committed the most hardened crimes." Carlos Stone responded by reminding the jury there was "no greater calamity than to make a man suffer for the commission of an offense which he could not help committing." It would be murder to hang Adin for killing his stepdaughter, Stone continued, given his family history of insanity and his severe "monomania" concerning his family problems. Henry McKinney continued in the same vein, stressing the bad strain inherited from "Crazy Jonas" and Aden's ill health as testified to by his sister. In his cleverest ploy, McKinney turned the prosecution's overwhelming evidence of Adin's oft-expressed malice and overt public violence on its head, arguing that his frequent threats and lack of dissimulation in performing the murders—his cold, calculated actions—matched *exactly* the way an insane person would act. Eddy closed for the state, emphasizing the evidence of premeditation and malice and insisting that the burden of proof for Adin's insanity rested with the defense—and the defense had clearly not proven it.

After Judge Hamilton's instructions, the jury went out at noon on Saturday, March 4. As the long hours of deliberation passed, Adin chatted freely with newspaper reporters, airing his opinions of how the trial had been conducted and his confident conviction that he would be found innocent. As afternoon waned into evening, he began hedging his conjectures toward a hung jury but maintained his overall optimism. As for himself, he averred, after his acquittal he might consider a career in local politics. Indeed, he fancied that he could perform ably as a professional juror, given his present experience, and that he "would do pretty well at that work." A *Cleveland Leader* reporter caught his mood of feckless, egotistical optimism perfectly in comments two days later:

> There was in his utterances neither the unthinking stupidity of a man who could not realize his peril, nor the bravado of a desperate criminal, but rather the philosophical coolness of a man who felt that he was right and was not fearful of the consequences.

Part of Adin's self-assurance, it was subsequently disclosed by his attorney, Carlos Stone, stemmed from his uncritical acceptance of a phrenological profile performed on him by a Professor O. S. Fowler in January 1875. The gospel according to Fowler could only have exacerbated Adin's already overweening megalomania:

> You, sir are one of the greatest workers anywhere to be found . . .
> you always appreciate the useful and substantial; are endowed
> with an uncommon amount of sagacity and discernment; are

eminently intellectual, a man of real, sound, strong sense and discernment . . . have an intuitive perception of truth and character . . . are calculated to make a good husband; are naturally fond of children . . . are trusted implicitly by all who know you . . . are just as honest and honorable as any man can be . . . have a terrible temper, yet you govern it well . . .

A less flattering portrait of the triple murderer, limned by a *Leader* reporter, may have taken Adin's measure with more accuracy. Commenting on Adin's picture in the paper, he noted:

The eyes set close together, give to the face a somewhat crafty look, which is called out far more distinctly when he is narrating some exploit in which his native cunning was brought into play, than when the face was in repose, as at the time the picture was taken. A side view, however, brings out more cruelty of expression, as the chin recedes and the mouth and nose set out together, strong and prominent, giving one an idea that, were the four large front teeth to once take hold, it would be hard to make them let go.

Apparently Adin's intuitive discernment was not working well that day, as his jury returned, just after midnight on Sunday, March 5, with a verdict of "guilty of murder in the first degree." It was subsequently rumored that they had spent the dozen hours of deliberation overcoming an initial 11-to-1 deadlock, but all 12 men refused to talk about it, then or later. As the verdict was read, Adin's face showed a deathly pallor and his stunned surprise was all too apparent. Seconds later, Judge Hamilton heard Stone's motion for a new trial and, after both sides waived argument, briskly rejected it. He then pronounced the death sentence, remarking, "The facts proven present a case of uncommon enormity and brutality . . . scarcely paralleled in the annals of criminal jurisprudence."

Which, of course, was not William Adin's opinion. Taken back to a death-row cell, he fulminated to anyone who would listen that the verdict was an outrage, a "premium on robbery and vice," not to mention a lost opportunity for his jurors "to rebuke women who rob their husbands, or young girls who will not obey their parents or guardians."

Recurring to his ambition to become a professional juror, he stated that had *he* been on the jury, he would have stood out for complete acquittal for at least three weeks. As ever, he demonstrated no remorse for his dead victims at any time. He told one auditor that he was looking forward to heaven but that he didn't expect to see Hattie, Barbara, or Mrs. Benton there, saying, "They are not fit to go to that place."

Adin's lawyers went through the motions of appeal, but the fight to save his life wasn't waged with much vigor. The main point of contention was the question of whether Judge Hamilton had acted legally in imposing a death sentence on a Sunday, but all parties concerned were well aware that a successful appeal would inflict two more murder trials on a city and a legal system that had already had a bellyful of William Adin. Adin, perhaps in reaction to his increasingly bleak prospects, soon dropped his ingratiatingly chatty style with newspaper reporters. As his days dwindled down to a precious few, he began to blame them for his predicament, insisting that they had biased the jury against him. Eventually, as the last week loomed, he physically assaulted a *Cleveland Leader* reporter who sought a jailhouse interview.

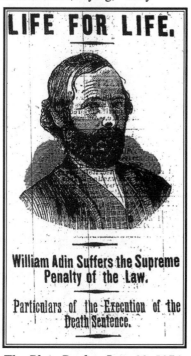

The *Plain Dealer*, June 22, 1876.

Meanwhile, the dreadful work of summary justice followed its wonted routine. Owing to the fact that the old county jail had been razed, Adin's hanging was held within the confines of the Central Police Station on Champlain Street. As his last days crept by, he could hear the timbers of the scaffold (the same reliable device used since 1855) being hammered into shape and the periodic *thunk* as sandbags used to test the drop mechanism fell to the ground. As had become the custom in Cleveland executions, Adin's spiritual counsel was provided by the Reverend Lathrop Cooley, assisted by the Reverend J. G. Bliss. To the end, Adin evinced no apparent response to Cooley's and Bliss's spiritual appeals. Neither did he yield, however, to morose despair. Just the night before his death, he caught a glimpse of the gallows while taking his regular walk and commented to his turnkey, "Look, Joe—there's my fly-trap!"

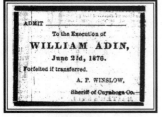

ADMIT
To the Execution of
WILLIAM ADIN,
June 2ʃd, 1876.
Forfeited if transferred.
A. P. WINSLOW,
Sheriff of Cuyahoga Co.

**Admission Ticket to
William Adin's Execution.**

Adin's execution was the usual coveted ticket for Clevelanders of enquiring mind and morbid curiosity. Although Sheriff A. P. Winslow had elaborate partitions built to screen the 50-foot-square hanging court from watchers outside the police station, he nonetheless issued hanging tickets to an audience of over 260 persons. One of them was George Benton, who stood at the foot of the scaffold until it was over, smoking a cigar and articulating his satisfaction with the proceedings. Another spectator was an anonymous Cleveland police lieutenant, who expressed his views in hanging-day versification:

> Adin, thy crimes will be remembered long,
> And son to son the tragic story tell.
> Three hapless victims in thy vengeance slain,
> And naught could stop thee in thy murderous spell.
> What was it led thee to commit the act,
> The powers that held thee in such fearful spell?
> We're ready to insinuate the fact
> 'Twas inspiration from the pit of hell
> With thy dark record of revolting crime.
> Thy hands imbued in helpless women's blood;
> You've expiated all you can in time.
> We leave thee to a just and righteous God.

Adin's last 24 hours were a perfect microcosm of his life. Meeting with Reverend Cooley on the afternoon of June 21, 1876, he prayed with him, asked forgiveness—and then launched into a lengthy tirade on how the three women "had driven him to it" and deserved their gory fates. After sleeping like a baby for seven hours, he awoke at 4 A.M. and breakfasted on coffee, ham, and bread, after which the Reverends Bliss and Cooley appeared for more prayers and photographer Jerry Green set up his cameras in the court to record Adin's last moments.

The crowd of lucky ticket-holders was admitted at noon. At

The execution.

12:40 P.M., Sheriff Winslow and his deputies went to Adin's cell. Declining to make a statement, Adin took the Reverend Cooley's arm and walked down two flights of stairs to the hall, out the door, and into the gallows area. Adin's last recorded words were an astonished "Oh, my! Look at this!" as he walked through the crowd to the gallows. Wearing a new black suit provided by the county, Adin mounted the scaffold with a firm step and sat down in a chair as Cooley read from the 51st Psalm. At 12:58 P.M., Sheriff Winslow asked Adin if he wanted to say anything; he just shook his head. Several minutes later, he was placed on the trap, his hands, arms, and legs secured, and the black cap pulled down over his head. At 1:06 P.M. Winslow triggered the drop. Adin fell down seven feet and hung there in sight of the crowd, not moving a muscle, his tongue grotesquely sticking out through a mouth slit. His pulse ceased at 1:20 P.M., and his body was cut down and removed at 1:27 P.M.

Before the burial in Woodland Cemetery, Dr. Proctor Thayer and some other physicians performed an autopsy on Adin's corpse. This had been Adin's last and dearest wish, as he was convinced that his brain would prove to be an abnormally large and impressive organ. He would have been disappointed: his brain, of unusually coarse texture, weighed a mere 43 ounces, about average for a man of his size, and the only medical anomaly noted in the postmortem was the unusual amount of blood—about two quarts—that the doctors found in his brain cavity. The autopsy also confirmed that Adin's neck had not been broken by the fall but that death had probably come quickly when the ligaments holding his brain in place were torn loose by the shock of the drop.

There was one final, appropriately macabre echo of the Adin tragedy. When his corpse was examined just before burial, it was discovered that his heart was missing. An investigation spurred by an irate Esther Hague revealed that one of the autopsy physicians, inspired by medical curiosity, had concealed it in a newspaper and spirited it out of the postmortem chamber. After some legal machinations, Mrs. Hague recovered the missing organ, and it is to be hoped that it rests to this day in the body of its owner. William Adin sleeps yet somewhere in the anonymity of Woodland Cemetery's potter's field. His three victims lie beneath a handsome stone monument nearby.

Chapter 16

DAMN THE TORPEDOES

The Fireworks Factory Horrors (1902–1903)

The 1908 S. S. Kresge fireworks explosion disaster is one of Cleveland's most poignant and celebrated disasters. In the century since it occurred, Clevelanders have taken justifiable pride in the impetus that tragedy gave to the "Safe and Sane Fourth of July" movement that eventually curtailed the annual carnage of American patriotic celebrations. Less well known, however, and less of a credit to the repute of the Forest City, is the story of the 1902 and 1903 torpedo factory explosions. Taken together, they killed and injured more persons and wreaked far more property damage than the 1908 dime store horror. Sadly, much as their stories are now forgotten, their lessons at the time were ignored, in a civic amnesia that made the 1908 horror almost inevitable. The story of the torpedo disasters provides yet more brutal evidence that the Forest City has had a very slow learning curve when it comes to protecting its citizens.

What was once the southwest corner of the intersection of Euclid Avenue and Fairmount Street is today but a modernistic component of the ever-expanding Cleveland Clinic campus. But in the spring of 1902 it was the site occupied by the Fairmount Manufacturing Company. Situated on the second floor over quarters occupied by the De Mars Bicycle Shop, the Fairmount Company factory consisted of a molding room fronting on Euclid Avenue, a mixing room in the center, and a storeroom at the rear. Communication with the street was by a rickety staircase, and all the second-floor windows but one were nailed shut with strips of wood. True, there was a "fire escape" adjacent to the one unbarred window.

Some fussy Cleveland city building inspector had insisted on that after a couple of previous, if inconsequential explosions at the Fairmount. What it was, in fact, was a flimsy wooden ladder nailed nearly flat against the side of the building. Not exactly the recourse one might wish if one were fleeing from a burning torpedo factory.

In 1902, a "torpedo" was exactly what the *Oxford English Dictionary* still defines as "a toy consisting of fulminating powder and fine gravel wrapped in thin paper, which explodes when thrown on a hard surface." There was great demand for torpedoes in that era of unregulated fireworks, and Fairmount Company owner-manager R. H. Opes and his crew of 16 women (mostly teenaged girls) and eight men had been working feverishly since the factory opened in March to meet the expected July Fourth demand. It was hard work with long hours, to be sure, but no worse than the lot of most working-class Clevelanders of the era. And, as owner-manager Opes constantly reassured his employees, the torpedoes were not dangerous, since they contained neither nitroglycerin nor dynamite, the only explosive substances prohibited by law in the densely populated residential neighborhood in which the Fairmount was situated.

Explosion Kills One and Injures Many in Factory of Explosives

Terrible Struggles of the Working People to Get From the Windows Which Were Barred Up--Grand Jury Will Fix Responsibility

Cleveland World,
March 15, 1902.

It happened just after work began at 7 A.M. on Saturday, March 15. The regular mixer of the critical torpedo formula was late, so chemist Frank Groch recruited 18-year-old Will Fisher to mix the starter mixture of potash and sulfur in a bowl. Fisher was new to the task, so Groch was careful to warn him about creating sparks by stirring too vigorously. Apparently, Groch wasn't careful enough. Several minutes after 7:00 a spark ignited the contents of Fisher's bowl. Attempting to carry it out of the mixing room, he spilled some of it into a barrel of volatile chemicals, principally sulfur. Seconds later, the barrel exploded, filling the second floor with flying debris, suffocating chemical fumes, and the screams of panicked employees. An instant later, flames sprang up, fed by the residue of sawdust and gunpowder on the floor. Chemist Groch made it out of the room just in time. With a dazed Will Fisher at his heels, he fled toward the rear, screaming, "Run for your lives! The building is all afire."

The torpedo workers in the middle and rear rooms escaped fairly quickly and easily by means of the tumbledown staircase. But the fire and the suffocating clouds of chemical smoke that attacked their lungs and made it impossible to see anything in the choking inferno of the second floor immediately trapped the dozen workers left in the front molding room. Eyewitness Walter Moffet, a trolley conductor, was passing by in his streetcar when he saw the building in flames. He immediately abandoned his car, grabbed a ladder, and climbed to the barred windows. He would remember what he saw through the nailed wooden slats for the rest of his life:

> It was an awful sight. The girls were pushing their arms through the windows and tearing at the wooden bars. Blood flowed from the cuts and their shrieks for help were heartrending. The hair on their heads was afire and they were trying to protect their faces and force the bars from the window at the same time.

That any of those trapped in the molding room were saved was owing to the heroism of several men. One was H. Gunthrie, a clerk at a nearby drugstore. He climbed the "fire escape," broke a window open and managed to pull two girls out through the opening. Fireman C. A. Spillman, who arrived with Engine Company 18 from the Doan Street station, got up a ladder in time to rescue Elizabeth Cotrell and her sister Lena Karpp, both of them badly burned. Several of the other workers who survived managed to leap unhurt from the broken windows before being overcome by smoke.

The entire explosion/fire sequence lasted no more than 10 minutes. When firemen finally smashed their way into the molding room, they found Anna Fritz, 17, dead from suffocation and atrociously burnt. Christina Schnitzer, 16, and Kittie Howard, 18, were taken out alive to Charity Hospital, but Christina died 20 hours later and Kittie succumbed to burns and sulfur inhalation at 7:30 A.M. on Tuesday morning. Anna Fritz had only been on the job two days, and Kittie had started work just that morning. There were seven serious injuries in addition to the three Fairmount deaths.

The subsequent official investigation did credit to no one. Owner-manager Opes denied under oath that there had been any explosion and insisted that it was only a fire. Investigating officer Cleveland Police captain Fred Kohler waxed eloquent on the infamy of the Fairmount factory, fulminating that it was a "sweatshop" where the "girls were packed in like sardines." But his opinion that the factory was simply a "deathtrap" did not preclude his agreeing with the ultimate finding of the official inquest, which found the Fairmount Company in violation of no existing laws and blameless for the events of March 15.

THE DEAD GIRL AND OTHER VICTIMS OF THE FIRE.

Victims of the Fairmount torpedo fire. *Cleveland Press*, March 15, 1902.

Apparently, nothing was learned from the Fairmount disaster. True, R. H. Opes's torpedo concern ceased operations, but that was due only to his completely uninsured $10,000 loss on the factory. Nothing was done by the city of Cleveland—much less the Ohio legislature—either to forbid the operation of torpedo factories in residential neighborhoods or to tighten restrictions on their use of inflammable or explosive materials. So when the next spring rolled around there were three torpedo factories running full tilt in Cleveland.

One was the Crescent Appliance Company on Case Avenue (East 40th Street) near St. Clair; the second was on Berlin Street (West 81st) near Madison Avenue. But the largest and most dangerous factory was the Thor Manufacturing Company at 647 Orange Street just a few steps from Case Avenue.

Owned by Joseph Raquett and Silas Cole, the Thor torpedo factory was a two-story wooden frame building, extending 60 feet back from the street and facing south on Orange Street. The concern employed eight women and seven men (mostly teenagers), plus managing owner Raquett and Cole's son Wilbur. The red, white, and blue torpedo "canes" that constituted the factory's chief product were small but noisy fireworks especially prized by small children too young for more powerful holiday armament. Owner Raquett would later claim there were no more than 100 pounds of dangerous materials—chiefly sulfur and potash—in the building, and he may have been correct. But the first floor was filled with boxes of finished torpedoes awaiting shipment, and the second-floor mixing area was covered with sawdust and accumulated powder debris from the torpedo mixture. The previous year, after several minor explosions at the Thor factory, John W. Bath, the state inspector of workshops, had ordered company officials to change the sawdust every two days to prevent dangerous buildup—but Raquett and Cole had failed to implement his order. Given the indifference of the Thor management to the safety of its employees and the location of the factory in the most densely populated area of Cleveland, all was in place for an unprecedented Forest City tragedy.

It came on Saturday, May 2, at exactly 12:16 P.M. The tragedy began as a practical joke. No one working with the flammable torpedo mixture was allowed to wear shoes in the second-floor mixing area. But Gusta Wolf, eating her lunch in an adjacent area, was wearing her shoes when a new employee, Mary Hollenen, gave her a playful shove. As Wolf slid across the floor into the sawdust, her shoes struck a spark. A second later, a flame sprang up, fed by the torpedo residue on the floor. Wolf quickly threw a basin of water on the blaze, but it was already too late. Joseph Katz, a laborer working on a new house next door to the factory, saw the developing scene through an open window. He screamed, "Run for your lives!" and immediately set the example. Smoke began to pour out of the windows, and within seconds the Thor building exits were streaming with panicked, fleeing employees.

Ironically, the Thor workers suffered relatively less than persons in neighboring houses or just passersby, because the initial fire provided sufficient warning for them to escape. But with the exception of the lucky Joseph Katz, the rest of the people in the crowded neighborhood had had no warning whatsoever when the contents of the Thor shipping room exploded at exactly 12:16 P.M.

It was the largest explosion in Cleveland history up to that time, and still probably the second-largest after the 1944 East Ohio Gas Company blast. It pulverized the Thor factory and a dozen adjoining houses and damaged hundreds of others within a half-mile radius. It damaged storefronts and residences for a half-mile stretch on both Orange and Woodland Avenues and knocked virtually everyone flat in that square mile of Cleveland. It smashed practically every pane of glass within 3,000 feet of the factory and was felt as far away as Doan Street (East 105th) and in Public Square.

The worst of it was in the new residential development just west and to the rear of the factory. Built by developer E. Brudno and leased mostly to Jewish families, the half-dozen or so homes took the brunt of the blast. Most were completely demolished, leaving but a precarious partition or single exterior wall in grotesque silhouette. The three deaths in the disaster occurred in the Morris Cohen residence, just 12 feet to the west of the Thor factory. Cohen had just brought his family of eight over from England to his new house the previous Monday, and the explosion caught his wife and two of his sons at their midday meal. Firemen quickly pulled the three of them from the splintered ruins of the house, but Mrs. Cohen bled to death from a severed neck artery in an ambulance on the way to the hospital. Five hours later, her son Solly, 12, died of a fractured skull at St. Vincent Charity Hospital, followed four hours afterward by Benjamin, 18, who had lost the top of his head in the explosion.

Another house hard hit was the Barney Quass residence directly behind the Thor factory. Mrs. Quass ended up in the hospital with her badly injured daughter Mabel and son Harry. They were joined there by Mamie Meyer, 14, of 1265 Case Avenue, whose left eye was taken out by flying glass and Wilbur Cole, son of the Thor co-owner, found bruised, cut, and horribly lacerated under the factory ruins. Many of the wounded had simply been walking in the area when the wave of the blast knocked them off their feet. Every ambulance in Cleveland was soon busy handling the casualties that jammed area hospitals through the weekend.

The Thor catastrophe produced the usual anomalies and heroics peculiar to such disasters. Mrs. Morris Weingarten was sitting in her rocking chair in the parlor at 12634 Case Avenue when the blast flipped her and the chair into a complete somersault. Miss Annie Sandrowsky of 1290 Case Avenue was so traumatized by the explosion that, although physically uninjured, she lost the power of

Ruins of a house destroyed by the Thor explosion. *Cleveland Leader*, May 3, 1903.

One of the wrecked buildings. *Cleveland Leader*, May 3, 1903.

A group of survivors of the explosion, *Cleveland Leader*, May 2, 1903.

speech. More inspiring was the experience of Arthur and Lizzie Conroy, Thor employees who were brother and sister. Lizzie escaped the burning building, only to go back inside to find her missing brother. Arthur, in fact, had also escaped, but he saw her reenter and risked his life to bring her back out again. They were just a few feet away from the factory when it exploded and knocked them senseless—but left them alive.

Amazingly, the final butcher's bill was only three dead and a couple of hundred injured. Unamazingly, the official sequel to the Thor tragedy followed the familiar script of public bravado and masterly inaction. Cleveland newspaper editorials shrieked loudly for punishment of the responsible parties and demanded an end to such lethal establishments in residential neighborhoods. Cuyahoga County coroner Thomas A. Burke, for his part, promised, "Someone is to blame and I expect to find out who it is." But his inquest, which commenced as the Cohen dead were tearfully buried in Fremont Cemetery and squads of police battled small boys searching for unexploded torpedoes in the Thor ruins, proved to be the usual empty civic ritual. Although Dr. Perry Hobbs of Western Reserve University testified that the torpedo mixture used was nearly as efficient as nitroglycerin as an explosive agent, Burke could not find any law prohibiting its use in city factories. True, state inspector of explosives Bath did bring up that little matter of his ignored order about exchanging the sawdust on the mixing floor, but he, County Prosecutor Harvey Keeler, and Coroner Burke agreed that it was too "technical" a violation of state law to pursue. Six days after the explosion, Burke issued his verdict, which was that the Thor explosion was purely "accidental" and that he held no one responsible.

The lesson of the second torpedo tragedy was not entirely lost on the city. On May 8, Cleveland fire chief George A. Wallace ordered the closure of the city's remaining torpedo factories. No more lives were lost or homes imperiled in the manufacture of "harmless" fireworks within the Cleveland city limits. But no one articulated the next logical step, which was to prohibit the storage of large amounts of explosive material in areas used by the public. Thus, the stage was set for the memorable tragedy of July 3, 1908, the last of Cleveland's three fireworks horrors. (For details of that disaster, see Chapter 1 of *They Died Crawling*.)

Chapter 17

"NO HOME, NOR NO MOTHER, NOR NOTHIN'"

The 1900 Death of Alfred Williams

You've probably never heard of him, but Alfred Williams is a Clevelander you should know. He was only 11 years old, he lived in Cleveland for only six months, and the only "significant" thing that happened to him here was his untimely death. But his story remains a moving one and reveals much that is both disturbing and uplifting about the Cleveland of a century ago.

No one even knows who his parents were. We know he was born in 1890 and that his family lived in Phillipsburg, Pennsylvania. Sometime in the late 1890s, Alfred's father died, and his mother was put in a charitable institution, probably an insane asylum. Alfred tried living with an older brother for a while after his family disintegrated, but he and his sibling couldn't get along. Then in June of 1899, an itinerant glassblower who toured the country giving demonstrations of his craft offered to take Alfred off his brother's hands. Perhaps Alfred's departure from Phillipsburg was voluntary, perhaps not. What is indisputable is that Alfred turned up in Cleveland in the spring of 1900 and that he decided to stay here.

Alfred naturally gravitated to what was then nearly the only unskilled occupation open to one of his tender years and puny physique: working as a newsboy selling the daily papers on the streets of the Forest City. Employed by the *Cleveland Press*, the frail-looking Alfred soon became a familiar sight at his regular selling post on Superior Street, on the south side between the Old Arcade (then still practically brand new) and Erie Street (soon to be rechristened as the more prosaic East 9th Street). T. J. Chase, a carpenter who had his shop in the old City Hall across from the Arcade, was one of the many adults who worried about young Alfred, a chronically unhealthy- and unhappy-looking urchin. Sometimes, Alfred's "newsie" peers would later recall, he was so weak that he could not stand up, and he would sit on the sidewalk or curb with his armful of afternoon papers thrust out at passersby with a pitiful plea to buy. Some of his newsboy friends pitied him and would sometimes offer to share their own scant supplies of food and money with the obviously ill and malnourished lad. But Alfred was notoriously proud about his poverty and would not accept their modest alms, although he often lamented his hard privations and lonely life.

The circumstances of Alfred's death would reveal that during his months in Cleveland he was informally "adopted" by a Mr. and Mrs. Joseph C. Loeb of 590 Superior Street. Whether the Loebs aggravated Alfred's unhappiness and ill health is unknown. They would later justify themselves to a hostile public with claims that they had valiantly struggled to reform an unruly boy who refused to obey or to attend school. But his perennial ragged state, his constant depression, and his obvious ill health spoke volumes to outside observers, and their subsequent verdict on the Loebs was a harsh one.

BOY OF 11 SUICIDES

Little Alfred Williams Takes Rough on Rats and Dies From the Effects—Took His Little Life Because He Didn't Want to Go to School—A Wild Child of Nature.

Cleveland World,
October 11, 1900.

Throughout the day of October 11, 1900, the news flew through the streets of Cleveland that Alfred Williams had committed suicide at the Loebs' house. The facts of his death were stark and simple. Sometime after returning from work the previous evening Alfred had swallowed a powerful dose of "Rough-on-Rats" (a potent rodent poison that frequently figured in press accounts of suicides among the poor). There were rumors that the violently sick Alfred had told Mrs. Loeb what he had done and that she ignored his parlous condition. Her version was that he simply said, "Mamma, I've eaten a little Rough-on-Rats," and that when she expressed disbelief, he replied, "If you don't believe me, go out into the pantry and see where it is spilled." Whatever really occurred that night, Alfred was incontestably dead when Dr. R. A. Kennedy was called to his bedside at 7 the next morning. Deputy Coroner George West exam-

"Boy Suicide Buried by Comrades,"
Cleveland Press, October 20, 1900.

ined his corpse, pronounced his death a suicide, and had the body
removed to the nearby undertaking rooms of Hogan & Company at
717 Superior.

Alfred's body languished in Hogan's establishment for six days
because he had left no funds for his burial. Finally, the management there informed a delegation of his concerned newsboy friends
that his corpse would either be sent to the city potter's field or
donated to a medical school for dissection purposes. This was a
horrifying prospect to the boys, many of whom were only a few
cents or an unlucky accident away from a pauper's grave themselves. On Thursday, October 18, at 11 A.M. they held a meeting at
the *Cleveland Press* offices and unanimously decided that they
would assume responsibility for Alfred's burial. Each boy was
allowed to contribute between one and ten cents to the fund, the
limit being set so that no one would feel that another boy was doing
more. The next day the boys, working with other newsies from the
Cleveland World, the *Plain Deale*r, and the *Cleveland Leader,*

completed the arrangements for the funeral and scheduled it for the next day.

It was a melancholy procession of newsboys that set off from the offices of the *Press* at 8 the next morning. Arriving in double columns at Hogan's, they were joined there by newsboys from the other papers, and they stood in somber silence as the Reverend J. D. Jones of the Floating Bethel conducted the brief, dignified services. After Miss Lou Beatty mournfully sang "There Never Is a Day So Dreary" and "Sometime We'll Understand," accompanying herself on the autoharp, Jones briefly commented on what he had learned about Alfred from his newsie friends. One weeping boy had told him, "They gave him a bad name but they hadn't out to a done it. He was a good boy and a hustler. He was a sick boy but he did the best he could." Moved by their memories of the forlorn child, Jones used the occasion to defend Alfred's reputation and to exhort the newsboys to rise above their grim circumstances:

> I will say to the living, now that I can't talk to this boy: Boys, aim to help your mother and keep your good name. There is no doubt in my mind as to whether this boy took his own life. I have conducted 200 funerals from this establishment and never before a case of a boy committing suicide. I don't believe this boy did. This is not the time or place to give my reasons . . . Perhaps, though, this boy's life was so full of sorrow and distress that his reason was dethroned and he couldn't bear it. Boys, you have no more right to take your own life than that of another. Attend Sunday School. I hope I have said something here that will aid you boys in forming a good resolution.

The service in front of the small, white plush coffin concluded with a prayer for the welfare of the newsies, and the boys reformed their double line for the march to Erie Street Cemetery. Much of Erie Street was torn up for sewer work, so it took the procession of more than a hundred newsboys some time to get there, marching in pitiful dignity and somber silence behind the sole carriage they had hired for the Reverend Jones. The heartbreaking scene at the graveside was well captured by a *Press* reporter, whose account appeared just hours later:

> It was a striking illustration of a truth sometimes forgotten—that newsboys have hearts. Surging around the fresh heap of earth were newsies who knew Alfred Williams. "China" and

"Alabama" were among the others. They were proud they had known him. They told their fellows so. "Nick" Abbey told the boys they must keep quiet and not talk while the preacher was speaking. A little colored bootblack and an Italian newsie crowded closer. A boy with bare feet, a soiled gray sweater and matted hair turned away and cried as though his heart would break. The sobs of some little girls broke into the preacher's reading of the brief funeral service.

It was newsie "Scrub" Smith who found just the right words in his epitaph for Alfred, muttered to "Limpy" Martin as they bent over the flower-covered mound at the conclusion of the service. Brushing some earth away from the wreath of roses on the coffin, he said, "He had no home, nor no mother, nor nothin'."

Much to their chagrin, the $105 raised by the newsboys for Alfred's funeral was not enough to cover the cost of a gravestone. But the example of their brave generosity melted the heart of at least one Clevelander. Two days after the funeral the head of the Newsboys Association received a letter from Joseph Carabelli, the proprietor of the Lake View Granite Works, where many of the most prestigious gravestones in Cleveland were produced. He had heard of their financial plight and his letter read:

> Boys: Send me the inscription you wish put on the headstone of Alfred Williams, and I will see that the poor unfortunate boy's grave is marked by a nice headstone free of cost. Yours, Joseph Carabelli, Proprietor, Lake View Granite Works.

The newsies immediately accepted Carabelli's offer and appointed a committee to prepare a suitable inscription. It read:

ALFRED WILLIAMS
Died October 11, 1900
Age 11 Years
He Was a Newsboy Without
Father, Mother or Home, And
Was Buried by His Newsboy Comrades

Sad to say, Alfred Williams was forgotten rather quickly. By 1910 his grave was so neglected and overgrown with weeds as to be invisible. But by an odd stroke of fate, spring of that year brought a new caretaker to Erie Street Cemetery. It was T. J. Chase, Alfred's old friend from 1900, and he saw to it that Alfred's grave was well kept during his tenure. By 1940, when an inquiring *Press* reporter sought it out, the grave's poignant epitaph had been completely effaced by time. And when Cleveland cemetery maven Vicki Vigil searched for the grave several years ago it was nowhere to be found.

The grave of Alfred Williams.
Cleveland Press, July 16, 1910.

Chapter 18

DEATH OF THE DANCE HALL GIRLS

The 1905 Anna Kinkopf / Eva Meyer Murders

PART 1: DEATH IN PAYNE'S PASTURES

Like many a terrible Cleveland story, the Anna Kinkopf murder announced itself innocently enough. Little Tommy Dorn was just playing tag with his cousin Tom Poland on the crisp Sunday afternoon of October 9, 1905. They were playing in "Payne's Pastures," several acres of grass and weeds lying north of Superior Avenue between Handy Street (East 19th) and North Perry Street (East 21st) that had remained undeveloped as Cleveland's urban frontier leapfrogged toward the East End at the turn of the 20th century. (This area is now, of course, the exact site of the new *Plain Dealer* building.) At 5 P.M. Tommy was only about 30 feet from Superior and running hard when he stumbled over something and fell down. Rising to his feet, he looked down to see a woman's leg protruding from a pile of grass. His first thought was that it just some drunken woman, passed out in the field. But then he saw the other leg, the torn clothing, and the blood, bruises, and scratches on the exposed parts of an obviously dead body. Screaming, he ran to his cousin Tom McLane's house on nearby Rockwell Avenue to spread the news.

Minutes later, McLane brought a Cleveland policeman and Dr. L. A. Osier to the scene. What Osier found there was the body of a young woman. She was five feet tall, well proportioned, and had dark, lush brown hair. Her face had once been angular and sharp, but it was now covered with scratches, bruises, and a thick coat of dried blood. She was wearing a small brown jacket and a skirt of dark blue wool, which had been pulled up over her waist. She lay face down, her eyes, nose, and mouth filled with dirt, as if someone had deliberately pushed her face into the muddy ground. Much of her body was covered with blood, as were her jacket and underwear.

The most horrifying sight, however, was her throat. Badly scratched, it clearly showed the marks of the powerful hands that had squeezed the life out of her: three deep fingernail gashes on the right side and two on the left. The condition of the corpse left little doubt that the victim had waged a ferocious struggle before going down.

Three hours later the victim was identified by laborer Max Konig at the Hogan & Company morgue. He said it was his sweetheart, Anna (sometimes Johanna) Kinkopf, a 22-year-old Hungar-

ian chambermaid at the Hotel Euclid (East 14th and Euclid). She had lived in the U.S. about two years, liked to drink and dance of a weekend night, but otherwise had a good reputation. Konig's story was that he had been with Anna on Saturday night at Nowak's saloon on St. Clair (on the north side, just east of East 34th Street). It was a tough place where young Hungarian immigrant males liked to go to drink and dance with immigrant girls who went there for the same reasons. The music was provided by amateur musicians, and sometimes Max himself played. But Max had not been feeling well that night, and he had left Anna there about 10:30 P.M. and returned to his

Anna Kinkopf, *Cleveland Press*, October 9, 1905.

home. According to other witnesses, including her sister, a reasonably sober Anna had left Nowak's about 12:30 A.M. walking west down St. Clair Avenue, bound for the Hotel Euclid. The last person to see her alive was Nowak's patron George Wolf, who lost sight of her near Alabama Street (East 26th Street).

No one knows how exactly how Anna walked from St. Clair to

death in Payne's Pastures. But the opinion of her autopsy physicians was that she had been dead for 12 to 18 hours, placing the time of her murder between midnight and 5 A.M. The police theory was that she had continued on her way home from the saloon when she was suddenly attacked by a muscular maniac hiding in the grass at Payne's Pastures. Getting more of a fight than he had bargained for from the feisty Anna (who had once successfully fought off *two* male attackers), her assailant had dragged her back in the weeds and strangled her to death. She had not been raped, although her attacker had deliberately shoved her face into the earth, as if making a final gesture of contempt.

Cleveland chief of police Fred Kohler's detectives contended valiantly with the glut of young Hungarian males their indiscriminate dragnet brought in over the next 72 hours. This measure was dictated by their operative theory that Anna had been killed by a jealous rival of Max

Anna Kinkopf's wake and location of her wounds. *Cleveland Press,* October 10, 1905.

Konig. (Other theories that it was a robbery gone awry or a revenge plot stemming from her Hungarian past were soon discarded.) But their vigorous interrogations were greatly hampered by the lack of Hungarian-speaking interpreters on the force and the general distrust of the Cleveland police shared by young Hungarian immigrant males. So Kohler's men made little progress as they attempted to bully confessions out of Max Konig, George Wolf, and a half-dozen other males known to have been at Nowak's saloon on the murder night. Nor did they succeed in apprehending such obscure, rumored suspects as "Collinwood Jimmy" and "Crazy Joe," suggested to them by impressionable tipsters.

A frustrated Chief Kohler was quick to pin the blame on the Hungarian community, rather than on the incompetence of his sleuths. The *Cleveland Leader,* his willing mouthpiece, echoed his excuses in its columns and appealed directly to its middle-class readers' deepest fears about Cleveland's enormous foreign population:

> In this instance the [Kinkopf investigation] has failed . . .
> because of the inability of those under suspicion to understand
> the English language and the Anglo-Saxon idea of right and
> wrong . . . "They lie," said Chief Kohler, "when the truth would
> serve them better. Why? I don't know, unless it is the fear of the
> police, which seems to be a part of the mental make up of a part
> of our foreign populations."

The police had better success in reconstructing the timeline of
Anna's murder. A canvass of the murder neighborhood turned up
George Downer of 222 Oregon Street (Rockwell Avenue), who had
heard some screams of distress from Payne's Pastures about 11:50
P.M. on Saturday night. He had been reading at the time, and when
the cries were not renewed, he decided it was just a mischievous
child. Mrs. Mary Johns of 266 Oregon Street came forward to say
that she had seen three men running on Superior about a half hour
later. And Mrs. Anna Newman of 216 Oregon Street told police
that she had been awakened at 1 A.M. by her agitated fox terrier.

Cleveland Press,
October 11, 1905.

She had let him out, and he had run
into the field and then returned. He
acted strangely, running back and
forth as if to invite her to follow him,
but Mrs. Newman wouldn't venture
into the lonely field.

By Tuesday morning, October 10,
the police had a quality suspect. It
was George Wentzel, a 33-year-old
machinist and habitual drunk. He
was known to hang around Nowak's
saloon, and he could not—or would
not—satisfactorily account for his
movements between Saturday and
Sunday afternoons. More importantly, he had deep scratches on his
face, and he lived in a shed just 125 feet from where Anna
Kinkopf's body was found. And the second and third fingers of his
right hand were missing—corresponding exactly to the pattern of
the finger marks on Anna's neck!

The climax of the Kinkopf murder investigation came on October 13, when the police released all of their suspects except

Wentzel. The police then put him in a lineup at Central Police Station with 20 other men. An unidentified couple who had seen a mysterious man at the murder scene about midnight viewed the lineup, in a moment recalled by *Cleveland Press* reporter Bob Larkin in 1930:

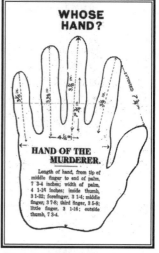

WHOSE HAND?

HAND OF THE MURDERER.

Length of hand, from tip of middle finger to end of palm, 7 3-4 inches; width of palm, 4 1-14 inches; inside thumb, 3 1-32; forefinger, 3 1-4; middle finger, 3 7-8; third finger, 3 5-8; little finger, 3 1-16; outside thumb, 7 3-4.

Cleveland Press, October 10, 1905.

> Several walked by and the couple betrayed no sign of recognition. Suddenly the woman started, her eyes dilated. She stared intently at one of the men. Her companion seized her by the wrist and commanded her to silence with a stern look. She became hysterical and was led from the room. Soon she regained her composure and the police had lost their chance of solution. Cross-examination by detectives failed to elicit any information from her. She denied she had recognized anyone in the "showup."

Chief Kohler's subsequent conclusion, echoed by Larkin, was that the couple had recognized the suspected killer—probably Wentzel—in the lineup. But they refused to commit themselves publicly, as they turned out to be a man and a woman who should definitely not have been together on Superior Avenue at midnight on October 9. Stymied by the couple's stubborn silence and the continued noncooperation of the Hungarian community, Kohler had Wentzel released from jail on October 18. For his part, Wentzel later explained his scratches as the result of injuries he had suffered due to his severe intoxication on the Saturday night in question.

Perhaps Wentzel was guilty, perhaps not. The circumstantial evidence against him was strong but imperfect. Moreover, the stumblebum Wentzel had many reasons to lie about his behavior other than to cover up a murder. But Cleveland moralists did not need a personal scapegoat for what had happened to Anna Kinkopf. They knew what had killed her, and they soon began an emotional public campaign against dance halls. The *Cleveland News* opened the crusade with a shrill blast only 24 hours after Anna's body was discovered:

> Johanna Kinkopf lies dead at the County Morgue. Two days ago she was a light-hearted, frivolous girl, willing to go where her conscience told her she should not go—if she was cheered on by jolly companions and surrounded by the temptations that allure [*sic*] thousands of girls in Cleveland today.

Then the real agenda of the *News* emerged in a sidebar that exploited the deepest anxieties of its white audience in its picture of interracial Forest City depravity:

> In a room over a saloon at 487 Erie street a dance was in progress. A score or more of men, all colored, waltzed with their arms around partners, not all colored. Down in the saloon, connected with the dancehall by a stairway, a crowd of colored men was drinking. The piano played in ragtime. The men hugged the women openly. The two white women in the place seemed to be enjoying themselves thoroughly.

The *News* continued in high dudgeon, excoriating the evils of dance halls that served liquor and condemning the city government (that is, Mayor Tom Johnson) for tolerating such civic disgraces. It ended its tirade, logically or not, with a call to close all saloons . . . to women. In the same edition, the Reverend Charles A. Eaton (Cleveland's most influential Protestant divine and an uncle of Cyrus Eaton) chimed in with a call for an end to all public dance halls, terming them "worse than the saloons themselves."

The final scenes in the Anna Kinkopf saga were suitably macabre spectacles. Five thousand persons, most of them strangers to the dead girl, turned out to gawk at her corpse on display at the county morgue. As was the custom in her community, Anna's body was then displayed in a shabby ballroom at 1395 Superior Avenue. Fortified by relays of drinks from the bar downstairs, the crowd of five hundred got their last good look at Anna, attired in a white silk dress, with a string of red and white roses festooning her casket. As the festive crowd walked by the bier, they flicked drops of holy water on her face, an Old Country custom. One inebriated mourner, unfamiliar with the gesture, saw the water on Anna's face and panicked, shouting "She's sweatin'! She ain't dead; get some water, here there—a doctor!" He grabbed Anna to lift her up, only to drop her in shock as he felt the cold stiffness of her corpse.

Downstairs, the beer soon ran out, and fresh supplies were rushed in from neighboring saloons. It is edifying to report that her final obsequies at St. Peter's Church and her interment at Calvary Cemetery were accomplished with greater decorum.

Meanwhile, the saloon dance halls stayed open . . .

PART 2: "SAY YOUR PRAYERS!"
THE ASSASSINATION OF EVA MEYER

Eva Meyer lived to dance. She had only been in the United States for 10 months, and she was already a fixture at the West Side saloon dance halls patronized by Hungarian, German, and Austrian immigrants living in Cleveland. Almost every weekend in the fall of 1905 found her dancing in such places, often accompanied by her sisters Katie and Lizzie. Like Anna Kinkopf, Eva was 22 and had a good reputation and no shortage of beaus, many of whom liked to pester the beautiful Eva for dances as she flitted from dance hall to dance hall. Whatever their blandishments, though, most dance nights now found her in the company of laborer Louis Hora. Hora had supplanted her previous suitor only a few months before, but Louis was already willing to tell anyone that he was head over heels in love with the lighthearted, fleet-footed, angelic Eva.

Sunday night, November 12, shaped up as a typical weekend night for Eva. Enjoying a day off from her stint as a domestic servant at the Griese mansion on Lake Avenue, she and Louis went to Mike Mongol's saloon and dance hall in the early evening. Located at 893 West Madison (now Madison Avenue), Mongol's saloon, like Nowak's East Side joint, served as both a watering hole and open dance space for young East European immigrants looking for entertainment at the fleshpots of Cleveland.

The evening went by in a whirl of happiness and laughter as Eva displayed the rhythmic abandon that had already moved all who saw her to call her "the dancing girl." There was only one odd incident to mar the pleasant evening. It came at about 10 P.M. when a young man suddenly bumped Eva's arm as he and his partner whirled by. When Eva turned to look at him, she noticed that he was staring at her in a way that made her uncomfortable. The next time Louis and Eva passed near the same couple, the man leaned over and whispered something in Eva's ear. Louis didn't hear what the man said, but he sensed that Eva immediately became nervous and apprehensive. Despite his entreaties, however, she refused to tell him what had been said to her.

Louis and Eva left Mongol's saloon about 10:30 P.M., a few dances before it closed for the night. She shook off Hora's offer of a streetcar ride back to the Griese mansion and declined to take her usual pedestrian route. Instead, at her insistence, she and Louis began walking down West Madison Avenue. It was quite dark, and Louis noticed that Eva seemed to become quieter and more nervous with every step they took. Several minutes went by, and then they turned north onto Hillsdale Street (West 69th Street).

Hillsdale Street was little more than a country road in 1905, flanked by fields of bushy grass and having neither lights nor houses on either side. As they walked along, Eva suddenly stopped. She seemed to think that there was someone following them and she asked Louis to listen. When he told her he heard nothing, she said, "I thought I heard someone on the other side of the bushes." "Nonsense," replied Hora and they walked on into the deepening darkness.

Several hundred feet farther, Eva suddenly clutched Hora's arm and whimpered, "Louis, I can swear I heard a voice whispering, 'Say your prayers! Why don't you say your prayers?'" Before Louis could reply, a shot rang out. By the time Eva screamed, the first bullet had already smashed into her brain. As she fell down dead, Louis looked up to see a man standing at the side of the road. His hat was pulled over his eyes, and his face was by concealed by his upturned coat collar. He looked at the prostrate Eva and laughed loudly. Then he lifted his revolver and fired twice at Hora. The first bullet drilled the top of Hora's black fedora hat, grazed his head, and kept on going. The second came nowhere near him, for by that time the panicked Louis was running back to West Madison as fast as his legs could carry him. He dashed to the trolley car barns there, blurted out his story in broken English, and waited for the police to come.

Hora was later criticized severely for running away from the shooter, but it is hard to fault his behavior in retrospect. The fatal bullet had entered the back of Eva's head, passing up through the right eyeball and killing her instantly. There was no aid Hora could have rendered Eva, and it is debatable whether honor would have

THE MYSTERIOUS WEST-END MURDER.

LOUIS HORA

EVA MEYER

JOHN LUDWIG

Cleveland Press, November 13, 1905.

been satisfied by his hanging around to become a target for more bullets himself. And, in any case, Hora was his own worst critic, as he revealed to a *Cleveland News* reporter:

> When I saw that man my teeth chattered, for I thought he was there to kill. I was afraid. Yes I was a coward. Then I saw the gun. My limbs quivered beneath me. The shot followed. I saw Eva place her hand to her head and stagger. Then I knew that if I was to live that I just run. I did.

Hora was immediately arrested by Chief Kohler's police, still smarting from the failure of the Anna Kinkopf investigation. Kohler was determined to break the case, and his men were given a free hand to sweat such members of Cleveland's male Hungarian population as they chose. Within 24 hours they had seven men in custody and were subjecting them to round-the-clock interrogation. As in the Kinkopf case, however, most of the "suspects" were window dressing to convince a skeptical Cleveland public that the police were doing *something*. As in the Kinkopf case, though, the police only had one real suspect, and it was upon his unlucky person that they concentrated their third-degree techniques.

His name was John Ludwig, and he was the suitor whom lovestruck Louis Hora had supplanted in early 1905. Given his personal history, it was inevitable that suspicion would fall on him. Further, police enquiries were no doubt accelerated by the statement of Katie Meyer, Eva's griefstricken sister: "A man whom my sister had rejected was at the dance Sunday night. I saw him there. I think he followed my sister and fired the shots."

Despite Kohler's blustering, the Cleveland police never had a real case against Ludwig. To begin with, he had at least six witnesses to support his alibi that he had been home at his Detroit Avenue rooming house when the murder occurred. And while he admitted that he was jealous of Hora, he denied shooting Eva and insisted that he didn't own and had never carried a revolver. An irate Kohler held Ludwig in jail for nine days before releasing him unconditionally.

As in the case of Anna Kinkopf, the frustrated Kohler soon found an alternate target for his wrath: Louis Hora. As in the Kinkopf case, the investigation was seriously hampered by the lack of interpreters on the force. Once again, Kohler found it convenient to blame the Hungarian community rather than his own bumbling officers. He insisted repeatedly that Hora, whatever his denials, had recognized Eva's killer and was refusing to tell for reasons of ethnic solidarity, a "code of silence" expected in the Hungarian community. An increasingly desperate Kohler fumed to a *Plain Dealer* reporter only three days after the killing:

> Except for the murderer himself, Louis Hora knows more about the crime than any other man. He was with the girl when the crime was committed, saw the murderer and knows who he is, but for some reason refuses to tell us his name. We will hold him

until we get something from him and in the meantime the police will do all in their power to run down the murderer. I am confident, however, that Hora could clear up the mystery and put us on the track of the man who murdered Eva Meyer, but we can get nothing from him. All our examinations have been conducted through an interpreter and this makes it very hard for us to corner the subject of the examination.

A day later, Kohler showed just how angry he was, threatening unlimited mass arrests until he got to the bottom of the mystery:

> I am making arrests in the Eva Meyer case because I am determined to force these foreigners to tell me the truth. I am going to arrest every man who, I find, is lying in connection with the case.

As good as his word, Kohler had his men arrest saloon keeper Mike Mongol that very morning.

In the end, Chief Kohler's bluster was all in vain. One by one, the arrested suspects were freed from jail for lack of evidence, the last of them being Louis Hora, who left his Central Police Station cell on November 21. Hora never changed his story that he did not recognize the man who shot Eva Meyer, and there is no reason to believe that he was not telling the truth. While still in jail, he was allowed to attend Eva's funeral on November 16 at 100 Winchester Avenue. When he saw her in the open casket he broke down completely and was still sobbing when detectives took him back to his cell an hour later. By the time Hora was released, Chief Kohler was beginning to hedge his bets, telling a *Cleveland News* reporter:

> I may have the murderer of Eva Meyer in custody in half an hour. But then again, I may never get the man.

No one knows to this day who killed the dancing girls, Anna Kinkopf and Eva Meyer. One theory never seriously pursued was the possibility that at least one of the women may have been killed by a jealous rival of her own—that is to say, by a woman. Cleveland detective Jake Mintz was particularly enamored of this hypothesis with respect to Eva's assassin. Mintz argued that if the killer had been a jealous man he would likely have fired at Hora first rather than Eva. But the years went by, and the female killer theory was forgotten with the rest. The Kinkopf and Meyer cases became just two more obscure entries in the bulging file of unsolved Cleveland murders.

Anna and Eva sleep forever in the pastoral peace of Calvary Cemetery. The rowdy saloon dance halls that lured them to their deaths are long since gone, replaced by more modern vices. The suspects in both cases vanished into the anonymity whence they had come. Fred Kohler went on to write his own personal pages of both triumph and disgrace in the annals of Cleveland history (see George Condon's amusing biography of Kohler in *Cleveland: The Best-Kept Secret*). And Anna and Eva and their unhappy and undeserved fates have been forgotten. It might behoove historically minded souls—perhaps members of Cleveland's Hungarian community—to create some more permanent remembrance of these unfortunate females.

Chapter 19

BURNING, BURNING, BURNING RIVER

The Cuyahoga River Fires of 1868, 1912, 1922, 1952, 1969, and...

June 22, 1969. Few Clevelanders would quibble with the designation of this milestone as Cleveland's undisputed day of infamy. For that was the day the Cuyahoga River caught fire, and soon thereafter Cleveland spontaneously combusted as a national laughingstock and byword for urban dysfunction. The received wisdom about that infamous blaze is that it signaled the nadir of the river's viability and ignited a sleeping citizenry to repair its badly compromised environment. True on both counts, in a general way, but there's much more to the burning Cuyahoga story than those simple facts. Sadly, like so many Cleveland stories, the full truth is much worse than you've been led to believe.

Nineteenth-century Clevelanders, like most Americans in the pre–*Silent Spring* epoch, paid little mind to the pollutants and poisons they dumped into their water supply. They did mind—and often complained about—the taste and smell of Cleveland water, which along with cholera and typhoid germs, carried the taste and odor of the petroleum refining refuse that John D. Rockefeller et al. were blithely pouring into Kingsbury Run, the Cuyahoga River, and Lake Erie. Rather than forbidding such uncivil practices, however, they coped with oily water by building the city's water intake cribs farther and farther out in Lake Erie—as the bloody history of water crib accidents attests. (See the title story of *They Died Crawling* for a chronicle of those melancholy events.)

The first serious hint that Clevelanders would be paying escalating costs for their indifference to the environment came on August 29, 1868. Waste oil floating near the Seneca Street (West 3rd) bridge on the Cuyahoga ignited a wide area and came close to burning down a dense strip of industrial

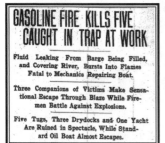

GASOLINE FIRE KILLS FIVE CAUGHT IN TRAP AT WORK

Fluid Leaking From Barge Being Filled, and Covering River, Bursts Into Flames Fatal to Mechanics Repairing Boat.

Three Companions of Victims Make Sensational Escape Through Blaze While Firemen Battle Against Explosions.

Five Tugs, Three Drydocks and One Yacht Are Ruined in Spectacle, While Standard Oil Boat Almost Escapes.

The *Plain Dealer,*
May 2, 1912.

firms on the river's east side. Despite some subsequent, if mild, suggestions that the unlimited discharge of oil waste into the river be curbed, nothing was done. Fifteen years later, in 1883, such persistent disregard earned its due reward when a raging oil fire on the surface of Kingsbury Run (by now containing more oil than water) came within seconds of burning down the entire city. (See the chapter "Cleveland's Burning!" in *The Maniac in the Bushes.*) More hands were publicly wrung, more suggestions for industrial waste regulation were offered—and the contamination of the Cuyahoga River by flammable liquids continued unabated. Despite another scare in August of 1887, when a grain elevator fire ignited part of the river, the turn of the century found the Cuyahoga River chronically and visibly tainted with petroleum products. The problem was generally worse during the long Cleveland winters, when blockage by lake ice in the harbor further retarded the normally sluggish flushing action of the river.

The accident waiting to happen occurred May 1, 1912, at a Standard Oil cargo slip just south of the Jefferson Avenue bridge. Standard Oil barge No. 8, containing 100,000 gallons of oil and naphtha, was being offloaded just across the river from the Great Lakes Towing Company's dry docks. Gasoline from No. 8 had been leaking into the river for some time, unbeknownst to anyone, when a spark from the passing tugboat *Superior* set off the first of six explosions at 3 P.M. Within seconds, oil and gasoline in the water likewise ignited, and an area of several hundred yards was inundated with flaming gasoline. By the time the fire was put out three hours later, it had incinerated five men, injured five others, destroyed five tugboats and three dry docks, and done additional damage to Great Lakes Towing. The dead men, working there as caulkers, had been trapped immediately between the dry dock flooring and the scow they were repairing. In the anguished civic postmortem, the *Plain Dealer* called for the flow of oil into the

CLEVELAND, THURSDAY, MAY 2, 1912.   PRICE ONE C

SCENES AFTER EXPLOSION OF OIL BARGE
THAT KILLED FIVE MEN; FOUR OF VICTIMS

1912 Cuyahoga River fire.
Cleveland Leader, May 2, 1912.

river to be curtailed but discreetly refrained from mentioning how it had gotten there in the first place. Cleveland fire chief George A. Wallace was, characteristically, more blunt. He stated that copious oil seepage from the Standard Oil works was the chief culprit and demanded that it be stopped. Cleveland city councilmen called for public hearings on the matter . . . and that, predictably, was the last heard about the riverine oil peril for some years.

Just 10 years later, on October 29, 1922, the 1912 disaster repeated itself, albeit with less lethal consequences. A fire of unknown origin broke out without warning at noon at the Great Lakes Towing Company's river docks on Jefferson Avenue. Although the blaze was contained within three hours, it damaged a lighter, a derrick, and a tugboat and for a while threatened the Jefferson Avenue bridge. Apparently, nothing was learned from the incident, as a similar blaze broke out in the Cincinnati slip of the

Cuyahoga on April 2, 1930. This time the cause was a film of alcohol and oil in the slip, supposedly ignited by smoldering debris from the Cleveland Grain Elevator fire some three months previ-

The 1930 Cuyahoga River fire.
Cleveland Press, April 2, 1930.

ous. Although there was no serious damage, safety forces got a bad scare as billowing clouds of ominous smoke blanketed downtown.

By the 1940s, public hand-wringing about the growing flammability of the Cuyahoga had become so chronic as to be comically repetitive. One year the *Cleveland Press* would caution: "Experienced [firemen] see the oil-covered river as the starting place for a conflagration which might easily sweep a large portion of the city." The next year would furnish the warning that an oil boat "could cause a lot of damage to…[a] vessel; fire under a railroad bridge would put the operating machinery out of commission." But not even a serious oil blaze that warped the plates of the ore carrier *Negaunee* in March 1941 motivated city officials to significant action. Nor was any decisive cleanup action taken after an intense petroleum fire almost took out the Clark Avenue bridge on February 7, 1948, and caused $100,000 in damage. Nor were any additional reforms initiated after a leaking Cities Service Oil tank spewed thousands of gallons of gasoline into the river on May 16 of the same year. Cleveland officials did, however, step up their public rhetoric—a crescendo of dire warnings that climaxed with Fire Prevention Bureau chief Bernard W. Mulcahy's tough talk in May 1952. Citing "definite proof" that Standard Oil was responsible for a two-inch oil slick under the Jefferson Avenue bridge, Mulcahy thundered that he would have Standard Oil officials arrested if they failed to alleviate the problem.

Apparently, Standard Oil officials did fail, as the worst river fire in Cleveland history broke out only six months later at that very site. The first alarm went in at 2:16 P.M. on November 1, and by the time firemen arrived at the scene, flames were roaring through the Great Lakes Towing Company's dock area, climbing the Jefferson Avenue bridge, and heading fast for Standard Oil Refinery No. 1. Before the flames could be extinguished, the conflagration became

The Cuyahoga River in flames, Jefferson Avenue bridge,
November 1, 1952.

a five-alarm fire, injuring one fireman and wreaking damage
amounting to $1 million. One tugboat was ruined, two more were
badly damaged, a workshop was destroyed, two dry docks were
ruined, and the Jefferson Avenue bridge was put out of commission
with charred flooring and a damaged lift mechanism.

The postmortems on the 1952 fire followed the familiar pattern.
Chief Mulcahy brandished photographs taken several months
before the fire showing six inches of oil on the surface of the water.
Mulcahy further noted that the greatest potential danger point was
where Kingsbury Run emptied into the river near Great Lakes
Towing—the exact locus of the catastrophic 1883 oil fire. And the
Cleveland Chamber of Commerce demanded that Mayor Thomas
A. Burke take steps to eliminate the danger of fire posed by the
Cuyahoga.

Meanwhile, river traffic resumed, the bridge was eventually
repaired after a month . . . and oil and kindred fluids continued to
pour unimpeded into Cleveland's crooked river.

Given this 100-year-plus back story of inflammable pollutants
and ensuing, periodic riverine infernos, it may seem surprising that
the 1969 Cuyahoga fire did not come as a mere anticlimax. By the

standards of 1912 or 1952, it was a very modest mishap. On the morning of June 22 an oil slick floating under two wooden railroad trestles at the foot of Campbell Road caught fire. Reported at 11:56 A.M., the five-story-high flames had been put out by 12:20 P.M., as firemen operating from shore and from a fireboat quickly responded to the alarm. The cause of the fire—aside from the perilous insanity of allowing industries to dump heavy concentrations of oil on the water—was never determined. The total physical damage wrought by the blaze amounted to only $50,000, most of it suffered by the Norfolk and Western double-track trestle, the single-line Newburgh & South Shore viaduct incurring only slight damage. The damage to the city's reputation, however, was almost incalculable. Only two days after the conflagration, the *Plain Dealer* cited the fire as a provocation for nationwide mirth at Cleveland's expense: "Cleveland, eh? Isn't that the place where the river is so polluted it's a fire hazard? Yuk, yuk, yuk."

It wasn't funny to Clevelanders then, and it remains a festering wound in the civic psyche, forever aggravated by the sound of Randy Newman's jeering commemorative anthem, "Burn On." Forest City residents, however, should be grateful to Newman and others who made the last Cuyahoga River fire a pretext for mortifying civic abuse. Given the apathy and abuse that had produced a century of river fires, only such national scorn was able to spark the resurrection of the Cuyahoga River in the years since.

Thick Coating of Oily Goo Lies on Cuyahoga River

Cleveland Press, December 19, 1961.

Chapter 20

THREE DISTAFF POISONERS

Elsie Bass (1917), Anna Kempf (1928), and Dorothy Kaplan (1956)

Poison is primarily a woman's weapon. Although some of the most notorious poisoners in the history of the world have been men—William Palmer, Graham Young, Thomas Neill Cream, and Dr. Crippen come to mind—even a casual perusal of accounts of such crimes offers compelling evidence that killing by poison is disproportionately attractive to women. The advantages of poison as a method of human disposal for women are obvious. Poisoning is generally furtive, an ideal quality for someone confronting an adversary of superior muscular strength or social power. No messy hand-to-hand combat, knowledge of firearms, or knife-fighting technique is required. Poison is easily acquired, hidden, and disguised: many lethal poisons have nonhomicidal uses and are part of the fabric of everyday life, as any amateur gardener or pest control professional can attest. It can be stealthily administered and difficult to detect—as many a delayed exhumation has shown.

A wide range of motives inspires the female use of poison. Some women use it simply as a tool for elimination, while others employ it for radical behavior modification. Still others use it to end not only the lives of those entangled in their personal miseries, but their own as well. The following are three case studies of female Cleveland poisoners whose stories illustrate the wide range of motives and results possible when ladies turn to Borgian methods.

PART 1: "I WOULDN'T EVEN KILL A RAT":
ELSIE BASS (1917)

Elsie Bass was angry. Three days in a row she had gone to the back porch of her house at 2045 West 32nd Street to get the daily bottle of milk delivered there—and each time she had found it gone. Today, Thursday, November 15, 1917, she was determined to do something about it. At first she thought it was the milk company's fault, but her milkman assured her he had delivered it and suggested that perhaps it was being stolen by mischievous boys. That made sense to Elsie. She told her husband John as he left that morning that she was determined to catch the milk thieves that very day.

Elsie Bass wasn't kidding. The first hint that she had taken decisive action came Thursday night at the home of John Perko, age 9,

Jury Gets Bass Case
Murder Verdict Asked

MRS. BASS PHOTOGRAPHED ON STAND

Mrs. Bass on the stand.

of 2025 West 32nd Street, just a few doors away from the Basses' back porch. John, a student at St. Mary's School, became violently sick shortly after he arrived home late Thursday afternoon. Vomiting, feverish, and tormented with an unappeasable thirst, John begged for water throughout the night. Shortly before 9 the next morning he died, just before the family doctor arrived.

Things were not going very well either at the homes of John's best friends, George Foley, 9, of 2100 West 32nd and Joe Pozsgai, 8, of 2051 West 32nd. Like John, both George and Joe became violently ill shortly after they got home from school on Thursday afternoon. John and Joe wouldn't tell their mothers what was wrong, but George's mother eventually wormed the truth out of her reluctant son. He told her that he had gotten sick shortly after stealing a bottle of milk off neighbor Elsie Bass's porch. He, John, and Joe had drunk it there at about 4 P.M. on Thursday, and George had vomited immediately after they ran from the porch and hopped over a fence. Mrs. Foley didn't know quite what to think about that, but she instinctively continued to dose George with the large quantities of salt water that apparently saved his life.

Mrs. Foley thought much more about it the next day when her older son reported the death of John Perko. After talking with Mrs. Perko and Mrs. Pozsgai, Mrs. Foley consulted family physician Charles H. Hay. Hay contacted District Physician T. G. Duncan, who notified Cuyahoga County coroner P. J. Byrne. An hour later Cleveland Police detective Charles H. Snyder knocked on Elsie Bass's door.

Elsie refused to admit anything at first, only repeating, "I didn't do anything to the milk." But when Snyder finally told her John Perko was dead, she screamed, "I didn't mean to kill anyone! I'll tell you all about it!" Several hours later, after an interrogation by Snyder, Lieutenant Edward Donahue, and Detective Henry Kiehl, Elsie signed a full confession and was booked for first-degree murder.

Elsie's account of the poisoning varied little in its various retellings, although she sometimes denied knowing the potency of her preferred substance. An immigrant girl from Hungary in 1911, Elsie had endured a hard life both there and subsequently as a Cleveland charwoman before marrying Jack Bass in 1913. She didn't like being taken advantage of—which is why she reached into her cupboard for some rat poison when she figured out what was happening to her milk. That Thursday afternoon, she retrieved the milk bottle as soon as it was delivered and brought it into her kitchen. There, she poured out a cup of the

GRAND JURY IS GIVEN CASE OF MILK POISONER

Woman Says She Didn't Intend Rat Poison to Kill Boy; Gets Bail.

HELD FOR MURDER OF BOY PILFERER

Elsie Bass, milk bottle poisoner. *Cleveland News,* November 17, 1917.

MRS. BASS IN COURT

Elsie Bass in Court.

milk, mixed it with a healthy dose of some old rat poison she had previously acquired at a Clark Avenue drugstore, and poured the mixture back in the bottle. She resealed it, set it back on her porch, and awaited events, concealed behind an adjacent window.

Elsie didn't have to wait long. This was the fourth trip to the Bass porch in as many days for John, George, and Joe. They laughed as they opened the bottle and took turns at swigging it down. George took the first drink, Joe followed, and John finished it off. Investigators later theorized that most of the arsenic poison had settled to the bottom of the bottle, which is why John Perko was the one to die from its effects. All three boys were terribly sick by the time they got home.

It is likely that no one in Judge Willis Vickery's Common Pleas courtroom believed Elsie Bass would be convicted on her first-degree murder charge. The all-male juries of the era were notoriously reluctant to convict females on capital counts, especially one as attractive as Mrs. Bass proved to be when her trial opened on January 29, 1918. The state's prosecution was led by County Prosecutor J. J. Babka and Stephen Young, while attorneys Lewis Greenfield and George S. Myers defended Mrs. Bass. The facts were not in dispute, although the defense tried to diminish the effect of her confession by charging that the Cleveland police had used "loud and threatening" language during her interrogation. After medical professionals testified as to the facts of John Perko's death, Elsie took the stand to repeat her assertion that she had not meant to kill anyone. As the rapt spectators scanned her pretty face, she plaintively insisted, "I did not know that it was poison that would kill anybody. I thought it would make their stomachs sick and they would not come back again."

Less persuasively, perhaps, Elsie also denied having any recollection of her detailed, signed confession. After Judge Vickery instructed the jury that a second-degree murder conviction was not an option, the conclusion of the Bass case became predictable. After less than three hours of deliberation, her jury returned a verdict of manslaughter at 5:20 P.M. on January 31. On February 7 an angry Judge Vickery, sourly noting the many letters he had received from Cleveland mothers seeking clemency for Elsie, sentenced her to an indeterminate term in the Marysville Reformatory. "To allow this woman to escape punishment," thundered Vickery, "would be to let down the bars for women to poison children." But during the next 10 days Vickery either changed his mind or decided to make glad the hearts of potential Cleveland child poisoners. For on February 18 Vickery nulled Elsie's prison sentence and put her on probation. Her last words for the public as she left the courtroom were appropriately grateful, even if they did not exactly strike a note of profound remorse:

> Oh, I'm so glad. They're not going to send me away. It has always seemed like a horrible dream to me. I would rather have died than to have been sent away. I can scarcely believe the awful thing really happened. I'm going to live right, now, always.

PART 2: "WHAT COULD A WOMAN DO?": ANNA KEMPF'S DESPERATE DEED (1928)

As Mrs. Julia Babel, Anna Kempf's mother, later put it, Anna looked "queer" when she came home shortly after eight on the night of Wednesday, October 3, 1928. Home was Mrs. Babel's house at 2803 Bridge Avenue, and along with divers boarders, it sheltered Anna and her three children: Julia, 7, Margaret, 6, and Mary, 3. And it wasn't just Anna's expression that was different— surpassing even the inner turmoil normally evident in her face, which reflected the travails of a hardworking 28-year-old mother with an estranged husband and three dependent children. Anna had brought home some decorative wax flowers, an unusual, frivolous, and even foolish gesture in a household where every penny counted.

Another oddity was the pint of chocolate ice cream Anna opened when she got to the kitchen. Ice cream was a special treat in the cash-strapped Kempf family, and even the children sensed that their mother was in some kind of rare mood. But they all waited

CHILD POISONING VICTIM

Child poisoning victim Mary Kempf and family. *Cleveland Press*, October 4, 1928.

patiently while Anna mixed up the ice cream in another room and spooned it into two bowls, one for her mother and the other for herself and the children. The ice cream was just as good as everyone thought it would be, and little Mary even got seconds. Then Anna did another unusual thing, which was to leave them all and go for a "walk" in the neighborhood.

When Anna returned almost two hours later, one of Mrs. Babel's roomers was just loading the children and Julia into his car. Shortly after Anna's departure, Mary had become violently sick, soon followed by her two sisters. When their frightened grandmother called the doctor, he told Mrs. Babel to get them to City Hospital (now Metro) as soon as possible. They were just leaving in the roomer's car when Anna showed up and became violently ill herself. Minutes later they were rushed to the waiting physicians at the hospital.

As she lay in pain on a cot there, Anna gasped out her dreadful confession to Cleveland police lieutenant John Luttner, who happened to be on duty at the hospital that night. Anna told him the details of how she had stopped at the grocery at 2528 Lorain on her way home from work and asked clerk Lucy O'Rhynare for some rat poison. Her first choice proved too expensive, so after some dickering, Anna settled on a cheaper, powdered version. Then she went to a nearby drugstore, bought the wax flowers and the chocolate ice cream, and brought them home to her mother and children. There, out of their sight, she carefully mixed the poison and most of the ice cream together, reserving an uncontaminated bowl for her mother. After they finished eating it, she left the house because, she told Luttner, she "didn't want to see them suffer and die." When she finished her confession, Luttner brought in Lieutenant Charles Timm, and she repeated her confession for a stenographer and signed it. When Timm asked her, "Didn't you realize the children might die of poison?" she replied, "I intended they should." Her purpose, she confessed to Timm, was to kill herself and her children, sparing only her mother.

Anna Kempf wasn't much of a success as a suicide and murderer. Owing to their stronger constitutions, both she and her two older daughters survived her dose of rat poison. But when little Mary Kempf died the next morning, Anna was placed under arrest. A month later a Cuyahoga County grand jury indicted her for first-degree murder. Just before she came to trial in December, however, additional charges of second-degree murder and manslaughter were added, at the suggestion of Chief Criminal Court judge Walter McMahon. Given the past squeamishness of Cuyahoga County juries when it came to convicting females on first-degree murder counts, McMahon has taking no chances that Anna would walk away scot-free from her heinous deed.

By the time Anna went on trial a month later, however, public opinion had surprisingly shifted strongly in her favor. Thanks to voluminous sob-sister coverage in Cleveland newspapers, especially the *Cleveland News,* most adult Clevelanders were familiar with the sad details of Anna's unhappy life by the time she sat in the criminal dock. With visiting judge George A. Starn of Wooster presiding and James Connell and Andrew Kovachy defending, it was clear that prosecutors Maurice Meyer and Jack Persky would be fighting an uphill battle against public sympathy for Anna Kempf's life.

And what a depressing life it was—as her lawyers Connell and Kovachy mournfully showed in their examination of witnesses to her doleful biography. Born in Hungary at the turn of the century, young Anna had been indentured out at the age of seven to a farm overseer who paid her nominal wages to her exploitative guardian. Anna had eventually escaped her serfdom by emigrating to America, but her lot here was hardly an improvement. In 1919 she married Joe Kovacs, a former Hungarian policeman. But when Joe found he couldn't get a job as a policeman in Cleveland, he refused to take any other job and Anna was forced to go to work to support herself and their children, Julia and Margaret. Anna finally divorced Kovacs in 1923.The next year she married Jacob Kempf, and they moved to what seemed like better prospects in Parma. Several years later, however, Jacob quit working too and after repeated estrangements left Anna for good in June of 1928. By that time Anna had a third child to support, and Jacob was remiss in his support payments. Anna was living at her mother's house on Bridge Avenue and working nine-hour shifts six nights a week for the Industrial Fiber Company, a rayon manufacturer. Anna told sympathetic journalists that she paid her mother her entire weekly wages of $12 for her family's room and board. By the fall of 1928, after Anna refused to help her mother propagate an eccentric religion concocted by Mrs. Babel herself, Julia told Anna to start paying her $15 or face eviction. At the end of her financial rope, Anna spent months trekking to every private and public welfare organization in Cuyahoga County, begging them all for some financial assistance. She even tried to give her children away to an orphanage, but everyone she talked to spurned her pleas for help. When she found out she was about to lose her job, she decided to kill herself and take the kids with her.

The challenge facing the prosecution became clear on December 3, the first day of the trial proceedings, when prospective juror Ralph Nellis was rejected because he had formed an opinion about Anna's guilt or innocence. As court clerk Frank Malley handed Nellis his $6 fee for jury duty, Nellis loudly said in court, "Have this cashed for me and give the money to Mrs. Kempf to buy Christmas presents for the other two girls."

Anna herself was most persuasive on the stand. Speaking through an interpreter in her native Hungarian, she reiterated the details of her excruciating life and convincingly articulated the desolation that had pushed her to attempted murder:

> I had gone everywhere for help and the grave seemed the only place left for me to go with my children if I wanted to be happy with them. What could a woman do? I went from office to office in the courthouse; talked to police; everywhere for months and months I look for help. And who is to help me? Nobody! Is it bad to leave such a life?

After her recitation of horrors, Anna's plea of temporary insanity must have seemed pretty persuasive to the seven men and five women on the jury, especially after Anna's mother calmly testified about her own religious "visions" and admitted that she had threatened to evict her own daughter and grandchildren over a matter of $3 a week. No doubt the jury was further impressed by Mrs. Babel's statement that she had enjoyed a precognitive warning of Mary Kempf's impending death. The court-appointed psychiatrists (then called "alienists"), Drs. H. H. Drysdale and John Tierney, further damaged the state's case with their muddled analysis of Anna's mental condition at the time of the murder. Tierney argued that Anna's disinclination to poison her mother argued against a state of temporary insanity. But Drysdale, who probably gave expert medical testimony at more Cleveland trials than anyone except Dr. Sam Gerber, then confused the jury with his report that Anna's state at the time of the poisonings had been sane but "ruffled," "panicky," and "agitated beyond normalcy."

MRS. KEMPF IS NEAR COLLAPSE

Mother on Trial for Poisoning of Daughter May Know Fate Tonight

Cleveland Press, December 7, 1928.

Prosecutor Maurice Meyer partially threw in the towel even before the case went to the jury. On December 7, he informed the Court that the state would not demand Mrs. Kempf's life, even if she were convicted of first-degree murder. Meyer needn't have bothered: after futile deliberations through the following day, the jury reported itself hopelessly deadlocked; Judge Starn dismissed them. The devastating effect of Drysdale's and Tierney's testimony became clear when it was subsequently reported that the baffled jury had requested a dictionary from Judge Starn. It seems they were confused by what the doctors meant when they used terms like "normal," "panicky," and "ruffled."

Undaunted, Prosecutors Meyer and Persky opened their second prosecution of Anna Kempf two days later, on December 10, 1928. It quickly mutated into her third prosecution when visiting judge Roscoe G. Hornbeck of London, Ohio, had to dissolve her second jury when one of the jurors came down with influenza. By this time it was, as presiding criminal court judge McMahon put it, "evident that no jury will convict or perhaps agree in a murder trial for Mrs.

Kempf." McMahon suggested a plea bargain to a manslaughter charge, but Anna initially refused, saying:

> If taking the life of my daughter was murder, then let God hold me to account. No one can ever get me to admit that what I did was wrong in the eyes of man or the law. I'll go on trial a dozen times before I could admit myself guilty of murder. It wasn't murder.

The following Monday, after some time to think it over and following her first visit to her daughters Julia and Margaret at the St. Joseph Orphanage on Woodland, Anna surrendered and pleaded guilty to the manslaughter charge. Judge Hornbeck immediately sentenced Anna to probation with palpable relief, remarking, "No jury would have found this mother guilty . . . There is no question but that she was temporarily insane when she gave the poison to her children but she is normal now." And, like others exposed to the details of Anna's life, Judge Hornbeck took the opportunity to criticize the social service organizations that had so signally failed to help Anna Kempf in her hour of desperate need. After Anna was released from jail she and her children disappeared into the obscurity whence they had come before the terrible events of October 3. In 1956, at the time of her mother Julia's death, Anna was reported to be married again and living in California.

PART 3: "I JUST WANTED TO SLOW THEM DOWN A LITTLE . . . ": DOROTHY KAPLAN DELIVERS THE MILK (1956)

Things should have been just peachy for Mr. and Mrs. Louis Elgart as the winter of 1956 waned toward spring. Louis was the proprietor of a men's clothing store, Elgart's Men's and Boys' Store at 4266 Fulton Road, and both he and his wife Ruth had worked hard to make it a success. But there was much more than business success to the attractive and talented University Heights couple. Louis, a cousin of nationally known big band leader Les Elgart, fronted a performing Cleveland band of his own, and Ruth was a pianist of the first rank. Studying with jazz legend Teddy

Cleveland Press, March 2, 1956.

Wilson, she had also performed with the Tommy Dorsey Orchestra and singer Frankie Laine, not to mention writing the Glenville High School fight song. Louis and Ruth were personable and cultured and often entertained other musicians and friends in their second-floor apartment at 14144 Cedar Road through many a night of music and conversation. And yet, as February 1956 arrived, they were deeply unhappy.

Things had started going wrong from the day they moved into that Cedar Road apartment in November 1954. Sure, the suburban neighborhood was all that it should be, and the apartment was just what they wanted. But their downstairs neighbor, Mrs. Dorothy Kaplan, was driving them crazy. She had been a thorn in their side from the day they moved in, and their relations with her just got worse and worse. Complaining about the "noise" of Ruth's piano playing, Dorothy, who lived in the flat beneath, often banged not only on her ceiling but even their walls from outside their apartment. When she wasn't doing that, she was arguing with her truck-driving husband, Thomas, creating a constant tumult of shouts, screams, and unbridled profanity. Then came the deluge of harassing telephone calls, with no one at the other end when they were picked up. It had gotten so bad by the end of 1955 that Ruth had begun circulating petitions throughout the building as part of a campaign to persuade the landlord to evict the Kaplans, but he refused to take any measures against them.

Things went further downhill in early February 1956. Several times after using the apartment building's laundry facilities, Louis and Ruth discovered that their washed garments were saturated with what appeared to be "grease." When the washer repairman informed them that it was brown shoe polish, Louis and Ruth learned from the building custodian that Mrs. Kaplan's regular rotation in the laundry schedule came just before theirs. Clearly, their living situation was deteriorating rapidly, and they began thinking about finding another place to live.

They were still thinking about it when events took a more drastic turn on the morning of February 16. Louis, as usual, drank a large glass of milk. He remembered thinking that it tasted kind of odd, but he attributed this peculiarity to some ice crystals. And he didn't give it much more thought, even after he became violently ill with stomach pains at his store a few hours later. He managed to drive himself to City Hospital, but after he was examined there the staff doctors told him it was just "muscle spasms."

Louis thought more about it two days later when he felt something peculiar in his first mouthful of milk. He stopped drinking it and decided to let the bottle of milk evaporate on a window sill. It did—and the next day Louis Elgart discovered definite shards of broken glass in the residue at the bottom of the bottle. He immediately called his milk supplier, the Dean Dairy Company at 3211 Mayfield Road.

After making their own tests, the concerned staff at Dean's Dairy immediately turned the case over to Cleveland Heights health inspector Dominic Tomaro. He personally tested the next bottle of milk delivered to the Elgarts' milk chute and discovered no fewer than 186 pieces of glass in it, not to mention a considerable amount of glass powder too fine to be picked up with a tweezers. After an interview with the Elgarts disclosed their long-standing feud with Dorothy Kaplan, Tomaro had a chat with the police.

Captain Harry A. Gaffney of the University Heights Police Department was not an impetuous man. He waited until three more glass-contaminated bottles were delivered to the Elgarts' milk chute before setting his trap. Early on the afternoon of March 1, he sent Detective Thomas Jarvis into the Elgarts' apartment building.

Jarvis, who was equipped with a newfangled "walkie-talkie" two-way radio, secreted himself in a custodian's closet with a discreet view of the Elgarts' milk chute, and Gaffney settled down to wait in the seat of his police car outside the building.

They didn't have to wait long. As expected, Mrs. Kaplan arrived at the milk chute shortly after the Dean's dairyman delivered a marked bottle and took it to her apartment. Minutes later she returned and was arrested by Gaffney and Jarvis as she put the freshly contaminated bottle back in the chute. Back in her kitchen, they discovered the hammer she had used to break up the glass from a small prescription bottle. She immediately confessed, saying, "I didn't want to hurt them. I just wanted to slow them down a little. They made too much noise up there."

Although Dorothy Kaplan was immediately charged with attempted poisoning, a serious felony that could merit a 2- to 15-year prison sentence, she almost as quickly posted her $1,000 bond and was released to await the consideration of the grand jury. A horrified Louis Elgart was moved to comment:

> I'm not going to return to that apartment until something is done about that woman. I stayed with relatives last night and my wife Ruth stayed away from the suite, too. Honestly, I think the police made a mistake in letting her out on bond.

Dorothy Kaplan was bound over to the grand jury on March 13, and it was already clear that her defense would stress her mental condition. During the 90-minute hearing conducted by Mayor Earl W. Aurelius, her defense attorneys Michael J. Picciano and Robert I. Koplow repeatedly drew attention to details suggestive of a plea of mental illness. These included (1) the phenobarbitol pills found in Dorothy's kitchen and purse; (2) her medical treatment for high blood pressure during the previous two years; and (3) the statements made by arresting officers Gaffney and Jarvis that she "looked sick" when taken into custody. Dorothy aided their strategy with a petulant statement that she had only poisoned the milk to make the Elgarts "sick" so she could "get some sleep for a couple of days."

The wheels of justice ground slowly in the Elgart poisoning case, probably to the satisfaction of no one but Dorothy Kaplan. After more than a year of legal delays, Dorothy Kaplan finally pleaded guilty to the poisoning charge on May 27, 1957. Judge Earl Hoover then had her jailed, pending a probation report. Three weeks later, Hoover sentenced her to two years' probation, on condition that she continue her ongoing psychiatric treatment. A tearful and grateful Kaplan commented as she left the courtroom, "I surely have learned my lesson."

Chapter 21

ORRVILLE'S "LITTLE BOY BLUE"

The 1928 Melvin Horst Mystery

As in so many tragedies, the crucial elements of the Melvin Horst mystery ultimately came down to commonplace objects and simple questions. They were mundane objects such as a child's broken toy truck, a pint whiskey bottle, a frozen orange with a bite out of it, and a two-year-old Christmas tree. Simple questions, such as whether the word of a mere child should send a man to prison, or whether his prior criminal record should be held against him in court. That was all investigators had to show for their efforts, two years after four-year-old Melvin Horst disappeared forever on a frosty winter evening in Orrville. Innumerable clues had been investigated, hundreds of witnesses interviewed, thousands of dollars spent, every square inch within a 10-mile radius of Orrville examined, five persons arrested, and two of them sent to prison for eight months. And after all that, they were no closer to a resolution of this baffling case than we are today, 74 years later.

Melvin Charles Horst was everything a 4-year-old should be. The middle child of Raymond Horst, a roofing artisan employed in an Orrville factory, and his wife Zora, Melvin also enjoyed the domestic company of his brother Ralph, 9, and sister Dora Elgie, 2. Tall for his age at three feet, one inch, and stocky at 49 pounds, Melvin was an attractive child with blue eyes, light-brown hair, a slightly upturned nose, and a ready smile for all of his 5,000 fellow citizens of Orrville. An active, outdoorsy child, not old enough for school, Melvin liked to spend most of his time playing outside his parents' home at the corner of South Vine Street and Paradise Avenue. Which is exactly what he was doing on the afternoon of December 27, 1928: the last day he was ever seen in Orrville.

Melvin left his home after lunch, about 1 P.M., with his new toy truck, a Christmas present from his parents. He soon fell in with Bobbie Evans, a seven-year-old crony, and they went in search of chum Bobbie Ellsworth. Unfortunately, Bobbie was down with the flu, then epidemic in Orrville, and they had to talk to him through the door. They then wandered into town, playing with other children at various locations and paying special attention to such smalltown excitements as a street bonfire and a manure wagon.

Melvin went home to leave his truck and pick up his little red wagon, returning to his playmates about 4 P.M., the last time his mother ever saw him. He and Bobbie Evans played some more, until about 5:30 P.M., when Melvin said to him, "Goodbye, Bobbie, I got to go home now." When Bobbie last saw Melvin he was trudging north on McGill Street, homeward bound. He was wearing a

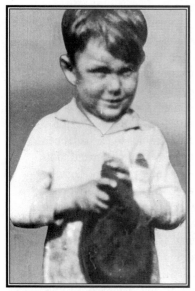

Orville's little boy lost:
Melvin Horst.

brown stocking cap, a brown overcoat, and a checkered sweater, and he was passing by the house of Orrville resident Elias Arnold.

When Melvin didn't show up for supper, Zora Horst went outside and called for him. When that failed to fetch him, she sent Ralph Horst to check the houses of Melvin's playmates, likewise to no avail. When Raymond Horst got home from work about 6 P.M., Zora sent him out to search the town for Melvin. Two hours later, after a fruitless search, an anxious Raymond and Zora notified Raymond's brother, Orrville marshal Roy Horst, who set off the town fire siren.

As many as 500 residents of Orrville turned out that night and over the next 48 hours to look for Melvin. They would be joined in the weeks that followed by thousands of Ohioans, methodically searching every nook and cranny of Wayne County and hundreds of other Ohio locations besides. Every street, lot, well, pond, thicket, and stack of wood within an area of 100 square miles was combed, and this was supplemented by painstaking house-to-house searches in the area where Melvin was last seen. Nothing valid was turned up

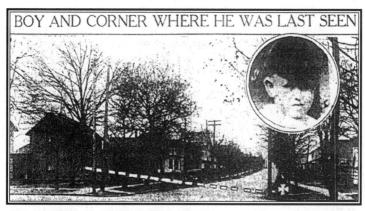

BOY AND CORNER WHERE HE WAS LAST SEEN

Cleveland Press, December 31, 1928.

then or ever after, although bogus tips and unfounded rumors sent many a lawman on wild-goose chases throughout Ohio and other states.

Somehow, inexplicably, Melvin Charles Horst had disappeared into thin air.

Meanwhile, the reward money for finding Melvin climbed to $1,600, and the entire school population of Wayne County was dismissed to aid in the search.

As was the case with most rural Ohio counties, Wayne County did not boast impressive law enforcement talent in the late 1920s. History would render a harsh judgment on the officials who investigated Melvin's disappearance. Led by Wayne County prosecutor Walter J. Mougey and Sheriff Albert Jacot, the investigation soon gained the services of prominent private detectives John Stevens and Ora Slater, the latter already famous for his work on the 1926 Canton assassination of crusading newspaper editor Don Mellett. But their investigation was handicapped from the start by lack of a discernable motive, much less any evidence as to how and why Melvin Horst had vanished.

The initial theory considered was that of a simple accident: Melvin had accidentally fallen down a well or drowned in an obscure pond. But when a painstaking search of such sites failed to turn up his body after three days, investigators began to explore more malign theories. One, briefly considered, was that Melvin had been hit by an automobile and that the panicked driver had removed and concealed his body, à la Alice Leonard (see Chapter 14). But when no evidence of or eyewitness to such a mishap materialized, Mougey, Jacot, and Stevens focused on revenge as the only plausible explanation for Melvin's disappearance. Inevitably, they began looking for someone with a grievance against Melvin's family.

Raymond Horst was a wage earner of modest circumstances and little property; no one who knew him could imagine he possessed an enemy malicious enough to kidnap his youngest child. But the Prohibition era of the 1920s had stimulated its usual animosities and corruption even in tiny Orrville, and Roy Horst, Raymond's brother, was a personal flash point for such unpleasantness. Known as an unusually vigorous enforcer of the dry laws, Horst had helped send a number of local bootleggers to jail and was reputed to have excited the hatred of more prominent liquor racketeers in Columbus. Could it be, Mougey and Stevens wondered, that some bootlegging enemy had kidnapped Melvin as a way of getting back at, or bringing leverage to bear on, Marshal Roy Horst? True, he wasn't the boy's father, but he had lived with Melvin's family until recently, was known to be especially fond of Melvin, and might even have been mistakenly identified as Melvin's father by his gangster foes.

Mougey and Stevens didn't have far to look for such foes—and they didn't look very far. Roy Horst had arrested many people for violating the Volstead Act in his one-year tenure as Orrville marshal but none so often as a Horst neighbor named Elias Arnold. Sixty-two years old, the tart-tongued, folksy Elias had been virtually unmolested during his bootlegging career until Roy took office on January 1, 1928. Thanks to Roy, however, Elias spent a good part of 1928 in the Orville jail on various liquor charges, as did several members of his extended family whom Roy also put behind bars. It was no secret in Orrville that Elias held a grudge against Roy, and during one of his recent sojourns in the Orrville jail, he imprudently said to a fellow prisoner, "I'll get even with that _____ marshal for socking me in jail." So, with all other theories and leads at a dead end within the first 72 hours of their investigations, Mougey and Stevens turned up the heat on Elias Arnold and his extended family.

Even Mougey and Stevens must have been surprised at how soon their efforts bore fruit. Elias's indiscreet vows of revenge provided a working motive, and their round-the-clock interrogations soon uncovered two eyewitnesses to the actual kidnapping of Melvin Horst by Elias Arnold. On January 2, 1929, Mougey announced the arrest of five suspects in the case and disclosed the identities of his key mystery witnesses to excited reporters. Seemingly, the hard-pressed lawmen had cracked an insoluble case. The five arrested and held on $10,000 bond apiece included Elias ("Nul") Arnold; his son William, 30, of Akron; his son Arthur, 17, who lived with him; his daughter Dorothy, 27, married to Bascom McHenry of Orrville; and Bascom McHenry, 35. A prosecutor's dream suspects, all of them were chroni-

Scene of the kidnapping according to Junior Hannah (revised standard version). *Cleveland News*, March 19, 1929.

cally jobless, linked by popular opinion with criminal activities, and already beyond the pale of respectable opinion in Orrville. Better yet, their chief accuser was a relative of the accused: Charles "Junior" Hannah, the eight-year-old son of Charles Hannah, a brother-in-law of Elias Arnold. After hearing the evidence accumulated by Mougey and Stevens, a Wayne County grand jury indicted the five suspects on charges of child stealing on January 9.

Young Junior Hannah seemed the perfect eyewitness. His detailed, calmly retailed memories just seemed to get better and better as the March trial date for the five accused approached. According to Junior, he, too, had been playing with Melvin near the Arnold house on the afternoon that Melvin disappeared. Then, just before 5:30 P.M., Arthur Arnold had sidled up to Junior and asked him to bring Melvin to the Arnold house. Minutes later, Junior brought Melvin to the alley adjacent to the house, and he heard someone say to Melvin, "Wait a minute; I want to give you something." That was the last Junior remembered seeing of Melvin, although his memory would later improve a great deal.

But that wasn't all. Mougey had found another witness, Tommy Johnson, 9, who corroborated Junior's story that he had been in the alley with Melvin around 5:30 P.M. On the circumstantial side, helpful physical evidence materialized on January 7, when an orange with one bite out of it and a pint whiskey bottle were found in the alley. After being told about the orange, Junior now conveniently remembered that someone in the house had passed something over the porch railing to Arthur . . . probably, Junior opined, an orange. The whiskey bottle, while irrelevant to Melvin's vanishing, nicely reinforced the immoral image of the Arnold clan.

A. D. Metz, a federal bankruptcy referee, agreed to defend the Arnolds. He was soon joined by attorney Clarence May of Akron. Events would show that the inexperienced lawyers were out of their depth in this kind of criminal trial. All five of the accused vehemently protested their innocence and denied knowing anything about Melvin's disappearance. Elias Arnold, the most eccentric of the suspects, proved good copy for newspaper reporters, and his analysis of his situation was both sensible and prophetic:

> I am innocent and will be found innocent. I make no secret of the fact that I don't like Roy Horst and I know he doesn't like me, but if I have a grudge against a man I take it out on him, and not on little children. But I don't blame the authorities for holding us. If the finger of suspicion points against us, it is their duty to investigate our actions. But I believe they arrested us because they had no clews and because of public opinion.

Everyone knew that Mougey's case against the Arnolds depended almost entirely on star witness Junior Hannah, and Junior did not disappoint the prosecution when the trial opened on March 12 before Judge George A. Starn in Wooster. By that time the whiskey bottle had become irrelevant, and the provenance of the orange highly suspect. (One newspaper reporter swore that it had appeared in the alley well after the area had been thoroughly searched several times.) Nor was the circumstantial evidence against the Arnolds overwhelming. Indeed, except for some minutes between 4:00 and 5:30 P.M. on December 27 that were unaccounted for by alibis, and Elias's unspecific threats against Roy Horst, there was little to connect the five Arnolds with Melvin's disappearance. Indeed, special prosecutor Mougey exposed the weakness of his case just before the trial opened, when he nulled the indictments against William Arnold, Dorothy McHenry, and Bascom McHenry. So all eyes were upon Junior Hannah when he

Sketches of figures in the Horst kidnap trial.
The *Plain Dealer*, March 14, 1929.

finally took the stand to tell his story to the seven men and five women of the jury on March 13.

Junior's memory had improved astonishingly since his rudimentary recollections of January. Attired in high leather boots with a double buckle, a plaid lumberjack shirt, gray knee breeches, and a black bow tie, Junior answered Prosecutor Mougey's questions for the most part in a deliberate, unruffled manner. He now distinctly remembered Arthur Arnold offering an orange to Melvin in the alley and then seizing him and dragging him into the Arnold house. Then, as he heard Melvin's fleeting cries of "Stop, quit, quit!" he watched as all the lights in the house ominously went out. Minutes later, as he watched surreptitiously from behind a telephone pole a block away, he saw Arthur Arnold carry Melvin out of the house, put him in an automobile, and drive him away.

Defense attorney Metz's cross-examination of Junior was a fee-

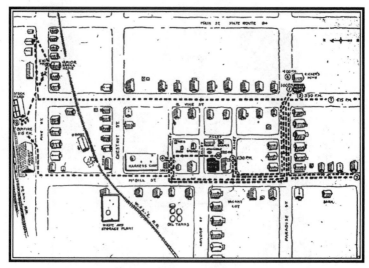

Map of area where Melvin Horst vanished.

ble effort. And Judge Starn, for his part, did little to expedite the lawyer's attempts to press Junior on the improbable aspects of his story. When Metz asked Junior why he had concealed his knowledge of the kidnapping for several days after it occurred, he cheekily retorted, "That's my business"—and Judge Starn allowed him to get away with such impertinently evasive behavior. When pressed a bit toward the end of his kidnapping narrative, he resorted to tears and was given ample time to recover himself becomingly in his mother's arms. When challenged to explain why he had initially accused Bascom McHenry instead of Arthur Arnold and then changed his story, he piously averred, "Well, I went to church where they talked about God and I decided to tell the truth."

Given such mawkish indulgence toward Junior Hannah by the prosecution, Judge Starn, and even the defense, it was an impossible task for Elias Arnold to make much of a countervailing impression on the stand. But he did the best that he could, often stunning everyone present with his eccentric candor. He readily admitted his bootlegging activities but categorically denied even knowing Melvin, swearing, "This boy was never in my house." From beginning to end he simply termed Junior Hannah's story "an unmitigated lie."

Prosecutor Mougey's final argument appealed directly to the kind of public sentimentality about children that had already shielded Junior from more analytical examination. Terming Junior and the other child witnesses (none of whom had directly corroborated Junior's accusations against the Arnolds) "messengers of God," he thundered:

> Do you prefer Junior, clear-eyed, a child who has been learning about God . . . to this to this iniquitous old man [Elias], burning with hate and a desire for vengeance? . . . We have proved beyond all doubt that the Arnolds committed the most dastardly crime on the calendar, a crime against childhood, against motherhood, against our dearest institution, the American home. And in this crime they used a little boy as the pawn in a bootlegging game.

Given the ugly public mood toward the Arnolds and their lackluster legal defense, the guilty verdict returned after seven hours and 20 minutes of deliberation on March 16, 1929, came as no surprise. What did surprise many observers, however, was how quickly the "solution" to the Horst mystery unraveled. Even as Judge Starn socked Elias with 20 years in the Ohio Pen and dispatched Arthur to the Mansfield Reformatory for an indefinite stay on March 26, new searches for the still-missing body of Melvin Horst commenced. Rumors of startling new evidence surfaced in the newspapers. Metz's appeal for a new trial properly dwelt on the delayed disclosure and evolution of Junior Hannah's kidnap stories; the Court of Appeals in Akron agreed on June 24, ordering a new trial. The Court of Appeals may also have been influenced by a photographic expose of Junior's testimony put together by *Cleveland News* reporter Dan Gallagher in the March 19, 1929, edition of his paper. Using detailed photographs of the alleged kidnapping site by the Arnold house, Gallagher proved that Junior Hannah could not have seen what he claimed to have seen from his alleged vantage points during the alleged abduction. The Ohio Supreme Court agreed on October 16, 1929, ruling that the Arnolds' jury should not have given such weight to the testimony of one so young.

The Arnolds' second trial in December 1929 was an entirely different affair. It was held before Judge Charles A. Turnbaugh, and the state's case was again handled by Wayne County prosecutor

Walter Mougey and his colleague, Marion Graven. But this time around, Elias and Arthur were represented by zealous Cleveland defense attorneys Nathan E. Cook and William F. Marsteller. They aggressively tore into the discrepancies in Junior Hannah's five different kidnap narratives and soon forced him into admitting the many times he had changed his story. At one point, the increasingly ruffled Junior snapped after one pointed query, "What the heck do you mean by that?" His credibility deteriorated further the next day, after the defense succeeded in having several of his conflicting statements read into the record. There wasn't much left of Junior's story by the time the case went to the jury of eight men and four women on December 7. It took them only a little more than seven hours to find both Elias and Arthur innocent. The jurors made no statements about their deliberations, but a good guess is that they agreed with the defense claim that Junior Hannah had made up his dramatic story—and changed it again and again— simply to get attention. As Marsteller put it in his final argument:

> I tell you that Junior Hannah has done what he set out to do—he has made himself the hero of one of the strangest cases ever tried in Ohio—he has put his name and picture all over the front pages of the newspapers.

Perhaps the most perceptive summation of his character appeared two months later when a *Cleveland Press* reporter noted that for all of his credulous defenders there were others who saw him as merely a "little Skunk."

Junior Hannah's subsequent behavior only served to confirm such negative opinions. A month after the Arnolds were acquitted, he recanted his accusations against them, only to accuse his father Charles and another Orrville neighbor, Earl Conold, 42, of having been involved in Melvin's death. The two men ended up accusing each other of the crime, an ugly exchange that climaxed on February 20, 1930, when Charles Hannah signed a confession for Prosecutor Mougey. In it, he admitted kidnapping Melvin at the behest of out-of-town bootleggers nursing a grudge against Roy Horst. Charles had then killed Melvin by accident and asked son Junior to blame the crime on Arthur Arnold, a ploy that evolved into Junior's mutating charges against Elias Arnold and his family. The sorry affair dragged on for two months, with all parties concerned making ever wilder and more improbable charges against the others.

Finally, in April, Wayne County prosecutor Marion F. Graven, disillusioned at last, quashed the child-stealing and first-degree murder indictments against Charles Hannah and Earl C. Conold. Not altogether coincidentally, but without comment, Graven simultaneously accepted the resignation of special prosecutor Mougey.

The years went by, and Orrville returned to its wonted calm. There were occasional reprises of the Horst tragedy, but they occurred less frequently. After Christmas of 1930, Raymond and Zora Horst took down the dried-out Christmas tree they had been keeping in their living room in the hope Melvin would return to see his toys under the tree. A number of cruel hoaxes promising the safe return of Melvin were perpetrated on the Horsts, the worst of which resulted in most of Orrville's population showing up at their house for his expected return on December 12, 1929. Mrs. Horst bravely kept up her hopes for as long as possible. In 1938 she admitted to an interviewer, "I like to think that he is still alive, but I am resigned to the probability that he is not." Ohio governor John W. Bricker briefly reopened the Horst case in March 1940 on the basis of a supposed new clue found in California, but the investigation came to nothing.

By 1943, Charles Hannah's whereabouts were unknown, as were those of Earl Conold. When last heard from in 1953, Melvin's parents were living in Eustis, Florida, where Raymond had started his own roofing business. He died there in 1961. Melvin's brother and sister remained in Orrville, now with children of their own and ever-dimming memories of their vanished brother.

What really happened to Orrville's "Little Boy Blue"? It is quite possible that Melvin was another Alice Leonard, a hit-skip victim whose body was spirited away and covertly disposed of. Alternatively, while it is unlikely the Arnolds were involved in his vanishing, that hardly precludes involvement by other bootlegging enemies of Marshal Roy Horst.

Cleveland Press crime reporter Bob Larkin proposed the most intriguing and, for my money, the most probable theory in a 1938 column on the Horst mystery. Based on information from contacts in the criminal underworld, Larkin believed that Melvin had been kidnapped in retaliation for Roy Horst's crackdown on liquor racketeers in the Orrville area. Melvin was subsequently placed with a farm family near Toledo and eventually forgot his family and his real identity forever.

Chapter 22

THE BODY
IN THE HARBOR

Samuel Smith's Fatal Jetsam (1904)

Sometimes the most entertaining murders aren't the solved ones or even the famous cases. For every homicide that reverberates for decades (for example, the Sheppard murder or the Kingsbury Run "Torso" killings), there are many others that furnish more diverting aspects and bizarre oddities of human misbehavior than their over-exposed competitors. It was the writer Richard Cobb who once said of such crimes that they "light up the years and give a more precise sense of period than the reigns of monarchs or the terms of office of presidents." Such a case was that of Cleveland's Samuel Smith and his sensational trunk murder of 1904.

Samuel Smith's neighbors in his rooming house at 5 Blee Court (a dead-end alley now occupied by the Chester Commons on East 12th Street) thought he had gone crazy. All that long day of Wednesday, September 7, 1904, they heard the constant banging of heavy trunks. They heard them banging as Smith hauled them into his shabby room. They heard the trunks as they went bumping heavily out his door. And they heard them again and again as Smith shifted them around his flat. They didn't know what he was doing with the trunks, but, as they later told Cleveland police, they gave no more thought to it after he stopped. Nor did they think much of it when Smith disappeared from Cleveland the next morning.

They gave much more sober thought to these matters a week later. About 7 in the morning on Wednesday, October 14, George Zimmerman, a professional salvage hunter, was searching for drift-wood in the commercial slips lining the Lake Erie shore at the foot of Front Street, just west of the Union Depot at Water Street (West 9th Street). As the autumn day began to lighten, he suddenly espied a boxy-looking object bobbing in the water under the J. W.

Ellsworth Company dock. It was near the shore, trapped under a crossbeam, and Zimmerman quickly rowed to it and tried to grab it with his hands. But it was too heavy, so he crawled out onto the dock's crossbeam, fastened a rope to the parcel, and hauled it into his boat.

It seemed a curious find even to the experienced Zimmerman. A cheap wooden trunk, it still had some shreds of a layered paper

The body in the harbor is delivered up. *Cleveland Press,* September 14, 1904.

veneer clinging to it and was held together by a heavier wooden strip that ran around it. Unlocked, its hinges and metal clasp were badly rusted by the action of the water. But someone, Zimmerman noted, had taken great pains to bind the trunk with high-quality rope, winding it repeatedly through the handles lengthwise and crosswise and securing it with heavy knots at the top. When Zimmerman couldn't untie the knots, he cut the rope with his clasp knife. The tightly bound lid flew open.

On top was a cheap quilt. At first Zimmerman thought he had salvaged a trunk of discarded clothing. He was soon disabused. Pulling back the quilt, he found himself looking into the badly decomposed and water-bloated features of a dead white woman. Her body had been doubled up to squeeze into the trunk—her head bent forward almost touching her chest. The horrified Zimmerman jumped onto the nearby wharf and hollered for the police.

They arrived soon after, accompanied by a coast guard lifesaving crew and undertaker Hogan & Company's "dead wagon." As usual at such events, the retrieval of the corpse was witnessed by several hundred curious Clevelanders who quickly gathered to gawk and get in the way of safety forces at the grisly scene. After retrieving the body with some difficulty, the police took statements from potential witnesses, collected the physical evidence, and then sent the corpse to the county morgue on Lake Avenue for a post-mortem.

The physicians who conducted the autopsy, John Darby and Curator Andrew "Keeper" Flower of the Western Reserve Medical College, could not discover the cause of death. There was no trace of a wound and they found no evidence of poison. But people don't end up floating in Lake Erie in tightly bound boxes through natural causes, so Cleveland police chief Fred Kohler assigned all of his detectives to the case that Cleveland's afternoon newspapers had already turned into an unprecedented sensation: Cleveland's first bona fide "trunk murder."

While Cuyahoga County coroner Thomas A. Burke's men remained stymied about the cause of death, Kohler's men had better success identifying the victim and her presumed killer. For reasons never explained, the death trunk also contained a great number of, well, extraneous objects. Jumbled in with the rotting, waterlogged corpse were a large number of photographs of black

people, a biography of P. T. Barnum, and what appeared to be old text-books and elementary school papers. On the flyleaf of an old geography book there, the police found this inscription: "Gertrude Lyons, 461 St. Clair, Cleveland, Ohio." Minutes later, Kohler's men were knocking at that door, a rooming house located in the heart of one of Cleveland's black residential communities.

The persons found at that address were not very cooperative, then or later. But after arresting almost everyone in the house and sweating them for hours, Kohler's detectives pieced together the human drama

She never got home; Inez Smith's residence at the time of her murder. *Cleveland Leader*, September 15, 1904.

that had led to the trunk murder. The victim, they learned, was Ernestine "Inez" Smith of 95 Oregon Street (now Rockwell Avenue). A hotel chambermaid at the Wellington Hotel on Ontario Street, Inez was 25 years old, five feet, two inches tall, and stocky at 160 pounds, with light chestnut hair. Until recently she had lived with her husband, Samuel Smith, who himself had vanished from Cleveland on September 8.

Matters beyond those basic facts proved murkier. Among those arrested at 461 St. Clair were Gertrude Smith and her grandmother Margaret Lyons. Despite the evasions of both women, the police

She loved not wisely but well: Inez Smith. *Cleveland Leader*, September 14, 1904.

soon discovered that Gertrude was the first wife of Samuel Smith, a 42-year-old laborer living at 5 Blee Court. Interviews with Inez's friends and a glance at court records disclosed that Samuel had also been "married" to Inez Smith. They had lived together in Cleveland until July of 1904, at which time Inez had learned of his previous, legitimate wife. She had then filed a bigamy charge against him, which she subsequently withdrew after he threatened her life. But three weeks before Samuel disappeared, Inez filed for divorce.

Over the next two weeks, Kohler's men painstakingly pieced together the events that had put Inez Smith in a cheap trunk in Lake Erie. On the morning of September 7, she had been lured to Samuel's room on Blee Court by this note: "Inez: Come to my room and get your clock. My girl has come back to me and has a clock of her own. I'm going away at 11:45. Let us part good friends."

No one knows exactly what happened to Inez after she arrived at Smith's room at about 7 A.M. But at 9:50 that morning, Samuel had expressman Hugh Doherty pick up a heavy wooden trunk at 5 Blee Court. He and Doherty dropped it off at 461 St. Clair, the home of Margaret Lyons, the grandmother of Smith's first wife Gertrude. Smith then called the Cleveland Transfer Company to pick up the trunk, but its driver never arrived. Then sometime before noon, someone picked up two trunks at 461 St. Clair and delivered them to 5 Blee Court. All that long afternoon, Smith's neighbors heard him dragging the trunks back and forth across his floor.

Around 10:30 that night, watchman Patrick F. Doyle saw two black men pushing a handcart on the dock of the Pittsburgh Coal Company, next to the Ellsworth slip. When Doyle accosted the suspicious-acting strangers, one of them told him he was looking for the Union Depot. When Doyle told him he was trespassing, the stranger simply said, "I am certainly a fool. I might have known it wasn't." Doyle then watched as the two men clumsily rolled the trunk away, rather than just picking it up and carrying it. When he last saw them, they had transferred the trunk to a wheelbarrow and were near the Union Depot. Sometime after that, they apparently dumped it into the harbor by the Ellsworth slip.

The police eventually found more eyewitnesses in the dock area, who in turn led them to Jesse Deggs, a plasterer who owned the handcart used to transport the death trunk. Deggs was no more cooperative with the police than Margaret Lyons or Gertrude Smith, but his interrogators were eventually persuaded that it was he who had picked up the trunk containing Inez at Blee Court and helped Samuel Smith dump it in the harbor. Cleveland lawmen accepted Deggs's explanation that he didn't know what was in the trunk, but they arrested him twice and held him in jail for almost a month. Other suspects held on "suspicion," including Samuel Smith's landlady Jennie Metzgar, received similar treatment.

And that was the inconclusive, frustrating end of Cleveland's trunk murder, except for the fleshing-out of Inez Smith's sad biography and Samuel Smith's successful evasion of the toils of justice. Inez's story was the familiar one of a young girl who married in haste against her family's wishes. Swept off her feet and into marriage by the handsome, smooth-talking, and "swell-dressing" porter while working with him at a southern Ohio resort hotel in 1899, the 21-year-old Inez Hall had endured a subsequent life of beatings and maltreatment, evidenced by the frequent black eyes and facial bruises seen by her friends. Smith himself best expressed the dynamic of their tortured relationship when he confessed to a friend, "I am bad. And she is good." The last straw for Inez came in June 1904, when she learned that Samuel had actually been married to Gertrude Lyons since January 1, 1896. Given Smith's propensity to violence, Inez's death became almost inevitable when she filed for divorce in late August 1904.

Looking back from the perspective of the 21st century, it seems unlikely that such a fuss would have been made over Inez Smith's death—either by the Cleveland police or the Cleveland newspapers—if Inez had not been a white victim caught up in a sordid black crime narrative. Readers desiring a perspective on how turn-of-the-century Cleveland authorities and newspapermen viewed the denizens of Cleveland's black ghetto are advised to look at the sensationalistic and racially tinged coverage of the Smith murder in Cleveland's newspapers of the time—the *Leader,* the *Plain Dealer,* the *World,* and the *Press.* The bullying contempt of Kohler's white police and the sullen uncooperativeness of the black suspects are almost palpable.

Ultimately, Samuel Smith got away with his trunk murder. The morning after he and Jesse Deggs hurled Inez's corpse in the Cleveland harbor, he left Cleveland on a Big Four passenger train bound for St. Louis. Samuel was last seen by a railroad detective as he sauntered down the midway of the World's Fair there. Chief Kohler would later castigate the St. Louis police for not apprehending Smith, but it should be pointed out that Kohler's telegraphed request for Smith's arrest neglected to specify the serious charge against him. With the World's Fair in hand, it is probable that St. Louis authorities rated the capture of an obscure black Cleveland fugitive a low priority. And in final fairness to Samuel Smith, too, it must be pointed out that it was never proved he killed the much-abused Inez. True, he disposed of her corpse and obviously did so in such a panic (attested to by his failure to remove the extraneous contents of the death trunk) as to imply a graver guilt. But there were no witnesses to her demise, and the experienced physicians who examined her cadaver never did come up with an official cause of death. Coroner Burke briefly flirted with the notion that she had been poisoned with picrotoxin (the active ingredient in a contemporary version of the "Mickey Finn"), but exhaustive tests found no traces of it or any other poison in her corpse. Chief Kohler and his men were convinced that Inez was strangled or smothered in Smith's flat at 5 Blee Court, but if so, it was done so delicately as to elude detection.

So there the Smith murder rests. Samuel Smith was no Winnie Ruth Judd (the notorious Arizona trunk murderer of the 1930s) nor was he quite the O. J. Simpson of his era, although he probably did kill his white paramour and escape deserved punishment. But the Samuel Smith trunk mystery remains an interesting puzzle and a fascinating glimpse into the social collision between blacks and whites in Edwardian-era Cleveland.

Chapter 23

A VICTORIAN SCANDAL

The 1888 Thomas Axworthy Affair

Thomas Axworthy is not exactly a household name in Cleveland, even among the sparse ranks of its historians. Neither the *Encyclopedia of Cleveland History* nor the *Dictionary of Cleveland Biography* mention him, and his name is absent from almost all other books touching on the history of the Forest City. That's a pity, as his melancholy story can be viewed from a number of potentially instructive perspectives. One is the historical view to be gained by a glimpse of his still pompous but rather weathered mausoleum in the northeast corner of Riverside Cemetery. Although of possible appeal to cemetery enthusiasts, it's not much of a legacy for a man who was once the most popular Democratic politician in Cleveland and a self-made capitalist all men were proud to call friend. Indeed, if you wish to contemplate the vanity of human wishes, the Thomas Axworthy tomb might well be your next stop after a look at the unfinished brick facade of the Ontario Street side of the Terminal Tower complex, still a stark visual memorial to the crash of the Van Sweringen brothers' empire.

Then there is the moral drama that resonates from the Axworthy story—the archetypal image of the damaged, disgraced man attempting to find redemption in "fortune and men's eyes." Thomas Axworthy was closer in moral fiber to Theodore Dreiser's Hurstwood in *Sister Carrie* than to Joseph Conrad's Lord Jim—but his disgrace was no less mortifying than Jim's, and his efforts at self-resurrection no less desperate. In the end, the result was the same: one moment's weakness and bad judgment forever canceled out the good character it had taken a lifetime to create.

There is an even more compelling and sensationalistic aspect to the Axworthy melodrama. The blunt truth is that Cleveland city treasurer Thomas Axworthy's 1888 defalcation of almost $500,000 was, and remains, the greatest theft of public funds—both in constant dollars and adjusted for inflation—in Cleveland history. The fact that Axworthy's theft financially embarrassed his prominent

bondsmen (Jeptha Wade Jr., Henry B. Payne, Truman P. Handy, Selah Chamberlain, et al.) to the tune of several hundred thousand dollars would only seem to amplify the gravity of his offense. [Under existing law, Axworthy's bondsmen were obligated to cover the entire amount of his defalcation—plus any interest accruing while the legal niceties of repayment were worked out.] Yet Thomas Axworthy was never criminally prosecuted, indeed never even seriously pursued or arrested for a crime that left his contemporaries grasping for a comparison. More astonishingly yet, Axworthy lived to prosper in Canada during the remaining years of his life and was even allowed to visit Cleveland without molestation. Nor were his bondsmen ultimately much distressed: despite a clear legal obligation to make good his stolen funds, they managed to stave off settlement of any claims for more than four years, in the end settling for a sum that did not include any interest on the missing city monies. Why Thomas Axworthy was not vigorously pursued or prosecuted and how his guarantors evaded their financial responsibilities are intriguing questions to be pondered in any history of Cleveland civic corruption.

Tom Axworthy sketch. *Cleveland Press*, October 27, 1888.

The Axworthy scandal exploded upon an unprepared Forest City sometime during the third week of October 1888. City officials and Axworthy's bondsmen would later claim they had no prior warning or inkling that anything was wrong, but that seems unlikely. Thomas Axworthy left Cleveland on the afternoon of September 28, telling friends and family he was going east for several weeks to look after his financial interests. Such trips were not uncommon for the city treasurer; it was generally known that he possessed considerable mining, shipping, and real estate investments that often required his presence elsewhere. But apparently more than one eyebrow was raised on October 15, when Axworthy failed to appear for the opening of bids from Cleveland banks. A new law had just gone into effect on October 1 requiring—for the first time—that city funds be placed in interest-bearing accounts in Cleveland banks at the highest rate of interest possible. It was odd, some thought, that the city treasurer was not present for the bid opening and, perhaps, odder still that only two of Cleveland's more than half-dozen national banks bothered to submit bids on the city fund accounts. After some consultation among city officials, the bidding process was reopened; discreet inquiries were made in Axworthy's personal and business circles as to his whereabouts.

These inquiries gained momentum several days later. Mayor Brenton D. Babcock's clerk, Sam Briggs, had been going over city accounts for the preceding years when he discovered a discrepancy of about $20,000 in city monies supposed to be on deposit at the American Exchange Bank of New York. This led to a more comprehensive investigation that eventually disclosed to Briggs and a horrified Deputy Treasurer Thomas McManus that there were about a half-million dollars of city money unaccounted for in Axworthy's accounts. Instead of the expected bank receipts or cash, McManus and Briggs found only slips of paper made out for sums totaling the missing amounts of money and bearing the name of Thomas Axworthy. As McManus later told officials, he was shocked to learn that Axworthy had long been substituting these slips of paper for whatever cash he needed for his own personal purposes. After failing to locate Axworthy in New York City, McManus diffidently approached Axworthy's family at their Lake Avenue summer home on Saturday, October 20. When they proved as ignorant as he about the missing treasurer's whereabouts, McManus apparently contacted Axworthy's current bondsmen, Jeptha Wade Jr. and United States senator Henry B. Payne. By Monday, October 21, the lights were burning furiously in the law offices of the bondsmen's lawyers: Estep, Dickey & Squire. Meanwhile, a worried Rebecca Axworthy, the treasurer's wife, asked her husband's confidential secretary, A. B. Conkey, to go to New York City in search of her absent husband.

It would later be said in Axworthy's defense that he was not entirely to blame for the civic financial catastrophe his peculations precipitated. There is some truth in that, and it derives from the amateurish level of governance Clevelanders enjoyed in 1888. At that time city money was not kept in official accounts at local banks; indeed, such a procedure was specifically prohibited by law. So the common practice was for the city treasurer to bank city monies paid to him under his own name in whatever banks he wished to patronize. And why not, reasoned Cleveland officials and politicians? The city treasurer's job only paid $2,000 a year, a miserabl. .ecompense for a successful capitalist like Axworthy or any man of like financial caliber the city was lucky enough to employ. Moreover, the treasurer was expected to pay his assistants out of his own salary. So, while it was not officially or legally recognized, it was common and accepted practice for Cleveland city treasurers of the era to treat city monies as their own, loaning cash out to their friends or investing it as they chose. The system had gone on in this way for years without apparent disaster, and most agreed it was only just that the city treasurer be allowed to make such profits on city funds as a reward for assuming the burdensome office. There was some concern about stricter bookkeeping and the question of the city earning some interest on its funds, hence the law passed by the city council and put into effect on October 1, 1888. Axworthy himself expressed no alarm about its provisions, and no one had reason to think it would help precipitate the disaster that now occurred.

By Monday afternoon, October 22, rumors were rife around Cleveland that Thomas Axworthy had absconded with $500,000 in city money and fled to a foreign land. Mayor Babcock was absent from Cleveland, but lesser officials fed bland assurances to reporters from the *Plain Dealer,* the *Cleveland Leader,* and the *Cleveland Press* that all was well with the city's finances. But the obvious bustle surrounding the machinations of officials and lawyers belied such seeming unconcern. By Tuesday, October 23, it was undeniable that the money was gone, Axworthy was missing, and his bondsmen and city officials were stunned almost into incoherence by what had befallen them.

The one note struck by virtually all who knew Thomas Axworthy was how unlikely a candidate he seemed for the role of villainous civic embezzler. As the *Plain Dealer* put it, "to believe that Axworthy, a man who had held the confidence of the general public for years, could stoop to a misappropriation of city funds was almost impossible." A veritable Who's Who of the Cleveland establishment echoed these sentiments of stupefied disbelief. Jeptha Wade Jr., prominent capitalist, one of Axworthy's bondsmen, and nobody's financial fool, said, "I don't believe a word of it; I can't." Charles Wesley, the proprietor of Weddell House, Cleveland's leading hotel, scornfully dismissed the rumors, saying, "I would bet my life that there is no truth in them." "Honest John" Farley, ex–Cleveland mayor and Axworthy's best friend, publicly burst into tears when he discovered his friend's crime, as did Axworthy's chief assistant, Thomas McManus. And Mayor Babcock probably spoke for the entire citizenry of the shocked city when he blurted out: "I couldn't believe it. I can't believe it now, even. If we can't trust Tom Axworthy, whom can we trust? I'll be hanged if I trust myself anymore!" How could Thomas Axworthy, of all people, have come to this pass?

No one has figured out the answer to this day. Up until the moment he walked out of his office with $500,000 belonging to his fellow Clevelanders, Axworthy was the golden boy of Cleveland politics. A self-made man, he was liked and admired by virtually all Clevelanders and elected city treasurer by them three times, always polling heavily, even in Republican wards. A gregarious, hail-fellow-well-met personality, Axworthy was known as a genial, generous man, possessing no "side" and always anxious and willing to help anyone in trouble. He was described as "jolly, sensible, and companionable" even by his Republican enemies over at the *Cleveland Leader*. Axworthy's short, sturdy, compact form was a familiar sight as he strode daily down the downtown streets on city business. It was no doubt meant as a compliment when that same paper went on to describe him as "a reduced duplicate, somewhat refined, of Grover Cleveland, or rather of the more flattering portraits of the president published in the periodicals of the day."

The known facts of Axworthy's biography only amplified the esteem of his Cleveland contemporaries. He seemed the paradigm of the self-made man, a miniature Cleveland version of the mighty capitalists so admired in the Gilded Age of the 1880s, such as Rockefeller and Carnegie. Born to humble parents in Devonshire, England, in 1836, Tom emigrated with them as a young child to a new home in Pennsylvania. His early American years must have been somewhat bizarre. His parents were working as nurses at the Kirkbride Insane Asylum in Philadelphia when Mrs. Axworthy sailed to England to visit family. On her return trip her ship foundered, the crew abandoned its passengers, and she was among those reported drowned. In fact, she had survived in a lifeboat, but she suffered so from exposure that she remained in a feverish coma for months after her rescue. When she returned to her senses, she learned that her husband, thinking her dead, had remarried. She decided to leave him alone, but her desire to see her infant son Thomas eventually led her to reveal herself to her surprised husband. Eventually, a compromise was effected with wife number two, who in return for Mrs. Axworthy's agreement to adopt her expected child, graciously effaced herself, withdrawing from the crowded domestic scene.

After attending Philadelphia public schools, young Tom Axworthy was apprenticed at 16 to the stonecutting firm of William Struthers & Son. Tiring of such rough toil after six years, he borrowed $500 to purchase a milk delivery route. Within two years Tom was able to repay the loan and sell the business at a profit. He now began his career as a proper capitalist and never looked back. After honorable service in the Civil War at the rank of major, Axworthy worked as an agent for the Powelton Coal Company, canvasing the Great Lakes region and in 1867 persuading Powelton to open an office in Cleveland. Moving there with his wife Rebecca, whom he had married in 1858, Axworthy prospered in minerals, real estate, and commodities while he dabbled in politics and helped rear his four daughters. Over the next two decades he became one of the most popular businessmen and politicians in Cleveland. Working tirelessly for other Democratic candidates, he long resisted the call to office before he was easily elected to the city treasurer's office in 1883. Reelected without struggle in 1885 and 1887, he firmly rejected strong pleas that he become the Democratic candidate for the local U. S. congressional seat in 1888. Best of all, as far as Axworthy himself was concerned, by 1888 his two decades of civic service had earned him the nickname of "Honest Tom," a rare political appellation in the moral squalor of the Gilded Age.

Although they later denied it, Axworthy's current bondsmen, Senator Payne and J. H. Wade Jr., obviously received news of Axworthy's theft from city hall sources well before the word was out on the street on Monday, October 22, 1888. After frantic legal consultation, their lawyers at the firm of Estep, Dickey & Squire showed up at Cuyahoga County clerk Levi Meachum's house on the South Side at 2 A.M. on Tuesday morning. Pulling him out of bed, they marched him over to his office to sign attachment writs, which Sheriff Sawyer and his deputies delivered early that morning to all the national banks doing business in Cleveland. And so it happened, that very afternoon when Deputy Treasurer McManus asked the banks to release to him the desperately needed remaining funds in Axworthy's accounts, that they informed him every cent had already been attached by the legal representatives of Henry B. Payne and Jeptha H. Wade Jr.

Meanwhile, where was Axworthy and the missing money? With Mayor Babcock out of town, official news on the matter was hard to come by; numberless and incredible rumors raced through the streets of the stupefied city for the next week. It was said that Axworthy was in Canada, that he was in England, that he had been arrested on an ocean-bound steamer, that he was hiding only seven miles from Cleveland. Reporters journeying to his pleasant West Cleveland summer home off Lake Avenue were refused access to his distraught wife. However, one of his sons-in-law, L. H. Presley, divulged the contents of a cryptic cablegram that had been received by one of Tom's daughters on Saturday, October 20. It read simply: "Papa is in Canada. Tell mamma. Don't worry. Will write mamma and Babcock." The cablegram did little to quiet the wild rumors, for there was no proof of Axworthy's presence in Canada, particularly as the cable had originated in Liverpool, England.

Almost a week went by before the hysteria generated by the discovery of Axworthy's flight began to dissipate. The actual shortage in Axworthy's accounts was eventually determined to be somewhere in the neighborhood of $460,000, of which $192,000 was owed to the Cleveland Board of Education, for which Axworthy had also been treasurer. As far as the citizens of Cleveland were concerned, that should not have been a problem, as there were ample sums of banked money still left to cover whatever funds Axworthy had taken with him in his flight. They soon found out otherwise, thanks to the timely, shrewd, and stubborn machinations of Andrew Squire and his fellow lawyers. It was true that the city of Cleveland still had existing balances totaling $467,550.05 at seven national Cleveland banks. It was also true that Jeptha Wade Jr. and Henry B. Payne had signed bonds guaranteeing Axworthy's accounts up to the sum of $500,000. But Payne's and Wade's lawyers, under Squire's direction, had effectively attached all available city funds pending disposition of fiscal responsibility for the mess Axworthy had left behind him. Moreover, it soon became clear, Payne and Wade were not inclined to pay the city any money, much less $500,000, without a protracted and costly legal fight. According to Squire et al., there was every reason to believe that Axworthy's embezzlements had been going on long before Payne and Wade signed their bond for his third term as Cleveland treasurer, beginning in 1887. Indeed, according to their accountants, at least $132,000 had been stolen by "Honest Tom" during his first term (1883–1885) alone. Which meant, lawyers for the city soon realized, that they would also be fighting with the lawyers for such Cleveland millionaires as Selah Chamberlain, W. J. Gordon (of Gordon Park fame), T. P. Handy, J. F. Clark, and John Tod, all of whom had served as "Honest Tom" bondsmen.

Meanwhile, desultory efforts to find Tom Axworthy commenced. A long-delayed query at the Hotel Windsor in New York disclosed that Axworthy had checked out of there on September 29, only a day after his departure from Cleveland. His trail was next picked up in Montreal, where in early October an unidentified man strongly resembling Axworthy had consulted with Canadian attorney A. C. Geoffrion concerning extradition law as it pertained to stolen public money. Receiving a pessimistic assessment from Geoffrion, Axworthy was seen for some days afterward at the St. Lawrence Hall Hotel in Montreal, drinking heavily and acting in a highly agitated manner. Sometime in early November he disappeared again.

The first solid clues to his fate emerged on October 31, when Mayor Babcock received a letter from Axworthy. Mailed from Canada on October 29, it contained the fullest (if not the frankest) confession of Axworthy's financial catastrophe and his motive for taking flight. Composed of equal parts self-pity and blustering self-justification, it painted a touching picture of the absconding treasurer as a victim of those he had trusted not wisely but too well:

> Respected Sir: There has no doubt been considerable comment concerning my absence. I arrived here some time since. I should have written before, but could not summon the courage to do so. I shall have to remain in some part of the dominion for perhaps all the time, for the following reasons: I went east, about Octo-

ber 1, for the purpose of collecting large sums loaned by me on call, from time to time during the last four years (at the suggestion of prominent Cleveland parties.) I have been receiving the interest regularly, but greatly to my surprise and horror, when I demanded the principal, I was answered, "We cannot pay it—in fact it would have been impossible for us to have done so within four months after we made the loans, etc., etc." In fact, investigation proved such to be the case, although I supposed the parties to be worth millions. I need not dwell on this matter, in fact, I cannot. It is too terrible for me to think or write about. You will know from the position I occupied in your community how my situation must affect me or any other man that has always been strictly honest to the letter, thus overwhelmed by circumstances which when too late he finds he cannot control. There was a combination to ruin me and it has succeeded. I am properly and deservedly, perhaps, the sufferer and an exile.

Axworthy went on to enumerate his remaining Cleveland assets and to vow that he had concealed nothing. He ended his lachrymose epistle with a promise to spend the rest of his life making good his theft, and closing with a heartfelt, "Goodbye! God bless the City of Cleveland and you all is the earnest prayer of THOMAS AXWORTHY."

The *Plain Dealer*, a partisan Democratic paper, greeted Axworthy's letter as a "manly and noble" document and darkly echoed Axworthy's charge that there had been some obscure plot to ruin him—as the *Plain Dealer* repeatedly hinted—for the purpose of embarrassing the local Democratic party. But the *Cleveland Leader* more accurately characterized it as a missive that "convicts him of being a liar as well as a thief." To begin with, Axworthy's assertion that his financial crash was caused by a sudden and unexpected inability to liquidate "large sums loaned by me on call" was belied by the evidence, later disclosed, that he had been systematically shorting city accounts since the day he first took office in 1883. He had also been quietly liquidating his Cleveland real estate interests for more than two years before October 1888, desperately converting his property into cash. Moreover, his list of alleged assets offered to cover his shortages—grotesquely overvalued, as it turned out—did not include, then or later, the "sums" supposedly lent at the "suggestion of prominent Cleveland parties." In short, Axworthy's "manly and noble" confession evaded the evidence

246 THE KILLER IN THE ATTIC

that he was a long-term embezzler and that his financial problems were not of a short-term, sudden-crisis nature.

There may have been some truth behind Axworthy's assertions about bad loans made at the behest of "prominent Cleveland parties." Like city treasurers before him, Axworthy loaned city money freely to whomever he liked—and it is likely that a number of well-known Clevelanders profited over the years from his largesse with easy credit and ample funds. Axworthy died without ever revealing who any of his alleged debtors were, and that may explain why no serious effort was made by either his bondsmen or Cleveland city officials to capture and prosecute him. In 1891, three years after Axworthy's flight, city solicitor Reynolds probably spoke for all those prominent Clevelanders when he said, "There are certain men who would rather see the devil in town than Tom Axworthy."

Which is not to say that certain men didn't want to see Axworthy's money. While Mayor Babcock left for Montreal in a secret attempt to find Tom, Andrew Squire more sensibly followed the money trail. He soon discovered that during the week before he left Cleveland, Axworthy had withdrawn over $100,000 in city cash from five banks and converted the money into bills of exchange drawn on Drexel, Morgan & Co. of New York. (No fool, Axworthy had carefully avoiding touching city accounts in the Merchants National Bank and the Bank of Commerce—banks in which his bondsmen Payne and Wade were heavily concerned.) During his one-day stay in New York, Axworthy had converted the bills of exchange into English pounds. Then, after consulting with attorney Geoffrion in Montreal, he had left on an England-bound steamer in early October. Arriving in London under the name of "Philip Anthony," he banked the remaining swag of over $200,000 at the National Bank, sent off the deceptive cablegram to his daughter, and entered into negotiations to buy a $100,000 English estate. Throughout all of these transactions, no doubt, he wore his special overcoat, an expensive, custom-made garment fitted with oversize pockets for bulky currency containers. As the *Cleveland Leader* sourly put it, it was an outfit "which would have done credit to the genius of a professional shoplifter."

Thomas Axworthy was smart, but Andrew Squire, befitting his legendary legal reputation, was smarter. On November 12, three weeks after Axworthy's flight, Squire succeeded in getting an English court to freeze the financial accounts of "Philip Anthony."

Discreet negotiations followed, and Squire subsequently crossed the Atlantic and met with Axworthy at a London hotel on December 7. Axworthy must have presented a pathetic sight to the canny lawyer, who remembered the ex-treasurer on that December day as exceedingly pale, 20 pounds lighter than when he had last seen him, and sporting a full beard in a vain attempt to disguise his identity. Three days later, Axworthy signed a document in which he agreed to the following conditions: (1) turn over $112,000 in cash and $46,000 in bonds to Squire for repayment to Payne and Wade; (2) name Jeptha Wade Jr. as trustee in charge of liquidating his remaining American properties; and (3) pay the English court costs of $10,000. It was a hard bargain, but, with most of his money frozen, Axworthy had no choice—not to mention the fact that the deal allowed him to retain perhaps as much as $100,000 of his ill-gotten gains. Ever the public victim, Axworthy took the opportunity of his settlement with Squire to send yet another whining letter to Mayor Babcock, ending with

> I hope that my life in the city of Cleveland was such for 20 years or more that when I have made every reparation possible, the good people there will realize that I have been the great sufferer and will be pleased to again permit me to come among them to visit my friends and family.

If, gentle reader, you think that the city of Cleveland ever got to the bottom of the Axworthy mystery or assigned proper blame, well then, you don't know much about politics. With the new depository law in effect, Axworthy's crime was unlikely to be replicated, and, in any case, Democratic mayor Brenton Babcock's officials were not interested in pursuing any other Cleveland politicos who might have been guilty of malfeasance, misfeasance, or nonfeasance in the Axworthy matter. Indeed, Babcock's main interest, abetted by his partisan friends at the *Plain Dealer*, was to distract public attention from Axworthy's three terms' worth of boodle by launching a highly publicized audit of the ancient accounts of his predecessor, Republican Sylvester T. Everett. And, when the *Cleveland Leader* had the temerity to accuse Democratic city auditor Jay Athey of dereliction of duty concerning Axworthy's accounts, the outraged Athey sued the newspaper for defamation of character. As "Mr. Dooley," Axworthy's contemporary and the most famous political pundit of the day, might have said: "Politics ain't beanbag—even in 1880s Cleveland."

The little matter of the missing $467,550.95 was ultimately disposed of in an even more ludicrous manner. The attached money was eventually allowed to flow unimpeded back into the city coffers by Messrs. Payne and Wade, but they refused to settle for the $279,413.21 remaining after the completion of Squire's London deal with Axworthy and the liquidation of the ex-treasurer's Cleveland assets. The Board of Education sued the city of Cleveland for its missing $192,000, claiming that Axworthy had used its funds to pay off city bills in the month before he absconded. The city sued all three sets of bondsmen for Axworthy's three separate terms, all parties involved claiming that *their* assessed share was far too much. Eventually, in late March 1893—over four years after Axworthy fled—all the bondsmen (or their estates, since Gordon, Chamberlain, and Tod had died in the meantime) agreed to a settlement with the city. In the end, the total shortfall after liquidation of Axworthy's Cleveland properties came to only $50,000. The bondsmen also agreed to pay the court costs, while the city agreed not to ask for the interest the funds would have earned if they had been paid promptly in 1888 (a sum of about $11,000). Probably the parties who fared the best in the settlement were the attorneys, especially Andrew Squire and William Lowe Rice. The terms of the settlement enhanced the already prodigious status of Squire's new firm of Squire, Sanders and Dempsey, and Rice's protection of his clients—Axworthy and the heirs of the James Clark estate— burnished his growing reputation as a cunning, reliable advocate.

Nor did Thomas Axworthy suffer much himself in the denouement of his shabby crime. Repudiating his original vow to start a new life in the West, he settled in Hamilton, Canada, acquiring a modest fortune in real estate and railroad development. An active officer in the social life of his adopted city, Axworthy became the vice-president of the Hamilton Trotting Association and was noted for the great pleasure he derived in showing off the luxurious attractions of his mountainside estate, Auckledun, to his many visitors from Cleveland. Although he continued to express ritual contrition for his defalcation, he also let it be known that he was highly displeased and impatient with the pace and competence of the Cleveland officials, bondsmen, and lawyers attempting to adjudicate the mess he had left behind in the Forest City. He must, no doubt, have been cheered by the many expressions of support and affection publicly tendered by such officials as Mayor George W. Gardner, who warbled this defense of Axworthy in 1891:

> Axworthy has been punished. He can be punished no more severely than he has been. He has tasted of brimstone and fire in his exile. I do not believe, in view of all of the facts, that he was in his right mind when he left the city . . . .Tom Axworthy is a good deal of a gentleman and I believe an honest man at heart. My opinion is that it would be in the interests of everybody—the bondsmen and the city—if Mr. Axworthy were allowed to return to Cleveland . . .

To which the *Cleveland Leader* aptly riposted:

> In the name of common sense and common honesty, we hope that no such compounding of a felony will ever be accomplished. Justice cries out against such a proposal, and there has been too much mawkish sentimentality wasted already upon a man whose generous and affable characteristics should never be permitted to hide the rapacity and meanness of his crime. It is entirely misleading to portray Thomas Axworthy as an unintentional embezzler betrayed by circumstances, who did his best to atone for his misdeeds by the surrender of his property . . . In view of these facts would it not be a shameful thing to permit Thomas Axworthy to return to Cleveland unmolested, while scores of men whose crimes were less serious, and whose repentance is as sincere as his can be, are confined in penal institutions?

Less than a week after the final settlement with Axworthy's bondsmen, Thomas Axworthy returned to Cleveland, on April 1, 1893. Greeted as a virtual hero by all who saw him, he spent a pleasant visit of several days' duration at John Farley's residence, where he was wined, dined, and reunited with his Cleveland friends and admirers—one of whom, it is recorded, was Jeptha Wade Jr. Forgiveness is a wonderful thing, and it would seem that the quality of mercy was never strained by Cleveland plutocrats and politicians when it came to the likes of Thomas Axworthy.

Axworthy's luck finally ran out on December 6, 1893, only eight months after his triumphant return to Cleveland. Surrounded by his wife and three of his daughters in his Hamilton mansion, he succumbed, at the age of 57, to the kidney disease that had wracked his body for several months. After well-attended funeral services in Hamilton, his body was returned to Cleveland, where it was met at the Union Depot by a group of sorrowing dignitaries that included John Farley, Mayor Robert Blee, and a phalanx of sorrowing millionaires. Today he sleeps in the stone mausoleum erected by his widow Rebecca in 1894. She herself died on November 6, 1920, and is buried with him.

No one really knows the whole truth of the Axworthy affair. The evidence is clear that Axworthy was using city money for his own speculative purposes as early as 1883—but how that differed from the practices of his predecessors in the city treasurer's office is an unanswered question. Why and how he fled Cleveland is another confusing tangle. Did he intend to abscond from the beginning—or did he take the funds as part of a failed effort to cover his shortages before the action of the new depository law disclosed his irregularities? Did he loan city money to powerful Cleveland capitalists and politicians—his bondsmen and fellow Democratic politicians, for example—and did they have a vested interest in not getting to the bottom of his defalcation? Was he part of a conspiracy to defeat the new depository law by colluding with local banks in a secret agreement to refrain from bidding on the city accounts? And why did he flee—as his liquidated assets quite nearly covered the amount of his defalcation and, in any case, his bondsmen would clearly have covered his losses if he had only asked them? All these unanswered questions died with him, but they are matters to contemplate, along with the vanity of human wishes, in the view from the Axworthy tomb at Riverside Cemetery. That is also the best location for reading the following lines of doggerel, penned by one of Axworthy's inveterate foes at the *Cleveland Leader*, whose deft parody of William Cullen Bryant's "To a Waterfowl" remains the best epitaph for Cleveland's most notorious treasurer:

Lines To a Dissolving Treasurer, by Another
Who Is About To Scrape The Safe for the Last Time:

Wither midst falling due
Of notes, and bets, and margins thou shouldst pay,
Far from the wrathful throng dost thou pursue
Thy Solitary way?
Vainly the Sheriff's star

Might dog thy distant flight to do thee wrong,
As dimly seen within a palace car
Thy figure whirls along.
Seek'st thou the plashy brink,
Of Ontario lake, or St. Lawrence wide?
Or where the rocking billows rise and sing
On the European side?
There is a fact most fair
To cheer thy anxious way to that far coast—
Of all who've heretofore lit out for there
Lone wandering, none were lost.
All year thy guilty breast
Hath beat and quaked with fear lest thou'd be caught,
Yet stopped not stealing with voracious zest,
'Til the rich vault held naught.
And soon that fear shall end,
Soon shalt thou find a welcome home and rest.
And strut among thy fellow's—friends will went
Soon toward thy feathered nest.
Thou'rt gone, th' Hague or Montreal
Hath swallowed up thy form, yet on my heart
Deeply hath sunk the example of thy gall,
And soon I too'll depart.
He, who from time to time,
Guides through the doctor'd books a fruitless search
When the full moment comes for me to climb
Will not leave me i' the lurch.
"EMULATE"

Chapter 24

SHOT IN HIS OWN BED

The 1868 Murder of David Skinner

There have been far gorier murders in Cuyahoga County's criminal annals than the slaying of David Skinner. But to citizens of the Forest City area in the mid-1800s the Skinner homicide was a truly appalling episode. It was bad enough that a peaceful, productive, and prosperous citizen should be murdered in a relatively rural setting, in his own home, and in front of his own family. And it was perhaps even more disturbing to Clevelanders of 1868 that when the evil threads of the Skinner murder were unraveled they revealed that Cleveland had grown and matured enough to have its own more or less permanent criminal class. More shocking still was the eventual disclosure, over the course of a numbing progression of criminal trials, that the men of Cleveland's police force—entrusted with the duty of protecting its citizens from the forces of evil and disorder—were themselves implicated in the murder of an innocent citizen and the cynically hasty execution of another.

The Skinner tragedy began sometime in the late summer of 1868. Acting on a tip furnished by a certain John Gannon of Independence, criminal circles in Cleveland began buzzing with rumors that there was a potential fortune waiting to be grabbed in that southern Cuyahoga County township. According to Gannon's information, there was a wealthy dairy farmer named David Skinner living there. Skinner, a well-known supplier of milk to Cleveland consumers, had 140 acres not far south from the Brooklyn Township line, plus 20 cows and a brand-new brick house. More importantly, Skinner was also reputed to keep $20,000 in cash in a small safe at that house. It seemed like a soft target to Forest City yeggmen, and sometime during the second week of September, Thomas Mulhall, a petty criminal well known to Cleveland police, was approached by another felon, John Kilfoyl, at a downtown bar frequented by local badmen. Other kindred souls were still mulling over the Skinner caper, but Kilfoyl had a well-thought-out plan that he now laid before Mulhall. Kilfoyl had reason to believe that the 36-year-old Skinner was going to be out of town that Friday night. There would be only an old man and an old woman present, maybe a hired man, too—but the job would be like taking candy from a baby for the right crew. All they had to do, Kilfoyl assured him, was come up with the right men and tools for the operation.

Tom Mulhall knew just the men, and by Friday, September 11, they had their crew. The first and most important recruit was 27-year-old Lewis Davis. Although known to most Clevelanders as a carriage maker and blacksmith, Davis was in fact a hardened career criminal, well known to Cleveland felons as a burglar and maker of expert criminal tools. He was also no stranger to Cleveland's finest, having been suspected in the $10,000 diamond heist at Hogan & Wade's downtown jewelry store in 1867. Another recruit was John "Hutch" Butterfield, a tough thug of some 50 summers who had served a term for manslaughter in the New York Penitentiary. Butterfield would later primly insist that he agreed to participate only after receiving assurances that no one in the Skinner house would get hurt by the robbers. Rounding out the crew was William Folliott, another practiced thief, who was recruited for his knowledge of the Independence area and his leadership abilities. Final planning was concluded at a meeting on Friday afternoon. They agreed to assemble for their mission at 4 P.M. sharp the next day at the corner of Seneca (West 3rd Street) and Michigan Street (now the site of the Terminal Tower).

A few last-minute details remained to be taken care of. Davis lacked a pistol, a defect that he remedied about 3 P.M. on Saturday, when he purchased a pistol and some cartridges at Richard Jennings's gun shop at 7 Broadway. (An irony never much pursued was that this pistol was the property of Cleveland police detective and future police chief Jacob Schmitt, who had left the pistol for sale with Jennings.) Then Davis and Butterfield went to Davis's blacksmith shop at 41 Michigan and picked up the evening's necessaries: a crowbar (known as a burglar's "jimmy"), some metal wedges, a fuse, some gunpowder, and a metal punch. In the meantime, Mulhall had been busy trying to recruit one more man for the caper. He wanted a reliable thug named Jack O'Neill but couldn't find him. Spotting an acquaintance, 20-year-old unemployed painter named Robert McKenna, he asked McKenna if he had a gun and wanted to make some easy money. McKenna went home to his house on Mulberry Street, retrieved an ancient Revolutionary War pistol from a trunk, and joined the gang at their 4 P.M. rendezvous at Seneca and Michigan Streets. None of the five men would later recall thinking it odd that John Kilfoyl—the originator of the Skinner caper—didn't show up for the meeting, having left word he was unable to come because of pressing last-minute business. Unconcerned at his absence, the five men began walking down the seven-mile towpath to Independence. All of them were armed with pistols, except for Butterfield, who carried a bowie knife.

Burglary was a relatively heroic business in that era; it took the gang over three hours to get to Independence, in part because they hid in the bushes to avoid being sighted whenever a canal boat drifted by. They had reason to be concerned: Folliott had insisted that they hide all of the criminal tools on their persons, and their awkward, stiff-legged gait might have been an hilarious spectacle under different circumstances. When they finally got to the eight-mile lock shortly after 8 P.M., they were delayed further as Folliott and McKenna left to steal a larger crowbar from a nearby shop owned by Independence blacksmith William Cash. When the two men returned cursing with the "sledge," the gang plodded on through the deepening dusk, only to discover that they had taken the wrong road. Folliott finally got them on the right track, and it was just about 9 P.M. when they came in sight of the Skinner house. Drawing handkerchiefs up over the lower parts of their faces to conceal their identities, they moved in for a closer look. They could see several lights on in the house and a few persons moving around. Thinking the occupants were just women and maybe a hired man or two, Folliott detailed Butterfield to act as a lookout. Sending Mulhall around to the front entrance, he turned to Davis and McKenna and said, "This is the house. Get ready to go in. Now, boys, if you can't get that money without hurting anybody, come away without it." Stepping through the back kitchen door, which had been left open on this warm, pleasant September night, they walked through the kitchen and burst upon the Skinner family group assembled in the adjoining sitting room.

Folliott's crew had been badly misinformed about the situation at the Skinner house. David Skinner's wife, her sister, and her sister's husband (David Skinner's business partner) were absent in Cleveland that night, taking in a performance of *The Rebel's Daughter* at the Rink. But 36-year-old David Skinner was home, half-dozing on a bed that stood in the parlor. With him were Mr. and Mrs. Charles T. Johns of Newburgh (Mrs. Johns was another sister of Mrs. Skinner), three or four children, a man named William Wood, and two hired men, who were sleeping upstairs. All of them except the hired men were in the sitting room, where they had been talking for the last half hour. Now, hearing the sound of footsteps coming from the kitchen, they looked up to see four masked men with guns appear in front of them.

Most present would later recall that they first thought this was a joke by some neighbors dressing up as burglars to frighten them, the imprudent frolic of a tedious late summer night. But such misapprehensions ended as William Folliott pointed his pistol at Mrs. Johns and shouted, "All keep your seats!" Things happened fast and veered out of control after that. Mrs. Johns started screaming, and as Folliott stepped forward to silence her, David Skinner, who had been reclining on the bed, suddenly raised himself up on one elbow. Skinner was probably asleep, and it is a good guess that he didn't even know what was happening as he started to rise. And he never had a chance to find out: even as his body was still rising from the bed, and before he could say a word, one of the robbers (later identified as Lewis Davis), who had been covering the hysterical Mrs. Johns with his weapon, stepped forward toward Skinner, pointed his pistol, and pulled the trigger.

The bullet hit Skinner on his left side. Ploughing through his chest, it shattered his collarbone, windpipe, and subclavian artery before coming to rest below his right shoulder. Immediately a jet of blood shot up from his fatal wound, even as Skinner lurched from his bed and stumbled into the hall leading to the front door of his house. There, he left a bloody handprint on the door sash before falling dead to the floor. He probably never even knew what hit him.

Lewis Davis's unexpected shot paralyzed everyone in the room for a few moments. William Folliott was probably the first to recover. Shouting to McKenna and Mulhall, "Come on, let's go. That damned son of a bitch has shot that man without any cause!" he fled through the kitchen door, followed closely by Robert McKenna. Meanwhile, as the screaming children dove for the floor, Charles Johns grappled with Thomas Mulhall. As they fought in the hallway, the handkerchief covering Mulhall's face slipped down, and as they fell together to the floor, he tried to shoot Johns. The bullet missed, ricocheting off the ceiling and wall before hitting the floor, where it was found the next morning. Mulhall got off another shot at William Wood, which also missed, and eventually broke away from Johns and headed for the front door. But Johns caught up with him again and knocked him down, while his redoubtable wife began hitting Mulhall with a chair. The last thing McKenna remembered hearing as he fled down the hill outside the house was Mulhall's plaintive cry, "Are you going to go off, boys, and leave me in this fix?"

Help for the undeserving Mulhall was on the way. Even as he gave himself up to despair under the combined assaults of Mr. and Mrs. Johns, "Hutch" Butterfield crashed

The Reign of Horror.

Another Horrid Murder.

A MAN SHOT BY BURGLARS.

They Make Their Escape.

FULL PARTICULARS.

THREE MEN ARRESTED.

The *Plain Dealer*, September 14, 1868.

through the front door and knocked Mr. and Mrs. Johns to the floor. Grabbing the bleeding and injured Mulhall, he pulled him out of the house and down the hill. Along with the other three robbers, they made their way back to Cleveland by midnight.

It is an ugly but predictable event when thieves fall out. The news that David Skinner had been shot by robbers in his own home reached Cleveland even before the last of the robbers returned there, and the identities of the likely perpetrators were on the lips of Cleveland's populous criminal fraternity very shortly thereafter. On Sunday afternoon, Butterfield talked to a man who mentioned that he had heard a rumor on Saturday—*before* the Skinner murder—that Butterfield had killed a man in a local robbery. Butterfield was not a cunning man, but even he began to scent the smell of a setup headed his way. As he later put it, he began to suspect that "there was to be a pressure to bear on me" and that such pressure would soon be coming from his disloyal confederates. The most likely scenario, he surmised, was that he would be lured to Cleveland's waterfront to become the victim of a watery "accident." That night, he went and had an interview with Thomas McKinstry, the superintendent of the Cleveland police.

The dramatic results of that interview were reported, seemingly,

in the pages of the next afternoon's *Plain Dealer*, where it was
announced that Lewis Davis, "Hutch" Butterfield, and Robert
McKenna had been arrested for the Skinner murder. All of them
were captured while asleep in the early hours of Monday morning
and brought in for round-the-clock interrogation, followed by
incarceration in the county jail. And while it appeared that Kilfoyl,
Mulhall, and Folliott had somehow eluded and, indeed, anticipated
the police dragnet for them by escaping to parts unknown, journalists and public officials joined in unanimous accolades for the

TERRIBLE TRAGEDY!

MURDER IN INDEPENDENCE.

A Man Shot by Burglars!

HE DIES ALMOST INSTANTLY.

Desperate Encounter with the
Villains.

THEY MAKE THEIR ESCAPE.

FULL PARTICULARS

Cleveland Leader, September
14, 1868

"promptness and skill" shown by
the Cleveland police in apprehending Skinner's killers. Justice, it
seemed, was about to be swiftly
done, and public opinion was
adamant that justice required the
execution of all the robbers
involved.

After six weeks of behind-the-
scenes maneuvers, the wheels of the
justice began their creaky rotation.
Lewis Davis, as the accused triggerman, was indicted on a charge of
first-degree murder, while Mulhall,
McKenna, Butterfield, and Folliott
were charged with conspiring to plan and carry out the robbery that
resulted in an innocent death—both capital charges. Cleveland was
electric with anticipation as the trial opened in Judge Samuel B.
Prentiss's courtroom on Monday, November 16, 1868. The capture
of Thomas Mulhall in upstate New York just before the trial opened
added to the popular excitement, as did expectations that the trial
would be a keen legal contest. And trial spectators were not disappointed by the struggle for Lewis Davis's life waged by prosecutors J. M. Jones and H. B. DeWolf (who would later help prosecute
Cleveland dentist Jay Galentine in the "unwritten law" murder of
his wife's paramour) and defense counsel Samuel E. Adams (who
saved Galentine from a hangman's rope), assisted by attorneys T. J.
and J. J. Carran.

Despite Prosecutor Jones's strong opening statement, the state's
initial case did not seem very weighty to discerning observers.
Davis himself made a good impression on all who saw him, with

his youthful appearance, his round, smooth face, curly auburn hair, and alert, restless blue-gray eyes, hardly the picture of the hardened criminal painted by the state. Also, the first few of the 40-odd witnesses called by the prosecution didn't support police identification of Davis as the triggerman. Although Charles Johns repeated his dramatic inquest testimony of what had occurred in the Skinner home on the fatal evening, he insisted he could not swear that it was Davis whom he had seen shoot his brother-in-law. Neither could his wife, who agreed that Davis had the right build, "same size and general appearance," but would not swear that he was the killer. Richard Jennings, who had sold the alleged murder weapon to Davis, likewise couldn't swear that he was the man who had bought Schmitt's pistol in his shop. And even the unexpected appearance of a hostile "Hutch" Butterfield on the stand during the trial's second day didn't put Davis much closer to a hangman's rope.

Butterfield, who minimized his own participation in the robbery as much as possible, testified that he had stayed outside the house as a lookout, and that the first sign he had that things had gone wrong were three pistols shots and some screaming, followed by the sight of McKenna and Folliott charging down the hill. He repeated his self-serving claim that he had agreed to go along only after receiving assurances that no one would be hurt and insisted he had learned of Skinner's death only after he was arrested on Monday morning. The state's presentation of the physical evidence—the burglary tools and abandoned weapons recovered from the Skinner house—added nothing more, as did the testimony of Patrolman Isaac Frank, who stated that he had found muddy pantaloons and boots underneath Lewis Davis's bed at the time he was arrested. True, it was muddy on the canal towpath Davis took back to Cleveland on the murder night, but that only made Lewis a member of the robbers' band, not the actual killer.

All that changed dramatically and unexpectedly on Wednesday. At noon, Davis's jailed confederate Robert McKenna sent for Cuyahoga County sheriff John Frazee. Two hours later, to the consternation of Davis and his lawyers, he was sworn in before a rapt and packed audience of courtroom spectators. And his tale did not disappoint. Heedless of incriminating himself—despite the apprehensive warnings of defense counsel Adams—McKenna related the real story of what had occurred on their ill-fated expedition to

Independence. After a long prelude, filled with persuasive detail, McKenna arrived at the crux of the fatal night:

> One of the women rushed in front of us and Davis pointed his revolver at her; the woman was holding her hands above her head and Mr. Skinner raised up on the bed to see what was going on; Davis then turned his revolver upon Mr. Skinner; pointed it directly and fired.

Little wonder that courtroom journalists noted the hitherto emotionless Davis was seen to strain forward in his chair, his eyes flashing as he listened to McKenna's dooming words on that Wednesday afternoon. His palpable rage, moreover, seemed to give credence to McKenna's subsequent assertion that Davis had told him just that morning, "Bob, if you swear against me I am going to kill you." It was subsequently related by inquiring journalists that when Davis returned to his cell that day, he "heaped upon McKenna all the vile epithets known to the blackguard's vocabulary." The next morning, some of Davis's fellow jailbirds obligingly testified under oath to the reality of his alleged jailhouse threats.

Davis's own appearance on the stand the following afternoon came as an anticlimax. Abandoning his lawyers' original strategy of a simple alibi for his whereabouts on the night of September 12 (for the support of which his lawyers had subpoenaed many willing perjurers), he baldly denied the testimony of Butterfield and McKenna, claiming, in fact, that he had never been inside the Skinner house. His story, suspiciously similar to Butterfield's, was that he had hung back while the others went in the house and that the first sign of trouble came when he heard a shot. He primly denied that he was a career criminal and swore that he had not threatened Robert McKenna's life, but only said that if McKenna testified against him, he would be guilty of Davis's murder.

Lewis Davis's defense counsel did its best under the circumstances. Attempting to magnify minor conflicts between the testimonies of Butterfield and McKenna, Samuel Adams convulsed the entire courtroom, including the beleaguered Davis, with his sarcastic indictment of Butterfield's self-exculpatory testimony. Skewering him as a "canting hypocrite," Adams thundered against the state's deferential employment of such a tainted witness:

[Adams] dwelt upon the utterly farcical nature of Butterfield's statements that he,—a hoary sinner, fifty years of age, his whole life reeking with corruption and crime—had been inveigled and seduced into this affair by the others who were merely boys. He had sanctimoniously declared that the only condition upon which he could be induced to join the party was that the robbery must be committed decently and in order, in a quiet and gentlemanly manner, and that nobody must be hurt, and then, said [Adams], he was brought from the jail to be put upon the stand. As he entered the room with his boots blacked, his face shaved, a clean shirt collar on and a good fresh chew of tobacco in his mouth, he is met with a polite bow by the attorneys for the prosecution and is courteously greeted with: "Good morning Mr. Butterfield! I hope you are well this morning! How's your family? Have the kindness to take that seat Mr. Butterfield." He did not ask him how long he had been *confined to his room*.

It was a masterly effort, but even Adams's rhetorical triumph could not save his entangled client. His final salvo, a specious claim that Butterfield's and McKenna's testimony was motivated by knowledge that Davis's conviction would free them from the shadow of the gallows, was refuted by prosecutor Jones, who reminded the jury that all of the other four robbers still faced capital charges and that there was a reward of $1,000 out for the two still at large. The jury went out on Monday, November 23, at 5:20 P.M. and returned a verdict of "guilty of murder in the first degree" at 11:15 the following morning. The announcement of the verdict momentarily shocked Davis out of his habitual courtroom torpor and into a wild vacant stare, but he returned to his usual passivity even as attorney T. J. Carran rose to make the obligatory motion for a new trial. On December 30, Judge Prentiss rejected the motion and sentenced Davis to hang on Thursday, February 4, 1869. When asked by Prentiss if he had anything to say, Davis replied, "Nothing."

In the weeks preceding the execution, Cleveland's three newspapers competed vigorously to discover details of Davis's shadowy biography. It was eventually disclosed that he had been reared by loving parents in the area of Fredonia, New York. Wearying of his apprenticeship as a carriage maker, he gave himself over as a young man to loose living and dissolute companions. When his parents relocated to Berlin, Wisconsin, they left him to sell their property and follow them later on. Davis sold the property but absconded with the money, afterwards pursing a life of crime as a brothel owner, burglar, and confidence man. When one of his bunko schemes resulted in the choice of either going to jail or the Union Army, he chose the latter, which served as the unexpected entree to a new career as a successful bounty jumper. When Buffalo became too hot for him at the end of the Civil War, he drifted down to Cleveland. More might have been known of Davis's life but for the understandable reticence of his kith and kin. When a brother who lived in Cleveland was solicited for biographical information about Lewis's early life by a *Plain Dealer* scribe, he played the reporter along for a while and then shouted: "Well, allow me to state, in language that can't be misunderstood, it's none of your God damn business what the facts of his early life were!"

Confined to the same death row cell previously occupied by Dr. John Hughes, Davis grew increasingly morose and haggard as his day of death approached. One by one his legal hopes crumbled, his first setback coming when Judge Prentiss rejected his motion for a new trial on December 30. Shortly after that, the Ohio Supreme Court turned down Attorney T. J. Carran's petition for a writ of error and sustained Judge Prentiss's sentence of death. The burden of Carran's legal argument was that the Davis jury had enjoyed improper access to the physical evidence, newspaper accounts, and Judge Prentiss's instructions during their deliberations—but the court upheld the verdict under the existing legal doctrine that a jury could not impeach its own verdict. Davis's last chance evaporated in early February when Ohio governor Rutherford B. Hayes refused to commute his death sentence.

Not that Davis had given up attempting to escape the law's penalty. The day after Governor Hayes turned down his appeal, a vigilant Sheriff Frazee discovered two steel saw blades and a ball of putty beneath Davis's jail mattress. They had been smuggled in to him by the wife of a prisoner. And the night before his execution, at 2 A.M., Davis took advantage of a guard's two-minute absence and tried to slash his wrists with the broken glass chimney of a kerosene lamp thoughtfully provided so he could read his Bible. His wound proved superficial, but Sheriff Frazee had him manacled until he vowed to die like a man.

The grim day loomed at last, a dark and stormy one of wind and lashing torrents of rain. Having been baptized the day before by his spiritual counselor, the Reverend A. H. Washburn of Grace Episcopal Church, Davis finished his earthly farewells, meeting with his brother and his forlorn wife. Utterly indigent and forsaken by all because of her connection to Davis, she left the jail weeping and moaning, "I'm left alone in the cold world now." Shortly after 8 A.M., Davis arose and was offered a breakfast of beefsteak, pork chops, rolls, buckwheat cakes, and coffee but partook only of a few sips of coffee. Trying hard to master his emotions, he would only say, "It is *very, very hard!*" To the surprise of onlookers, he encountered his prosecutor, J. M. Jones, who warmly shook his hand and whispered something in his ear that seemed to make him very happy. At that very moment, Sheriff Frazee's deputies were soaping the noose with soapstone and soft soap to make certain it did its deadly work well.

At 12:23 P.M., Davis walked to the gallows before a small crowd of invited witnesses and hundreds of others gathered in balconies and perches outside the jail yard. Dressed in black pantaloons, a dark vest, and fine boots, he displayed little hint of his inner state, save a slight quiver of the lip and an occasional involuntary tear. Kneeling on the steps of the scaffold, he listened while the Reverend Washburn intoned the moving words of the Episcopal service for such occasions. Then he climbed the steps and submitted calmly to the grisly procedures, offering his hands up to be manacled by Sheriff Frazee and his assistants.

Asked if he wished to say anything, he merely shook his head and whispered, "Nothing." His arms and legs were pinioned and the black cap placed over his head. At 12:28 P.M., Sheriff Frazee shouted, "Hats off!" and the crowd suddenly silenced itself, in impressive contrast to its unseemly, carnival-like behavior during the preliminaries. Four minutes later, at 12:32 P.M., Sheriff Frazee touched the spring, and Davis fell through the drop. He twitched but little, there being no movement after four minutes and no pulse after eleven; the consensus of the seven doctors present was that his neck was broken instantly. Davis's body was taken down at 12:47 P.M., placed in a plain pine coffin by undertaker D. W. Duty, and turned over to his friends. After a funeral from the widow's house on Broadway two days later, it was returned to Westfield, New York, for burial.

Unexpectedly, the end of Lewis Davis was just the beginning of the unraveling of the Skinner murder skein. No one except the Cleveland police authorities was satisfied by the execution of Skinner's alleged killer. Many wondered why his life had not been spared until at least some of his accomplices had been put on trial. Still more began to entertain doubts about the suspicious ease with which the Cleveland police had solved the violent crime.

The real story began to leak out after Thomas Mulhall was captured in Albany, New York, where he was discovered working as a railroad brakeman in November 1868. Brought back to Cleveland, he was briskly convicted of murder in the first degree and sentenced to hang. But his verdict was overturned by presiding judge Prentiss in April 1869, when it was argued that one of the Mulhall jurors had been prejudiced. By the time his second trial commenced, his partisans had made enough of a stink to bring about the arrest of John Kilfoyl, who had been back in Cleveland, living unmolested for several months. Kilfoyl's subsequent indictment opened up the complete can of worms at last. Heavily publicized testimony revealed to a stunned Cleveland public that Kilfoyl—the primary instigator of the robbery that took Skinner's life—had been employed for some years as a "secret detective" by Superintendent Thomas McKinstry of the Cleveland police. It was obvious to most citizens that "secret detective" was merely a euphemism for stool pigeon, and it was further suspected—if not legally proven—that Kilfoyl had long since crossed the line from police informant to become an agent provocateur in the Cleveland underworld. Testimony by Mulhall, Kilfoyl, and others disclosed that McKinstry had known all about the Skinner robbery within hours of its occurrence, thanks to the voluble Kilfoyl—and *may have even had advance knowledge* that it was going to happen. McKinstry stoutly maintained his innocence and insisted that he had simply followed good police procedure. But the whole mess stank in the nostrils of the public. When it was found that Kilfoyl had been carrying a pistol given to him by McKinstry at the time he was arrested, McKinstry resigned in disgrace.

The final box score after a half-dozen trials and several years of legal maneuvers was a complex and ultimately unsatisfying record. Thomas Mulhall was convicted of first-degree murder a second time but had his sentenced commuted to life imprisonment. Eventually pardoned after he lost some fingers in an Ohio Penitentiary accident, Mulhall returned to Cleveland before disappearing after a bitter stove moulders' strike. John Kilfoyl was tried as an accessory to the murder and earned a long prison term. Later pardoned, he was active in the Y.M.C.A. for some years but was reported in 1889 to have returned to a life of crime. Butterfield and McKenna served three- and five-year penitentiary terms, respectively, for their participation and then disappeared from sight. The last to be captured was William Folliott, who received a 20-year term but was said to be working in a Cleveland bakery in the late 1880s. Whether justice was served by the varying results of these trials and the corresponding failure to punish implicated parties among Cleveland's Finest are questions still unresolved.

It was rumored but never proven that Lewis Davis wrote out a 140-page confession before he died, hoping that the sale of his testament would provide financial support for his impoverished wife. It was said to include his admission that it was his gun that fired the fatal bullet into David Skinner that September night. He hadn't meant to kill Skinner, but he had underestimated the sensitivity of the trigger on Jake Schmitt's pistol, and he was as surprised as anyone present when it unexpectedly went off in his hand. If so, Davis's confession died with him, perhaps destroyed by his despondent and disgraced wife, along with some photographs taken the day before he died. Future researchers in the annals of Cleveland crime might well wish to unearth these items, not to mention the full story of just what Thomas McKinstry knew about the Skinner murder—and when he knew it.

It would be remiss, before taking leave of the Skinner tragedy, not to relate an irresistible anecdote about David Skinner's father gratuitously included in the news coverage of his son's murder. Nothing else captures quite so well the casually discursive and defamatory flavor of the journalism of the age as this item from the *Cleveland Herald,* which appeared on the Monday following Skinner's Saturday-night murder:

> The deceased, David P. Skinner, was about 36 years of age, a strong healthy man, hereabouts, and possessed of many eccentricities. His father, Ichabod L. Skinner, was an old settler in the county, living on the farm to which David succeeded. The old man died on a winter night eight years or more ago. He had been out two or three miles, and coming back a little the worse for liquor, slipped partially under the broken ice as he was crossing

Quarry Creek, not far from his home. He was found in the morning, frozen to death, in a sitting position, his legs and body up to the waist under the ice, a huge cake of which was before him like a table, and on this his elbows rested and supported his head, while by his side was a bottle.

Chapter 25

RAMPANT CRIMINALITY

The Legend of Shondor Birns (1906–1975)

"Do you know who I am?"
"Yes, I've heard tell of you."

—Shondor Birns in conversation with Cleveland policeman Carl Delau, on the occasion of Delau arresting Birns for speeding at East 40th and Shore Drive

It's not surprising that no one has written a biography of Shondor Birns; what's astonishing is that no one has composed an opera about this larger-than-life gangster. To three generations of Clevelanders, spanning half a century, Shondor Birns was *the* Public Enemy Number One. And it was a role he played to the hilt: invariably outfitted in expensive, impeccable suits, perennially accompanied in public by spectacularly beautiful women, always driving late-model, luxury automobiles (usually Cadillacs), and ever lavish with an open-handed hospitality that furnished gourmet meals and free drinks for legions of Cleveland newspaper reporters, politicians, and policemen—many of whom denounced him publicly. More than any other Cleveland hoodlum of any era, Shondor had a reputation for (as a Cleveland prosecutor once aptly put it) "rampant criminality"—and he made the most of that repute until the moment he died in the blasted ruins of his aqua-blue 1975 Lincoln Mark IV Continental. So let us now praise one infamous man.

In his mature years, Shondor liked to boast that the miseries of his childhood rivaled the grimmest pages of Charles Dickens. He told a U.S. immigration board trying to deport him in 1943, for example, that he "came up from the gutter" and that his earliest bed was a "pile of newspaper." It wasn't quite as bad as that, although it wasn't fun. Born to Hungarian Jews Hermann Birn and his 22-year-old wife Selona in 1906 in Hungary, the 10-month-old Sandor (old-country equivalent of "Alexander") arrived in the United States with his parents, brother, and sister on March 18, 1907. (Shondor's birth date is commonly given as February 21, 1905, but his age at the time of his entry was 10 months, which would place his birth sometime in May of 1906.) Sandor's name would eventually be Americanized to "Shondor," and it is said that he added the "s" to his surname to spare his family embarrassment through association with his criminal repute.

Shondor's neighbors would recall that from his earliest days in the Woodland Avenue neighborhood, he was an unusually tough, aggressive kid, one who demanded respect and got it—or else. At Outhwaite School, where he attended elementary school, he was remembered both for his athletic ability and his implacable ruthlessness. One anecdote told about him concerned the time he missed the school marble-shooting contest because he was absent. The day he came back to school, he simply took the medal from the actual winner, informing him, "See, I would have won it anyway if I was here." Another oft-old tale was that the muscular Shondor was so strong, even as a youth, that he could swim out to the Five-Mile Crib and back. These traits served him well when he graduated to Kennard Junior High School and in his activities at the Council Educational Alliance, a settlement house on Woodland. Even then, perceptive observers noted that Shondor Birns liked to win and wasn't happy when he didn't.

Things changed very much for the worse when Shondor turned 14. Like many struggling immigrants of their era and neighborhood, Shondor's family made ends meet by bootlegging alcohol in the family flat at 2447 East 59th Street. On November 9, 1920, a 10-gallon mash still exploded, showering Selona Birn with burning alcohol. Following her death the next day, Cleveland police raided the Birn apartment and arrested Hermann Birn for violation of the Volstead Act.

The years just after his mother's death were probably the worst for Shondor. After stints at East Tech High School and Longwood High School of Commerce, he quit school for good after completing the tenth grade on June 16, 1922. He spent some months at the old Jewish Orphans' Home on Woodland, and he may have subsequently enlisted in the navy, although there are no records to prove it; the story goes that he was discharged when officials discovered Shondor's real age and sent him home—back to the streets of Cleveland. There he scuffled for a living as best he could, selling newspapers and engaging in petty theft to help support his family. It was during his newspaper-selling days that he met Mickey McBride, kingpin enforcer in the newspaper circulation wars and future owner of the Yellow Cab Company and the Cleveland Browns. McBride liked tough kids like the scrappy Shondor and would later remember the boy he befriended by leaving him a legacy in his will. Many of the men like McBride whom Shondor met during these years of struggle would later have starring roles in the drama of his mature criminal life.

Shondor Birns mugshots (from top to bottom): February 6, 1932; October 14, 1925; September 20, 1949.

By the mid-1920s, Birns had perfected the persona that would become notorious to generations of Clevelanders. Already involved in prostitution and games of chance in the Woodland–East 55th Street area, the public Shondor sported flashy clothes and, more often than not, a large, expensive cigar sticking aggressively out of his mouth. He also cultivated a well-earned reputation for a volcanic temper, which usually culminated in sudden violence and a readiness to inflict rapid, savage hurt. It was this brutal repute that led the black criminals with whom he dealt to call him "Shin-do," and tread warily when on his criminal turf, an empire of vice that stretched from Woodland Avenue to St. Clair along the axis of East 55th Street.

Shondor's official criminal record began on November 14, 1925, when he was sentenced to the Mansfield Reformatory for auto theft. Released on February 1, 1927, he won his final parole in August 1928. Exactly a year later, Birns, already a quick hand with a knife, was arrested and charged with "cutting to kill." Although the charge was boosted to manslaughter after his victim died, Birns was exonerated by a sympathetic jury. In August 1931, Shondor shot a man after insulting him in a speakeasy near the Central Police Station. When no witness to the shooting was willing to be found, the case was dismissed. On February 12, 1932, Shondor was arrested for assaulting a woman and taking $1,480 from her. He was again found not guilty by a jury. Arrested a month later as a fugitive from a Pennsylvania warrant for armed robbery, Shondor escaped when the governor of Ohio refused to sign his extradition papers. On June 3, 1932, Birns went berserk during an argument with a cab driver about his slow driving and broke his jaw. It was at the ensuing trial that prosecutor John Butler (later to become one of the most famous criminal defense attorneys in Cleveland and the occasional counsel of one Shondor Birns) made a plea that many a future judge would hear from many a frustrated prosecutor: "It is time the courts put away this man whose reputation is one of rampant criminality." Alas, the judge did not heed Butler's plea; after giving Birns 30 days in the Warrensville Workhouse and a $25 fine, he courteously offered Shondor the exact legal advice he needed to avoid having to serve his sentence.

Birns's pattern of violence, arrest, and escape continued to intensify as the Depression wore on in Cleveland. In January 1933, Shondor was arrested and released in the nonfatal shooting of gangster Max Diamond. Several days later, on January 30, he was arrested on an assault and battery charge and again released. In July he was fined $50 and given a 30-day term in the workhouse for assault and battery. In September, it was discovered that he had left the workhouse early on August 9, and he was returned there as a parole violator to serve out his sentence. Shortly after he finished his term, he was arrested for shooting to kill during a wild melee of gunfire at East 49th and Central Avenue, and was again acquitted. But the first chink in Shondor's legal armor developed unexpectedly out of that acquittal. When Herbert Burman, a state witness to the shooting-to-kill charge, failed to show up for the trial, outraged Cuyahoga County authorities hunted him down in Georgia and brought him back. Retribution came on December 22, 1933, when Shondor, his associate Alex Cohen, and Shondor's attorney Max E. Lesnick were all found guilty of bribing Burman not to testify. The legal penalties suffered by Birns were slight: 60 days in the workhouse and a $500 fine. But it was the first real setback for Shondor after beating three felony raps in a row and encouraging news for those Cleveland lawmen who were determined to destroy the growing legend of Shondor Birns's invincibility.

Shondor's behavior during his workhouse term provided ample evidence of why working newspapermen loved him. He was always "good copy," unpretentious, voluble, and willing to help reporters make their editors happy. The verbal sketch he now drew for them of Shondor The Hard-Working Stiff disappointed none of them, as Shondor bragged of how he had turned down a soft job in the workhouse library:

> I didn't like that stuff. I never had to lift anything heavier than a dictionary. I want to work and get my health back. Look at 'em dukes—look at 'em. So I'm living the life of Riley, huh? Phooey! Who started this stuff about me having it easy out here? Some of them wise guys, I guess. Say, this is the hardest work I ever did—and I like it.

Birns's proverbial luck bounced back in 1934. In the spring of that year Birns got into an argument one night with Rudy Duncan, the bouncer at the Keystone Club at Euclid Avenue and East 24th. Shooting ensued, and when the police arrived they found both Birns and another man wounded. Birns, who was arrested for carrying a concealed weapon, piously claimed he didn't know who had shot him. He also disclaimed ownership of any of the many guns there, the most suspicious of which had been dipped in perfume. But it is a matter of fact that Rudy Duncan was found dead in his car on June 25, 1934, just a few days after a jury acquitted Birns on the weapons charge. It was becoming clear that it didn't pay to mess with Shondor Birns.

In fairness to Shondor it should be noted that he did more during the Depression than kill people, run prostitutes and policy [the numbers racket—the traditional, illegal, and still-flourishing ghetto lottery], and beat innumerable raps. Shondor had grown up poor, and he always had a soft spot for those who were up against

it. One such beneficiary of his charity recalled Birns The Philan-
thropist for Michael Roberts in a 1975 *Cleveland Magazine* profile
of Birns: "He simply gave my parents money so we could eat. I
worked a little bit around the pool room that Shon ran and we
pulled through." There were plenty of other Clevelanders, especially from Shondor's old Woodland neighborhood, who could tell
similar stories of how this undeniably vicious gangster helped save
their lives and families during the Great Depression.

Not that Shondor himself was much depressed during the later
1930s. Although arrested by the Cleveland police with increasing
frequency during periodic anticrime crusades, he was released
from jail, usually only after a few hours, with the same frequency.
When things got a little hot for him in early 1937, he tried to take
a vacation in Miami. Florida authorities, apparently alerted to his
presence by Cleveland lawmen, immediately rousted Birns at his
luxury hotel. A good idea of the rancor toward Shondor flourishing
in the columns of Louis Seltzer's *Cleveland Press* can be gleaned
from its front-page news his Florida troubles provoked in the edition of February 3, 1937:

> Shed a tear for Shondor Birns, kingpin Cleveland racketeer. Not
> for him the breeze, the sun, the golden sand of Florida. Doubt-
> less it will come as shock to the cream of Cleveland crimedom
> to learn that the land of the finger-printed bellhop has asked the
> irrepressible Shondor to return to the windy North. They are
> aware that those without money or jobs are barred at the border,
> and feel that is as it should be for bums should not be permitted
> to clutter the beaches. But they feel that this should not apply to
> the redoubtable Shondor Birns, into whose pockets flows the
> bulk of the proceeds of prostitution in the Woodland Avenue-
> East 55th street area. Perhaps the Miami Beach police were not
> aware what a big shot they were trifling with when they invaded
> Shondor's apartment, seized his pistol and his cartridges (injury
> to insult!) and hauled him into court for failing to register him-
> self as a felon.

> Perhaps the judge who suspended Shondor's 90-day sentence on
> condition he leave Miami Beach and never return was not aware
> of what high esteem is held for Shondor in the courts of his
> native Cleveland, where he has been often tried but almost never
> convicted of anything more serious than failing to tie his neck-
> tie properly . . . You can bet your boots that judge never heard of

Rudy Duncan or Artie Miller or John Consorte. They trifled with Shondor's dignity, too, at one time or another. All got shot. Rudie and Artie are dead . . . Ignore the insult, Shondor! You'll find things just as you left them in Cleveland . . . Come to Cleveland, Shondor! Spend your money where you make it.

Two days later, Shondor did return to Cleveland, where he was immediately thrown in jail by Inspector Joseph Sweeney, who blandly insisted, "We just had a few questions we wanted to ask him." That official attitudes toward Shondor had noticeably hardened under the regime of Safety Director Eliot Ness was made clear when Shondor was put in a police lineup the next day and introduced to his viewers by detective Emil Smetana thusly: "This is Shondor Birns. He is 29 and lives at 3605 East 149th Street. He is known as a plain racketeer."

There was more rough banter at Shondor's expense only three days later, on St. Valentine's Day, when he was caught in a police raid on a house where he was running prostitutes at East 55th and Carnegie Avenue. Shondor was nowhere to be found when the police broke in, but a loud sneeze alerted them to his presence in a woodshed out back. There they found him, hiding under a large winter coat with three females of questionable occupation. Birns blamed his untimely sneeze on a cold contracted due to his recent change of climate, a change he blamed on the Florida Ku Klux Klan.

Eliot Ness kept up the pressure. On June 19, 1937, detective Ernest Molnar (later convicted of taking bribes from criminals) led a raiding squad to the door of Birns's suspected policy operations room at the Alton Hotel at 2573 East 55th. When a peep through the transom of Room 313 proved uninformative, Molnar called in Hook and Ladder No. 3 from a nearby fire station and sent Patrolman John Sullivan up the truck's ladder for a look. When Birns and the men inside Room 313 saw Sullivan at the window, they ran for the door, only to be greeted by Molnar and his men. Just three weeks later, Birns beat the rap when his associate, Charles Oddo, admitted ownership of the wager notebook confiscated by the police. A smirking Birns told reporters, "They're just menacing me . . . Honest, I'm a good boy."

Area law enforcement officials had another go at Shondor in 1942. Belatedly pursing criminal indictments handed down in

1939, they tried Shondor on a charge of extortion, saying he had shaken down policy operator Oscar Williams for $4,000 in "protection" money. Thirteen persons had already been convicted on the 1939 indictments, and it looked bad for Shondor. But on August 7, Cuyahoga County Common Pleas judge Frank S. Day acquitted Birns, stating that the testimony of Williams was "grossly insufficient" and lacked any corroboration. Birns's acquittal, naturally, only brought more billingsgate from his editorial enemies at the *Cleveland Press*:

> So, another close call for the town's easiest spending, most brassy, bedizened and bespangled racket man goes up on the right hand side of the blackboard. The glittering Mr. Birns, whose penchant for flashy clothes, bizarre entertainment, high-powered cars, and highly amusing conversation are combined with a rather whimsical attitude, has the ability to make many folks like him in spite of everything.

Even as Shondor reveled in another miraculous legal victory, a new and more deadly nemesis appeared. An alien since his entry into the U.S. as a Hungarian infant, Birns had never bothered to become an American citizen. More critically, he was a felon who had been convicted on prostitution-related charges, which, along with his repeated failure to confide his criminal record when crossing the U.S.–Canadian border on multiple occasions, made him technically liable for deportation as an "undesirable alien." So Birns was arrested on September 18, 1942, and federal officials began preparing the paperwork that would return him to the land of his birth.

Like many a trap laid for Shondor, the deportation snare misfired badly. Even as his fellow hoodlums held a hastily arranged two-night fundraiser for the beleaguered Shon at Willie Langer's Hickory Bar-B-Cue on Carnegie Avenue ($1,500 was raised for the worthy cause), federal lawyers discovered the unhappy fact that Shondor had been born in an area ceded to Czechoslovakia by the Treaty of Versailles after World War I. The upshot of this legal conundrum (not to mention the difficulty of deporting Shondor to any country in wartorn Europe) was that Shondor was ordered interned as an enemy alien for the duration of the war. This greatly pained the sentimentally patriotic Shondor, who boasted to reporters of his repeated attempts to enlist in the U.S. fighting forces and went on to contrast his stepmother Sadie's war work with the slacking of his adversaries in law enforcement: "If some of the people that put me in this trouble did one half the work that my people do in regard to this war effort, I think I would call them real honest-to-goodness patriots."

He also disclosed that he had undergone a painful hernia operation just so he could meet the physical requirements of the United States Army, although cynical souls recalled that the operation had been timed to delay some unpleasant legal proceedings.

To the consternation of Cleveland lawmen, the luck of Shondor Birns continued its relentless course. After several months in an alien internment camp in McAlester, Oklahoma, Birns was released by order of United States attorney general Francis Biddle in March 1943. Returning soon thereafter to Cleveland, Birns flourished a glowing letter of praise from the camp superintendent extolling his "proper attitude to the authorities." Shondor

Happy days are here again: Shondor Birns leaving jail, late 1940s.

also now vowed to settle down to legitimate toil as a towel supply salesman.

Whether Birns could have made good on his improbable vow is debatable. By the end of World War II he was indelibly etched in the public mind as the most notorious hoodlum and scofflaw in Cleveland history. The columns of all three Cleveland newspapers were frequently filled with denunciatory columns, editorials, and brutal cartoons detailing his evil intentions and wicked deeds. Shondor himself would always claim that he tried to go straight many a time, especially as a restaurant entrepreneur, but his enemies in local law enforcement and the press (especially Louis Seltzer) just wouldn't let him. No matter what he did, no matter how clean he tried to be, they were always waiting to trip him up.

They used him as a criminal scapegoat to explain away their own failures, corruption, and incompetence. (Shondor had some grounds for his charges of police incompetence—in a 1942 *Cleveland Press* poll of Cleveland policemen seeking promotion, it was discovered that 13 out of 19 above the level of captain could not identify photographs of the most notorious Cleveland hoodlums—including Shondor Birns.) So, in the end, following the Gospel According to Shondor, he was forced, out of sheer financial necessity, to return to the underworld realm of prostitutes, policy, and the divers other vices at which he excelled so famously. Maybe so—but there is really no evidence to dispute the assertion of Safety Director William F. Smith, who opined to a newspaper reporter in 1947: "Id like to have one person show me where Shondor Birns ever made an honest penny—up to this hour."

Whatever the truth of Shondor's frequent justifications of his behavior, there's no question that undesirable-but-undeportable alien Shondor was soon in hot water again. One of the swankiest nightclubs of postwar Cleveland was Shondor's Ten-Eleven Club located at 1011 Chester Avenue. Although it was heavily patronized by high-ranking policemen and other law enforcement officials of the Greater Cleveland area, repeated crackdowns there soon made it an uncomfortable investment for Birns, who also had an interest in the Theatrical Grill on Short Vincent. It didn't seem to matter that many of his enemies felt comfortable freeloading at the Ten-Eleven, nor did Shondor get public credit when the Ten-Eleven stayed open round the clock during the terrible days of the East Ohio Gas Company explosion in October 1944, feeding legions of exhausted fireman and police for free. There are still many Clevelanders alive who remember Shondor at his best during his restaurant days, always sitting with his back to the wall, his eyes shifting nervously as he scanned the door and his patrons for possible opportunities or potential mischief. A cynical Birns would later remember those officials who exploited his restaurant hospitality in a conversation with writer Michael D. Roberts:

> If I'm the city's biggest crook, why do they all want to be my friend? I'll tell you why. Most of them are worse than I am, and they know that I know. Write that sometime.

Shondor's nightclub troubles only escalated after he acquired the Alhambra Lounge and Restaurant at 10309 Euclid Avenue in the late 1940s. Again, there are Clevelanders yet living who will swear that Shondor Birns was a born restaurateur and that the Alhambra was the best-run nightclub in Cleveland history. But that didn't matter to Birns's enemies, led by Louis Seltzer of the *Cleveland Press*, who exploded in public wrath when the Ohio State Liquor Control Board renewed the Alhambra's liquor permit in April 1947.

Birns's foes were spoiling for a fight after their failure to shut down the Alhambra, and they soon got it from the feisty Shondor. On September 15, 1948, Shondor was arrested after a brawl with a policeman behind the Alhambra. Patrolman Edward J. Kirk accused Birns of beating him and resisting arrest after an argument about a parked car. After a trial featuring unseemly revelations about police drinking habits (the Fifth District Headquarters was located within a drunk's roll of the Alhambra) and charges of witness intimidation, Birns was convicted on Kirk's charges on November 1, 1948, and sentenced to seven months in the workhouse. While Shondor's lawyers successfully stalled his workhouse term, a further scandal erupted the following May, when Assistant Safety Director Alvin Sutton saw Shondor being chauffeured away from the Cleveland Stadium by two detectives in a police car. A grinning Shondor explained that he was just trying to make it easier for the two detectives, who were supposed to have him under constant surveillance.

Birns finally began his workhouse term the following summer, but even there he couldn't stay out of the limelight. On September 12, 1949, a powerful bomb exploded at the home of policy kingpin Joe Allen at 2131 East 100th Street in Glenville, destroying his 1947 Cadillac and badly damaging his home. Four days later, unsavory workhouse guard Charles ("Kingfish") Billingslea came to the Cleveland police with a bombshell story. He told them that he had been the go-between in a Birns scheme to extort protection money from Joe Allen, threatening the policy mogul with dire consequences if Allen didn't give Birns 25 percent of his weekly numbers profits. "I'll soften him up," Billingslea recalled Birns saying. "[We'll] hit Allen's car first, then his house, then his new house. If that [isn't] enough, then we'll get him." When Allen refused to fork over the 25 percent, Birns engineered the bombing, involving mobsters Nick Satulla, Charles Amata, Joseph Artwell, and Angelo Lonardo in his plot. Billingslea further charged that Birns had been virtually running the workhouse during his sojourn there, having cases of whiskey and beer delivered to him, enjoying the company of women at a private house on the grounds, having a private phone at his disposal, meeting freely with his criminal associates, and even leaving the workhouse grounds at will. It seemed an implausible story, but it gained credibility when workhouse superintendent Raymond J. Walsh resigned in disgrace less than a week after Billingslea's charges became public. Shondor's comment was simply that he was being "framed by a screwball."

From the police perspective, Billingslea's allegations were almost too good to be true—and so they proved to be at Birns's ensuing trial. After two months of argument and testimony, a jury of seven men and five women was dismissed by Judge Edward Blythin after being deadlocked for 37 hours. Following widespread criticism of their reasoning, 10 of the 12 jurors disclosed that they just couldn't believe Charles Billingslea, a self-confessed liar, criminal, and pervert. Nor did it help the state's case when Joe Allen—the victim of Birns's alleged plot—contradicted Billingslea's story on the stand. The rage of those hoping for Birns's conviction was best expressed by Al Sutton, who sputtered, "The dirty pigs jumped with joy when this jury was hung." An interesting aftershock came several days later, when U.S. postal official Arthur Forsberg admitted trying to fix the jury on behalf of Birns's codefendant Charles Amata. Despite his own signed confession, Forsberg was acquitted of the jury-fixing charge on January 28, 1950. An angry Judge Blythin got the last word when he slapped both Amata and Forsberg with contempt of court charges, resulting in 10-day jail terms for each of them.

Birns's second trial on the Allen bombing charge proved even more amusing than the first. It had barely gotten under way in late March of 1950 when it, too, erupted in a jury-fixing scandal. It was a complicated mess, the gist being that Shondor had persuaded Joan ("Vicky") Kanezic, a jaw-droppingly beautiful Alhambra Tavern waitress, to approach one of the prospective jurors on Shondor's behalf. Although Birns's plan to have Vicky sway juror Albert Brichacek over lunch was sabotaged by a flirtatious newspaper reporter who entertained Vicky himself, Vicky did manage to telephone Brichacek and tell him that Shondor Birns was interested in a "fair trial" and that Shondor would make it "worth his while." When Judge Joseph H. Silbert discovered Birns's contact with Brichacek and two other prospective jurors, he boosted Shondor's bail from $60,000 to $120,000, a slight that prompted Shondor, against the advice of his lawyer, to write a letter to Silbert. Insisting that he had the right to investigate prospective jurors in the interest of insuring a fair trial, Shondor tried to pass off the bribery attempt as the innocent behavior of an enthusiastic girl:

> I know it is hard to get an unbiased jury and all I wanted is a fair jury and a fair trial. And I still believe I have to right to investigate . . . As far as a gift being promised to any one, I did promise Vicky a present in taking my interest to heart, never realizing how far she went. I think her anxiety in trying to help overwhelmed her better judgment and maybe my judgment also. Please be fair to me, your honor. I finally realize this girl is sick in her mind and would appreciate a doctor or psychiatric examination and I am sure you will realize that I am right at the present time . . . In my heart I still believe I have done no wrong.

Birns's second bombing trial continued on its eccentric course. On April 19, a man named Charles T. Ferguson, who identified himself as a visiting circuit court judge from St. Louis, was allowed to sit next to Judge Silbert as a matter of professional courtesy. Judge Silbert wasn't pleased when he found out Ferguson was just a curious businessman, and he slapped him with a 10-day suspended sentence. Meanwhile, attorney William J. Corrigan, representing Birns's codefendant Angelo Lonardo, chipped away at the remnants of Billingslea's ragged credibility with a ferociously effective cross-examination. An uncharacteristically low-key Birns played it cool for a change, telling the jury that, rather than plotting violence against his numbers rivals, he habitually acted as Shondor The Peacemaker between rival policy factions. And as for that alleged jury tampering, well, Shondor felt he had "a right to check out" jurors he suspected were prejudiced, but if he had "stepped out of bounds" he was sorry.

Cleveland lawmen were not pleased when the jury acquitted Birns on the extortion bombing charges on May 17, 1950, after less than three hours of deliberation. Some of the jurors later stated they thought Billingslea was a liar and that there simply wasn't enough evidence. Nor was there edification over at the *Cleveland Press*, which reacted with a fulminating front-page editorial entitled: "Who Runs This Town—Birns Or The Law?"

> Well, here is Shondor Birns loose on the town again. What dirty
> work will he be up to next? Whose reputation will he ruin? What
> laws will he smugly sneer at, and break, and go his way believ-
> ing he is above all laws. What witnesses will he bribe. What
> jurors will he try to fix? . . . What decent people will Shondor
> next pull down into the gutter with him?

An appalled Judge Silbert had the last word a week later, when
he slapped Birns with a six-month sentence for trying to tamper
with juror Brichacek. "In all my years on the bench," Silbert
steamed, "I've never seen a more brazen act. I don't know of a
plainer case of contempt than this. The defendant doesn't even
deny it." Further proof of Judge Silbert's adamant contempt for
Birns came in September, when he loftily spurned Shondor's offer
to leave Ohio for 10 years in return for a reduction of his sentence.

The term Shondor served for jury tampering proved to be an
augury of his fortunes during the 1950s. His misdeeds were beginning to catch up with him, and it was a plaintive Birns who spoke
to reporters before the end of his incarceration in November 1950:

> I've been locked up so long that I don't know what I'm going to
> do. [Birns had been in jail almost every day since May of 1949.]
> The close air in here doesn't do anything for a guy's thinking . . .
> I'd like to get a job managing a small restaurant down South, but
> who would hire me? Are they going to let me work for a living
> like a human being, or are they going to cat-and-mouse me to
> death . . . My stomach is on the blink. This confinement and lack
> of exercise gave my stomach trouble. I've been x-rayed and I'm
> going on a diet when I leave.

As if to confirm his bleak misgivings, the State Liquor Department refused to renew the liquor permit for the Alhambra Tavern
just five weeks after Shondor got out of jail. He emerged just in time
to suffer a further indignity, his unwilling appearance before the
Kefauver Crime Committee hearings, a televised congressional
roadshow that brought federal legislators and lawmen to Cleveland
to interrogate notorious hoodlums in public sessions. Birns's federal questioners ran out of time before they could put him on public display, but he is said to have had a most uncomfortable private
interview with them. That same year, Birns lost a rumored $65,000

to $70,000 in the Alhambra debacle. Eventually it reopened under new management, retaining Birns as a "public relations consultant."

Nor did the Cleveland police relax their efforts to discourage Shondor, even if they couldn't make any charges against him stick for long. The long-standing pattern of arresting Birns as frequently as possible on "suspicion" charges intensified after Mayor Anthony Celebreeze took office in 1953. Two incidents soon made Celebreeze aware of what a brazen figure Shondor cut in the Forest City. The first incident came only a week into the new mayor's term, while he was standing in a drugstore at Kamm's Corners. Celebreeze was horrified when he overheard a teenaged boy there talking about how he wanted to be like Shondor Birns when he grew up, because "he could get away with anything." The other disquieting episode came at a Cleveland Browns game in the fall, where an incensed Celebreeze witnessed Birns verbally abusing a rookie policeman with arrogant impunity. During the following months Celebreeze did all he could to make it virtually illegal for Shondor to be in Cleveland, moving Birns to moan publicly, "I can't even take my wife out to dinner without the cops following me." Ultimately, Celebreeze's campaign didn't work, although it did move Shondor to flirt briefly with the idea of relocating to Miami—until Florida officials made it clear they hadn't forgotten his 1937 vacation there.

Meanwhile, the federal government tightened the screws on Shondor. Although continuing efforts by the Immigration and Naturalization Service to find a country willing to take Cleveland's most undesirable alien off its hands proved fruitless, the Internal Revenue Service had more success. After relentless scrutiny of his nightclub finances, the feds, led by IRS agent F. Leo Baumgardner, finally moved against him in September 1952. It took them two years, but they were able to convince a jury that he had systematically skimmed thousands of dollars from the Alhambra Tavern. He was given a three-year sentence in a federal prison by federal judge Charles McNamee on July 28, 1954. There he was known as a model prisoner, which is probably why he returned to Cleveland almost a year early, in the fall of 1956.

Shondor was now technically free, but in fact he would be hounded for the rest of his life by tirelessly vigilant IRS men, who relentlessly stalked him and continually impounded any cash, valuables, or automobiles found in his possession during their incessant rousts. It was legend among Shondor's acquaintances that he might suddenly and silently shove a wad of bills into your pocket in anticipation of an impending IRS visitation. The author's father, Peter Bellamy, once saw Shondor running a broken foot race in the middle of a morning rush hour on Chester Avenue in University Circle, hotly pursued by IRS agents only scant feet behind the fleet-footed Birns. As Shondor dashed by the car, he spotted my father, shouted, "Hiya, Pete," and continued his desperate flight. Over a quiet drink later at the Theatrical Grill, Shondor explained that he had been holding $10,000 in cash, and he needed to sequester it somewhere before the feds caught him with it.

The Cleveland police soon knew that Birns was back in town. Birns had long been involved in the numbers racket, and he moved aggressively now to regain his former clout. That was getting harder to do in the black neighborhoods where policy traditionally flourished, as Shondor once explained to a fellow criminal:

> The niggers have the idea since they organized clearing house [the financial infrastructure that provides cash flow to the policy organizers] and policy, it should belong to them. If you don't keep the niggers in line, the first thing you know they will be running the city.

One of the men who thought it should belong to them was an up-and-coming policy operator named Donald King. (Yes, *the* Don King—now better known as a successful boxing promoter.) Violence in the Cleveland numbers racket began to escalate following Shondor's return, and no one was much surprised when a dynamite bomb exploded on the front porch of King's home at 3713 East 151st Street early on the morning of May 20, 1957. Birns and four other likely suspects were charged with the bombing, but once again Shondor escaped the net woven for him. King proved to be a poor prosecution witness, especially after he was shotgunned with pellets in the back of his head before his trial testimony. (King was dubbed "The Talker" by court wags, who could not interpret much of what the motor-mouthed King said on the witness stand.) Another trial highlight came when Birns's attorney, Fred W. Garmone, admonished the jury to follow the Biblical injunction in acquitting Birns: "Remember that the Bible says 'Thou shalt not condemn a man from the mouth of one witness.'" The King case ended in another hung jury, and the charges were eventually dropped. The inevitable *Cleveland Press* headline followed: "Another Break For a Bum."

Not that Shondor's myriad enemies didn't stop trying. Sometime in March 1959, someone fired a rifle round at Shondor as he was leaving his house at 16913 Judson Drive. The shot missed, but both the police and Shondor were convinced that it had been fired by rival numbers operator Clarence ("Sunny") Coleman. It was imprudent of Sunny to miss Shondor, and it was even more unwise to boast of his near miss in East Side criminal circles.

That made Shondor mad, and, as Prosecutor Michael Pusti had once remarked, "When Birns gets mad, he does something about it." "Something" proved to be three shots from a .357 Magnum, which were fired at Sunny through a window of his house on East 124th Place. Shondor—or whoever it was—did not miss, hitting Sunny twice in the legs and once in the left arm. When Sunny identified Birns as the man who had driven the shooter's car, Birns piously retorted he'd been home watching the Jack Paar show on television when Sunny had his untimely mishap. And when Sunny's memory of the shooting proved elusive during his testimony before a curious grand jury, Birns escaped from yet another legal embarrassment. No doubt even Shondor was amused when a chastened Coleman told the jury:

> I can't testify with any degree of moral certainty that Birns was in the car. In the initial heat of passion, fear and anger, I thought perhaps it was Birns . . .

As the 1950s gave way to the 1960s, Shondor Birns remained one of the last of the real independents. With no family ties to the traditional Mafia clans, his relative outsider status made him particularly useful to organized crime circles when they needed a delicate job done. One such job came Shondor's way in 1963, when he was apparently recruited to do something about Mervin Gold. Gold was a Cleveland financier who had used some stolen Canadian bonds to secure a government loan and then tried to flee to Israel to escape the consequences. When he had to return to Cleveland to face the music, the investigation of his activities promised to be one full of potential embarrassment for interested criminal parties, including Birns.

That potential for embarrassment ended on July 8, 1963, when Mervin Gold was found in the trunk of his car on Chagrin River Road in Solon. Shot once in the back and thrice in the head and strangled with a clothesline, Mervin had also been beaten so brutally that his wedding ring was bent out of shape. An impressed Coroner Sam Gerber characterized his killers well: "It would seem they most certainly weren't happy with Gold and that he didn't give them whatever it was they wanted." A police chat with Gold's wife Lily revealed that Mervin had been on his way to see Shondor when he disappeared from his Pepper Pike home several days earlier. Moreover, the apprehensive Mervin had left behind affidavits in which he stated he had gotten the stolen securities from Birns. Better yet, the police discovered tapes of telephone conversations between Birns and Gold in which Shondor had threatened Gold:

> Listen, Merv, you're gonna keep talking to me like that—you think you're talking to a fool? I'll come up there and make you talk the way you're supposed to talk.

Following a dramatic nationwide manhunt for Birns, Shondor surrendered himself to Cuyahoga County sheriff James McGettrick three days after Gold's body was found. Now, Cleveland authorities gloated, Shondor's luck had finally run out.

They should have known better. Police had narrowed the time of Gold's death down to around 11:30 P.M., July 5—and Birns now produced an unlikely alibi witness who claimed he had been far from the scene of Gold's demise. She was Allene ("Ellie") Leonards, a demure 24-year-old of unimpeachable reputation, who taught second grade at the Garfield Park School. She insisted that she had been feasting on frogs' legs with Shondor at Kandrac's Steak House in Oakwood Village on the evening of Mervin Gold's murder. And when officials proved flexible about moving up the time of Gold's murder, Miss Leonards obligingly moved with them, admitting to spending the entire night of July 5 with Shondor. And that was that. Although Leonards stuck to her basic story, she ended up invoking the Fifth Amendment 75 times at the inquest into Gold's death, most memorably when she refused to answer the question "Is Garfield Heights in Ohio?" on the grounds "that it may tend to incriminate me." The more practiced Birns, of course, bested her, invoking the Fifth Amendment a total of 90 times. The following year Birns divorced his first wife Jane to marry Miss Leonards.

The Gold murder was probably the highlight of Birns's improbable career, but he continued his usual activities in the years afterward. His main preoccupation remained the policy rackets, which led to his arrest in 1964, after Parma and Cleveland police surprised Birns with policy evidence in a July 23rd raid on his "office" at 5715 Brookpark Road in Parma. Eventually, the charge was thrown out on a technicality—lack of a valid search warrant—but Shondor, as was his wont, couldn't leave well enough alone. Before the case went to trial, Shondor met Clarence Bennett, one of the Brookpark raiders, in the Beef & Bottle bar. They had what Birns thought was an amiable conversation about gambling. But the next time they met at the Beef & Bottle Bennett was wearing a wire. Money changed hands, and Shondor was subsequently convicted of attempted bribery, although he testified that the money given to Bennett had just been the soft-hearted Shondor's way of expressing sympathy for the low salaries paid policemen. Simultaneously, Birns found himself again the target

Shondor walks again: Birns leaving Central Police Station, 1960s.

of the IRS. When its agents managed to convince a jury in 1965 that Shondor had repeatedly perjured himself about his real financial assets, Shondor elected to serve his sentence on the federal rap instead of the Parma bribery conviction. In 1968, he won a moral victory when the U.S. Sixth Court of Appeals threw out his tax conviction, but he was immediately transferred to the Ohio Penitentiary to serve out his term for the bribery charge.

As was his custom when incarcerated, Birns proved to be a model prisoner, both in Columbus and at the Marion correctional facility where he was eventually transferred. He was especially good at running the prison commissary—no one ever stole anything on Shondor's watch—and his sterling behavior earned him a parole in 1971.

By the time Shondor returned to the streets of Cleveland at the age of 65, he had become something of an anachronism. The numbers game was becoming an increasingly black-dominated racket, and such white involvement as still persisted was dominated by the likes of Danny Greene. Greene was a younger, tougher, and more sophisticated version of Birns, and it was inevitable he would become a protégé under the aging Shondor's tutelage. But it was likewise inevitable that the ambitious Greene would fall out with Shondor, and by 1975 it was well known that they were gunning for each other. While walking in downtown Cleveland in February, Shondor and a female companion were almost taken out by shooters who fired several near-miss shots from a car. Shortly thereafter, Greene discovered that someone had wired a C-4 bomb (a highly potent explosive used by the U.S. military) to the undercarriage of his car. When Greene found it, he supposedly said, "I'm going to return it to the old bastard that sent it to me." And no one doubted that the "old bastard" was Shondor Birns.

In retrospect, it would be clear that Birns had become careless in his old age. The wary gangster had finally become a creature of habit, and when he wasn't spending quiet evenings with his wife Allene at their home in Orange Village, Shondor's social life was predictably spent in various haunts where men of the world relax, bend elbows, and engage in the kind of worldly conversation with which Shondor was comfortable. One of them was Christy's Lounge at West 25th and Detroit Avenue, which is where destiny took Shondor on the evening of Holy Saturday, March 29, 1975. After buying everyone in the house a drink, Shondor talked quietly at the bar with his acquaintances, who would remember his final hour as a wistful one. He talked of his impending Florida vacation, of trying to shake a persistent cold. He even spoke of his eventual retirement, telling at least one person that this was his "last month in the rackets." Everyone remembered that he looked like the stylish Shon of old, dapperly attired in a white turtleneck and maroon pants, with an enormous cigar jutting out of his mouth.

Just before 8 P.M., Shondor stepped outside Christy's and walked to his car. After a brief conversation with lounge employee Edward Kester, he opened the door of his Continental Mark IV, sat down, and turned the ignition key. A second later, the package of C-4

Wreckage of Birns's Lincoln Continental, March 1975.

explosive under his seat exploded, blowing him to pieces that scattered all over the neighborhood, not to mention the horrified parishioners of nearby St. Malachi's Church, who had gathered for the Easter Vigil Mass. Whoever placed the bomb there was good—it is estimated that he must have gotten into and out of Shondor's car within 30 seconds to avoid setting off its sophisticated electronic security system. It is said, perhaps apocryphally, that a veteran Cleveland police officer who was one of the first to arrive on the scene looked at the far-flung panorama of car debris and human remains and commented, "It's only fair. For more years than I can remember, Shon owned a piece of every part of Cleveland through his rackets. And now every part of Cleveland has a little piece of Shon." Not to mention the ever-watchful agents of the Internal Revenue Service, who immediately pounced on the $843 in cash found fluttering amid the bomb debris.

Shondor left no legacy, except for the gaudy legend of an arrant criminal who escaped most of the usual consequences of a career such as his for almost half a century. Only 70 persons attended his funeral before he was planted in Hillcrest Cemetery on April 1, 1975. He left behind a son, Michael, and his wife, Allene, who mourned him sincerely. Two years later, Danny Greene got his comeuppance, when he suffered a fate virtually identical to Shondor's, blown apart by a bomb in a suburban parking lot while returning from a dental appointment. Shondor, wherever he was, would no doubt have been pleased. Shortly before he was killed, he had spoken to one of his associates about Greene and said, "If anything happens to me, make sure they get him."

Perhaps, though, like Big Jim Morton, Shondor Birns regretted his life as misspent in the end. In a 1954 interview, he disparaged the reputed glamour of his gangster lifestyle and yearned aloud for the secure pleasures of regular working-class life:

It's not worth it. It just doesn't pay. I think I must have spent close to a quarter of a million bucks on attorney's fees, bond money, and fines. And what do I have to show for it? Not a blan/kety-blank thing. The guy I admire is the steady plugger, the nine-to-five guy. He'll never get rich, but think what he can own. He can buy a house, furnishings, a car, support his family and not have a worry in the world. He probably even likes the work he's doing, too.

Chapter 26

WHEN NATURE FROWNS

The 1924 Lorain Tornado

Even great disasters abound in small ironies. After the dead were buried and the debris hauled away, the surviving victims of the brutal 1924 Lorain-Sandusky tornado couldn't even agree on what it was or exactly where it came from. Some said it was a hurricane. Others insisted it was a cyclone, tornado, or maybe just a Lake Erie waterspout that crawled ashore and got out of hand. (For the record, the Reverend Frederick L. Odenbach of John Carroll University called it a "line squall" or waterspout.) Those who insisted it was a tornado—as we shall here—couldn't agree whether it was a single funnel or four separate storms that fatally converged to batter Ohio. But whatever it was, some facts about it are certain: it killed at least 72 persons in Lorain (85 in Ohio), injured 300, destroyed hundreds of houses and vehicles, caused $12.5 million in damage ($1 billion–plus in 2002 dollars), and was likely the most powerful storm that ever hit Ohio. To offer some perspective: the better-known twister that hit Xenia, Ohio, in 1975 caused only $100 million in damage and killed 34 persons. A more significant fact is that the Lorain storm ranks tenth on the all-time list of storms in the United States.

Most meteorologists believe the Lorain tornado began as a barometric depression on the morning of June 28, somewhere over northeast Iowa and southeastern Wisconsin. Moving quickly eastward, it evolved into a family of violent storms, which deluged much of the Midwest and caused widespread damage in Iowa, Illinois, and Indiana. By the time it hit the western end of Lake Erie, it had become an "F4 force" storm (winds of 207 to 260 miles per hour on the Fujita Tornado Intensity Scale). Some contemporary observers thought the Lorain tornado reached its final lethal form

Wreckage in downtown Lorain, looking north on Broadway
Avenue.

just off Pelee Island and then roared westward. Others would argue
that it reached its peak just north of Sandusky about midafternoon.
Like the category of the storm (tornado? waterspout?), its origin
doesn't matter now. What matters now—as it did then—is that the
storm came ashore at 4:35 P.M. and slammed straight into the heart
of Sandusky.

As was the case in Lorain, the death toll would have been much
higher had it been a weekday. But it was Saturday afternoon, which
meant that many of the commercial and factory buildings in downtown Sandusky were empty when the wedge-shaped, rotary funnel
of wind passed within 1,000 feet of the main business area and
plunged into an area circumscribed by Market Street, Adams
Street, Washington Park, and the Lake Erie shore. Smashing
through nine city blocks, it left a path of destruction a half-mile
long and a quarter-mile wide, killing eight persons and injuring
100. Five of the eight dead were found later in the ruins of the
three-story Groh Coal Company building.

One of the injured was three-year-old Robert Wolf, who was
watching his mother board up the upper windows of their house on
Castalia Street. He ignored her warning not to look up at her, and

when the storm hit it slammed one end of a nail-studded board into his forehead and the other into the wall. Seventy-four years later, still bearing head scars, Robert would remember how she bound his head with used tape in lieu of stitches after the storm passed by. Just before leaping back into Lake Erie, the tornado knocked down the city's tall standing waterpipe, leveled 100 homes, and totaled 25 businesses.

A hero of Sandusky's unprecedented catastrophe was Associated Press telegraph operator Jack Vance. Working at the office of the *Sandusky Register*, he was at his telegraph key when the twister hit the city. Refusing to leave his post, he managed to file a bulletin on the AP line before all the wires went down. Unsure that his message had gotten out, he stumbled through downed wires and debris to get to an auto, drove to a New York Central Railroad telegraph wire, and sent out the first storm dispatch on a line to Columbus.

The most dramatic Sandusky storm scene occurred at the lakefront. Thirty-five persons were on the tugboat *Columbus* when the storm picked up a drilling rig from a nearby dock and rammed it into the tug. The *Columbus* soon sank, but all 35 passengers managed to struggle their way to safety on the deck of a car ferry that the tugboat had been towing when it was hit.

Just a half hour later, sometime between 5:08 and 5:11 P.M., the storm came ashore at Lorain. Coming from a northwest direction, it touched down immediately at the lakefront and drove southsouthwest for just over three miles through the city's main business district centered along Broadway Avenue and adjoining residential areas. Most witnesses there experienced it visually as a funnel-shaped storm of rotary winds, visually preceded by green, blue, or yellowish clouds. Like most violent storms, it was capricious, leaving some buildings undamaged adjacent to those it completely destroyed. But wherever it did touch down, with its varying breadth of 500 to 4,000 feet, it left a horrific path of smashed houses, dead victims, maimed survivors, and ruined lives.

The storm's first target was the Municipal Bathhouse in Lakeview Park, at the shoreline. Many apprehensive bathers and spectators had gathered there for safety and were defenseless when the storm lifted off its roof, swept it out into Lake Erie, and then pulverized the stout brick sides of the structure. The physics of its destruction, common to all tornadoes, would be replicated many times throughout Lorain that afternoon. After it removed the roof, the tremendous vacuum at the center of the tornado descended, causing the walls to implode—nature abhorring the vacuum—as the equalizing external pressure rushed in. A nearby skating rink was also demolished and its astonished skaters hurled into the lake, along with six automobiles and their terrified passengers. Pausing only to level every tree in Lakeview Park, the storm moved on.

The tornado took only 104 seconds to do its work in Lorain, much of it concentrated along Broadway and Colorado Avenues. Its prime target on Colorado was the Colorado Hotel. Twenty persons had just sat down to dinner there when the roof collapsed, pinning many of the badly injured diners under heavy steel girders and debris. More fortunate was the family of a tailor who lived above his shop on the same street. No sooner had they fled to the basement for safety than the tailor remembered he had left his cashbox

Some small survivors.

in the shop. He returned to get it while his son held the door shut. They had just reached the top of the second-floor landing when the storm hit the house. Seconds later they landed in the basement alive, standing next to the tailor's wife.

A more awful outcome was simultaneously occurring at the home of C. E. Van Deusen across the Black River on Fifth Avenue. The Ray Richards family had just arrived from Columbus for a visit (they wanted to show off their new car) when the tornado leveled the house completely. It also caught both families in the basement, where they had lined up against the wall for safety, killing six of them and putting the horribly injured C. E. Van Deusen in the hospital. The tornado had picked him up and thrown him 30 feet into a neighbor's porch.

The bathhouse and Van Deusen horrors were but preludes to the main tragedy. As in Sandusky, most of the Lorain office buildings were empty that late Saturday afternoon, but there were perhaps 80 persons on Broadway that summer afternoon, most of them young teenagers in the State Theater. It was between shows, and house pianist Mary Herst was playing a tune called "The Sacrifice" when the tornado hit. The house lights flickered momentarily, and then there was a sound like a tin roof being rolled up. It was probably hundreds of loosened bricks falling. Mrs. G. L. Eiselstein of Lakewood would recall that she thought the sound must have been coming from the stage, perhaps part of a magician's trick to entertain the restive children gathered there. Her husband, who had ducked into the theater with her to escape the violent rain, was not deceived. "That's a tornado," he said, and began pulling his wife through a rain of falling bricks, wood, and glass toward the exit through the lobby. When the Eiselsteins got to the lobby they found it blocked with fallen bricks. Looking up they saw the sky; looking back they viewed scenes of unimaginable suffering as smashed and suffering children writhed in the ruins of the collapsed walls and three balconies. A *Cleveland Press* writer summarized what had happened there with almost poetic power:

> The tip of the tornado rested above the theater, tore the roof from the structure and pressed the walls together like some giant accordion. Only a sharp roar was heard by the audience before they felt the swish of the roof as it was torn from its moorings and the tornado tip, rotating like a huge revolving door, descended into the theater. A moment of suspense and the tornado was gone, leaving a huge vacuum, which sucked the walls of the theater together. Then pandemonium. Hoarse cries of men. Shrill shrieks of women. The soprano wails of small children. All rising in an indescribable roar of supplications and fear as they fought in a frenzy to escape from the accordion that was swiftly pressing together and squeezing out all hope of life and safety.

Two experiences that were typical for those caught in the State Theater were the ordeals of Arthur Fosity and Margaret Powers. Fosity was talking to pianist Herst when the tornado descended and was trapped by a falling door as he ran for the exit. He eventually crawled out from under it to safety and met Herst, who had escaped by another exit. Margaret, age 5, was not so lucky. Although she survived the theater collapse, she was trapped for hours in the wreckage after she witnessed a heavy beam sever the head of her

Wrecked and damaged houses.

friend Audrey Pressick, 10. But it could have been worse. Early and erroneous reports of the carnage at the State Theater listed 80 to 100 dead; the final toll was only 15, most of them young children.

The deadly twister was no kinder to smaller groups it found at two other nearby locations: the Crystal Restaurant on Broadway Avenue and the Dinery Restaurant on Erie Avenue. Two victims died in the flattened Dinery, and two more were found in the ruins of the Crystal. One of them was 12-year-old Dorothy La Londe; still clutched in her hand was her bank book, showing a balance of $3.26.

The rest of Lorain's 72 dead were scattered amid the wreckage of hundreds of smashed houses, crushed automobiles, and pulverized buildings. As the stunned survivors emerged in the aftermath, they confronted hellish scenes not unlike the vistas of ruined villages that some of Lorain's World War I veterans had seen on the Western Front in 1918. Thousands of trees were down; in some areas virtually everything above the level of a weed was flattened, and thousands of pieces of straw were found rammed into tree trunks like nails. At least 500 homes were completely destroyed, with three times as many damaged, some of them lying on their sides or upside down. Many electrical and telephone lines were down, with virtually all power and communication cut off to the

Wrecked autos.

outside world. Along Broadway, for a run of 35 city blocks, stretched a grotesque parade of smashed automobiles pitched helter-skelter along a street entirely filled with debris. *Plain Dealer* reporter Fred Charles described the unsightly mess well:

> Nameless, vague objects cluttered the streets, articles of furniture or merchandise, torn by the storm, sodden in the rain and ground into the mud by countless feet until they defied the imagination to conjecture what useful purpose they might have served.

Just outside the city limits lay the derailed and upended cars of a 78-car Nickel Plate freight train, casualties of the storm's high winds. Some of the heavy cars were blown as far as 300 feet from the tracks. Inside the city, a similar sight could be seen in the Black River, where a B.&O. train, its conductor unaware that the railroad bridge was open, had hurled itself into the river just hours before the storm hit. Perhaps one flippant flapper best expressed the incredulity experienced by those who first gaped at the ruins of the once-thriving city of 37,000. Looking at the wreckage of a substantial home, she turned to her girlfriend and commented in the slang of the day, "Gosh, Mabel, pipe that shack! Isn't it funny?"

One wonders what she might have said about the steeples of Lorain's churches, a half-dozen of which were missing, rearranged, destroyed, or damaged.

As with most disasters, the Lorain tornado was replete with odd incidents and bizarre sights. Two-year-old Myrtle Wood was standing on the front lawn of her grandmother's house when the tornado picked her up, blew her 12 feet into the air, and then deposited her 100 feet away with only a lacerated cheek. The storm picked up a truck, smashed it against the fourth-floor exterior wall of a downtown building, and then conveyed it elsewhere. One freakish sight was a completely demolished house, in the shattered roof of which hung a sign still proclaiming, "For Sale. Inquire Within." Another oddity was a canoe, found wrapped around the top of a telephone pole 1,000 feet south of the wrecked bathhouse. Personal objects picked up in Lorain by the storm were later found as far away as Chardon and points just west of the Pennsylvania border.

As news of the Lorain catastrophe spread throughout Ohio over the next 24 hours, columns of organized relief rushed to the aid of the stricken city. They had a tough time getting in, as fallen trees and crowds of both outgoing refugees and incoming voyeurs blocked most of the highways. But by the next day, hundreds of troops from the 112th Engineer and 148th Ohio National Guard units, under the command of Brigadier General John McQuigg, were patrolling the wrecked city. No one without a pass was allowed into the restricted area, curious gawkers were forcibly press-ganged into crews cleaning up wreckage, and McQuigg announced that all looters would be shot. There was a report later in the week that a "Mexican" had been killed in the act of looting a store, but this was never confirmed; it is likely that the threat of forced labor was the more effective tool in keeping undesirables away from the disaster area. Meanwhile, physicians and skilled nurses poured into Lorain, treating those who had not ended up in the temporary morgues established at South High School, the Reichlin-Reidy-Seanlum Company, and the Wickens funeral home. Eventually most of the dead were buried in either Elmwood Cemetery or the Catholic Calvary Cemetery, neither of which was damaged by the tornado. The tenor of such interments may be gathered from press coverage of the July 1 funeral of little Wilbur Van Deusen, whom the officiating minister pictured as a "little candle in the window of heaven, lighting the way for those he loved

Lorain in ruins, June 30, 1928.

down here." Meanwhile, medical and safety forces struggled to
prevent additional deaths from epidemic diseases made possible by
the ruin of Lorain's sanitary system and contamination of its water
supply. They were mostly successful, although 30 cases of lockjaw
were reported in the two weeks after the disaster.

Considering the widespread damage, Lorain made an astonishingly rapid recovery from the storm. Within three days, two-thirds
of the city had its lights back on, and over half its telephones were
restored to service. The worst of the extensive ruins were demolished and carted away within two weeks, and the Lorain community recovered completely within just a couple of years. A conflagration that destroyed 12 businesses along Broadway Avenue at
6th Street in 1928 was an unpleasant reminder of the 1924 tragedy,
but the city persevered and continued to flourish—and to forget.
Sixty years later there was little memory of the tornado, except in
the stories of aging residents and occasional references to its fury
in meteorological textbooks.

One who didn't forget, however, was Carolyn Sipkovsky.
Although unborn at the time of the tornado, she grew up vividly
conscious of the disaster that had killed her grandfather Joseph
Michaelek, a young shipwright and father of five children. Her
long campaign to memorialize Ohio's worst tornado finally ended
on June 28, 2001, when officers of the Black River Historical Soci-

ety placed a historical marker at the site of the former State Theater in downtown Lorain. Long may it stand as a monument to the incredible suffering of June 28, 1924—and a reminder of what terrible things may happen when Nature frowns.

PHOTO CREDITS

For all newspaper reprints, the date of the featured headline is listed under the image.

Auth—Author's collection
CSU—Cleveland Press Collection, Cleveland State University Archives.
CPHS—Cleveland Police Historical Society
WRHS—Western Reserve Historical Society
PD—*The Plain Dealer*
Press—*The Cleveland Press*
News—*The Cleveland News*
Leader—*The Cleveland Leader*
World—*The Cleveland World*
Herald—*The Cleveland Herald*

Chapter 1   p. 18, *CSU*; p. 19, *CSU*; p. 20, *CSU*; p. 20, *CSU*; p. 22, *CSU*.

Chapter 2   p. 24, *CSU*; p. 24, *News*; p. 26, *Press*; p. 27, *News*.

Chapter 3   p. 30, *CSU*; p. 31, *Press*; p. 32, *Press*; p. 33, *Press*; p. 35, *Press*; p. 41, *Press*.

Chapter 4   p. 44, *Press*; p. 45, *World*; p. 45, *PD*; p. 46, *Press*; p. 48, *PD*.

Chapter 5   p. 50, *CSU*; p. 51, *News*; p. 56, *News*.

Chapter 6   p. 64, *Press*; p. 66, *News*.

Chapter 7   p. 70, *CSU*; p. 71, Auth; p. 72, *Press*; p. 74, *News*.

Chapter 8   p. 76, *Press*; p. 77, *Press*; p. 79, *News*.

Chapter 9   p. 105, *PD*; p. 82, *Leader*; p. 83, *Leader*; p. 95, *Herald*; p. 98, Auth.

Chapter 11 p. 118, *CSU*; p. 119, *News*; p. 120, *News*; p. 121, *Press*; p. 122, *News*; p. 124, *Press*; p. 125, *News*; p. 127, *News*.

Chapter 12 p. 132, *Press*; p. 133, *Press*; p. 134, *Press*; p. 135, *Leader*.

Chapter 13 p. 143, *CSU*; p. 144, *Press*; p. 145, *Press*.

Chapter 14 p. 148, *News*; p. 150, *News*; p. 151, *News*.

Chapter 15 p. 155, CPHS; p. 157, CPHS; p. 158, CPHS; p. 159, CPHS; p. 166, *Leader*; p. 169, *PD*; p. 170, *Leader*; p. 171, WRHS.

Chapter 16 p. 174, *World*; p. 176, *Press*; p. 178, *Leader*; p. 178, *Leader*; p. 179, *Leader*.

Chapter 17 p. 182, *World*; p. 183, *Press*; p. 186, *Press*;

Chapter 18 p. 188, *Press*; p. 189, *Press*; p. 190, *Press*; p. 191, *Press*; p. 195, *Press*.

Chapter 19 p. 200, *PD*; p. 201, *Leader*; p. 202, *Press*; p. 203, *CSU*; p. 204, *Press*.

Chapter 20 p. 206, *News*; p. 207, *News*; p. 208, *News*; p. 210, *Press*; p. 213, *Press*; p. 215, *Press*.

Chapter 21 p. 220, *CSU*; p. 221, *Press*; p. 223, *News*; p. 225, *PD*; p. 226, *Press*.

Chapter 22 p. 232, *Press*; p. 233, *Leader*; p. 234, *Leader*.

Chapter 23 p. 238, *Press*.

Chapter 24 p. 257, *PD*; p. 258, *Leader*.

Chapter 25 p. 269, *CSU*; p. 275, *CSU*; p. 285, *CSU*; p. 287, *CSU*; p. 287, *CSU*.

Chapter 26 p. 290, *CSU*.p. 292, *CSU*; p. 294, *CSU*; p. 295, *CSU*; p. 297, *CSU*.